Accessible Elements

# Accessible Elements
## Teaching Science Online and at a Distance

**DIETMAR KENNEPOHL**

AND

**LAWTON SHAW**

AU PRESS

© **2010** Dietmar Kennepohl and Lawton Shaw
Second printing 2010

Published by AU Press, Athabasca University
1200, 10011 - 109 Street
Edmonton, AB T5J 3S8

**Library and Archives Canada Cataloguing in Publication**

Kennepohl, Dietmar Karl, 1961–
    Accessible elements : teaching science online and at a distance / Dietmar Kennepohl and Lawton Shaw.

Includes index.
Issued also in electronic format (978-1-897425-48-0).
ISBN 978-1-897425-47-3

    1. Science--Study and teaching (Higher). 2. Science--Computer-assisted instruction. 3. Distance education. I. Shaw, Lawton, 1972– II. Title.

Q181.K46 2010       507.1'1       C2009-906647-5


Cover and book design by Natalie Olsen
Printed and bound in Canada by Marquis Book Printing

This publication is licensed under a Creative Commons License, Attribution-Noncommercial-No Derivative Works 2.5 Canada, see www.creativecommons.org. The text may be reproduced for non-commercial purposes, provided that credit is given to the original author.

Please contact AU Press, Athabasca University at aupress@athabascau.ca for permission beyond the usage outlined in the Creative Commons license.

We wish to express our gratitude and appreciation to those who have contributed to this book. The authors graciously gave of their time and expertise to make this book truly come alive, and were also very patient through the review and production process. Many reviewers and colleagues from around the world provided helpful comments and suggestions. The AU Press editors and designers — Erna Dominey, Peter Enman, Kathy Killoh and Natalie Olsen — demonstrated exceptional professionalism and creativity.

Dietmar Kennepohl thanks his loving wife, Roberta, for help with redesigning some chapter figures and for her patience in listening to innumerable discussions around delivering science courses at a distance.

Lawton Shaw thanks his wife, Tanya, for always being positive and encouraging about this project.

# Contents

**ix** Foreword
**xv** Introduction

## Learning

**1** CHAPTER ONE
Interactions Affording Distance Science Education
  Terry Anderson

**19** CHAPTER TWO
Learning Science at a Distance: Instructional Dialogues and Resources
  Paul Gorsky and Avner Caspi

**37** CHAPTER THREE
Leadership Strategies for Coordinating Distance Education Instructional Development Teams
  Gale Parchoma

**61** CHAPTER FOUR
Toward New Models of Flexible Education to Enhance Quality in Australian Higher Education
  Stuart Palmer, Dale Holt, and Alan Farley

## Laboratories

**83** CHAPTER FIVE
Taking the Chemistry Experience Home—Home Experiments or "Kitchen Chemistry"
  Robert Lyall and Antonio (Tony) F. Patti

**109** CHAPTER SIX
Acquisition of Laboratory Skills by On-Campus and Distance Education Students
    Jenny Mosse and Wendy Wright

**131** CHAPTER SEVEN
Low-Cost Physics Home Laboratory
    Farook Al-Shamali and Martin Connors

**147** CHAPTER EIGHT
Laboratories in the Earth Sciences
    Edward Cloutis

**167** CHAPTER NINE
Remote Control Teaching Laboratories and Practicals
    Dietmar Kennepohl

# Logistics

**191** CHAPTER TEN
Needs, Costs, and Accessibility of DE Science Lab Programs
    Lawton Shaw and Robert Carmichael

**213** CHAPTER ELEVEN
Challenges and Opportunities for Teaching Laboratory Sciences at a Distance in a Developing Country
    Md. Tofazzal Islam

**235** CHAPTER TWELVE
Distance and Flexible Learning at University of the South Pacific
    Anjeela Jokhan and Bibhya N. Sharma

**247** CHAPTER THIRTEEN
Institutional Considerations: A Vision for Distance Education
    Erwin Boschmann

**267** Author Biographies
**275** Index

# Foreword

**PROFESSOR MICHAEL GRAHAME MOORE, PH.D.**
The Pennsylvania State University
Editor: *The American Journal of Distance Education*

I first became aware that there were special problems in teaching science at a distance some forty years ago when Charles Wedemeyer asked me to write (in those days on a typewriter to be delivered by surface mail) to a selection of distance teaching institutions around the world. What he wanted to know was what solutions, if any, they had found to the problem of enabling people who studied at home to undertake scientific experiments as part of a distance learning program. One of Wedemeyer's core beliefs was that if teachers applied enough creative intellectual effort, any learning outcome that could be achieved in a classroom should be achievable outside also, and he would not accept the popular assumption that people who studied at home, usually in their spare time, could not study science simply because they should have to undertake experiments. The question was not if it could be done, but how best to do it, and particularly, how to accommodate the need for experiences that were usually undertaken in a laboratory. In his Articulated Media Project (Wedemeyer & Najem, 1969) he had already come up with one answer to this particular problem, in the form of mobile laboratories that traveled around his state, an idea based on what he had heard about a common practice in the Soviet Union, where laboratories for distance learners were shunted around the country on railway trains. Looking for a simpler and less costly solution, my assignment was related to his work on the concept of the home experiment kit. This would be a package of materials and equipment that could be loaned to the student, who would use it in conducting science experiments at home. It was one of many ideas that Wedemeyer had been discussing with friends in the United Kingdom who were in the process of setting up the Open University, where it became extremely successful as sophisticated and ingenious home experiment kits were developed on an industrial scale (see Chapter 10).

Forty years after those early initiatives — and in spite of the example of the Open University, which has not only shown that science can be taught at a distance, but has become a world center of high quality science — the prejudice that science can only be taught face-to-face is still widespread, especially in the United States. Indeed, innovative course and program proposals frequently fail to get off the ground because of very ill-informed assertions by classroom teachers that distance teaching of science is not possible.

It should be a matter of some surprise — now that we have Dietmar Kennepohl and Lawton Shaw's book before us — to realize how long it has taken for someone to produce a book to challenge this prejudice, indeed to begin to describe the problem and to document some of the ways in which it has been tackled. Further evidence of the slowness of the educational community to deal with the challenge — and opportunity — of distance teaching in the sciences is provided by the number of articles that have appeared in the quality research journals. In more than twenty years, the *American Journal of Distance Education* has received only one publishable research-based article having "science" in its title; this was an article on the subject of science teaching in high schools (Martin & Rainey, 1993). Added to this, there have been descriptive, i.e., non-research based reports, in the Journal's "Grassroots" section describing isolated experiences in science teacher education (Jaeger, 1995), and another about an attempt to deliver a biology laboratory (Naber & Leblanc, 1994). A recent research article (Abdel-Salam, Kauffmann & Crossman, 2007) reports an experiment to provide laboratory experiences in engineering courses.

Given this dearth of information, the arrival of a whole volume on the subject of science education at a distance is an extremely important event. The book is not a final answer to the challenge of science teaching, and of course none of its contributors would imagine it to be so. (Personally, I would have liked the editors to have found more evidence about the use, or potential use, of virtual reality as a powerful alternative to the real-world laboratory; it is presumably a topic that will follow as this book inspires others to experiment and report on their progress in this approach.) The book is, however, an excellent overview of the state of the art, revealing where we are today, and pointing to the problems and opportunities now opening up to us, especially the opportunities for using, as I have just indicated, Web 2.0 technologies. As such it provides an excellent foundation for teachers, researchers, and students who are preparing themselves to come to grips with the exciting opportunities in this field.

The book provides the global perspective, the editors having searched globally for their contributors — as indeed in such a neglected area they would have to. Thus, while the majority of contributions come from their own Athabasca University and Australia's Monash University, these are complemented by experiences from other North American universities, from Israel, Bangladesh, the University of South Pacific, and the United Kingdom. Represented here are physicists, biologists, and chemists, an astronomer, a microbiologist, and a geographer, among others. All of course, are engaged in teaching their subjects, but — and this is the core strength of the book in my opinion — they have been well complemented with a team of *educational* scientists, people who I am fairly sure are like me in knowing little or nothing about biology, chemistry, or physics, but who know quite a lot about how people learn and how best to teach them. In this regard, I was very impressed by the editors' forthright explanation of the reasons that teaching science at a distance has been such a neglected part of the field of distance education, particularly the fourth of their five points. But all five bear repeating; they are: first, that it is particularly challenging to construct an effective learning environment for the study of the sciences; second, that science teachers suffer as do others from lack of resources, combined with the expectation of their employing organizations that they teach at a distance in the same "lone-ranger style" they use in the classroom; third, that the literature that might inform innovators in this area is hard to find, being scattered in a variety of both scientific as well as educational journals; and fourth, and perhaps most difficult to cope with, the educators of science students at post-school levels invariably bring very strong disciplinary and research backgrounds to their teaching but have no training in teaching or in-depth study of the philosophies and methods of teaching and learning; finally, there is the problem of providing laboratory experiences that I have already referred to.

Based on this analysis, the editors have brought together a team of teaching and learning specialists to complement the experts in the disciplines. By so doing they have provided a series of responses to the problem of teaching science that is based on pedagogical theory and research, which helps move the quality of analysis and then the level of debate several steps beyond anything we have seen on this subject until now. I particularly enjoyed seeing the first chapter deal with the challenge of managing instructional development teams. What a revolution in the quality and efficiency of distance education there would be if we could move from rhetoric to reality in the application of the team concept in course design and delivery! The book goes forward then with leading experts on the subject of interaction and dialogue revisiting and developing this relatively well known part of the field, though here very interestingly approached through the lenses of the specialists in teaching subjects that have not always, until recently, been seen universally as lending themselves to a constructivist pedagogy. The big question, of providing laboratory experiences, is the subject of a full section, in my opinion one of the core questions in this book, and then a final section deals with some issues of the logistics and infrastructure of program delivery.

This book will, I hope, be read by everyone with an interest in education. This is not only for science educators or distance educators alone. Certainly one hopes that teachers of science in the classroom — most of whom are likely to be called on in the future to teach at a distance at least in blended learning conditions — as well as those who already do teach at a distance, and also the administrators and policy makers who have to allocate and manage the resources that are available for science education will study this book carefully and glean from it some of the valuable ideas it provides for the expansion and improvement of distance education in the sciences. Surely our students deserve better programs, the out-of-school population needs more opportunity of continuing education in the sciences, and society deserves and needs a better return on its education and training investment in the sciences than it has enjoyed until now.

If this book goes even a short way toward sensitizing these populations to the challenges of teaching science at a distance and also the enormous potential for society and the individual of upgrading our response to that challenge, it will indeed prove to be a most important work — besides being a thoroughly enjoyable read.

REFERENCES

Abdel-Salam, T.M., Kauffmann, P.J., & Crossman, G.R. (2007). Are distance laboratories effective tools for technology education? *The American Journal of Distance Education*, 21(2), 77–92.

Jaeger, M. (1995). Science teacher education at a distance. *The American Journal of Distance Education*, 9(2), 61–75.

Martin, E.D., & Rainey, L. (1993). Student achievement and attitude in a satellite-delivered high school science course. *The American Journal of Distance Education*, 7(1), 54–61.

Naber, D., & Leblanc G. (1994). Providing a human biology laboratory for distant learners. *The American Journal of Distance Education, 8*(2), 58–71.

Wedemeyer, C.A., & Najem, C. (1969). *AIM: From concept to reality. The Articulated Instructional Media program at Wisconsin.* Syracuse, NY: Center for the Study of Liberal Education for Adults, Syracuse University.

# Introduction

**DIETMAR KENNEPOHL AND LAWTON SHAW**

*We've arranged a civilization in which most crucial elements profoundly depend on science and technology.*
• Carl Sagan

The importance of science education and science literacy is rising rapidly. As a society and as individuals, having access to it has become absolutely vital. Established educational routes of the past have served us well, but their limitations are becoming more apparent. There is very real and growing demand by students for more flexible approaches to learning science. Online and distance delivery offers practical alternatives to traditional on-campus education for students facing barriers such as classroom scheduling, physical location, and financial status, as well as job and family commitments. In short, it is becoming a viable and popular option for many on- and off-campus students in meeting their educational goals.

As educators in science and science-related disciplines, we recognize that pursuing online and distance delivery not only provides equal access for students, but also gives us several more teaching options that can lead to quality learning. This book embodies the experience of educators around the globe and presents approaches that have been successful in teaching science online and at a distance. We hope it will inspire a positive change in science and science-related education.

## The challenge

Teaching science online and at a distance is more demanding than and certainly not as common as in many other disciplines. There are a variety of reasons why this might be the case. First of all, the concepts and skills that a student must master are numerous, complex, and often build on each other. Crafting an effective learning environment for a science student is not trivial for any mode of delivery. Secondly, science teachers do not necessarily always have sufficient technological savvy or logistical support to create their courses. The myth of free multimedia resources that can be created out of thin air is alive and well. To make matters worse, many teachers still want to go it alone with a sort of 'lone ranger' attitude. While this might be okay for a chalk talk in the classroom, many modern courses with multimedia resources really do require a team approach to develop. Thirdly, the literature available specific to online and distance delivery of science courses (especially the laboratory component) has appeared in widely scattered sources. There is frankly little organized pragmatic information readily available in the sciences for distance educators. The fourth reason is primarily found at the post-secondary level. Science educators, who bring with them very strong disciplinary and research backgrounds, often do not have any formal pedagogical training. To develop their teaching skills faculty rely on their own learning experiences, model colleagues, and research the literature. This self-taught and learning-on-the-job approach brings variable results at best. Finally, there is the very real problem surrounding the practical or laboratory component. A strong laboratory component is at the heart of many science courses, but it is also one of the more difficult components to deliver effectively at a distance.

The challenge of teaching science online and at a distance is very real. There are no simple answers or silver bullets for any of these concerns. However, as you go through this book you will quickly see you are not alone and many problems will sound familiar. You will also discover some interesting approaches and clever solutions that might be adapted to your own science courses.

## Who is this for?

This book is aimed at teachers and administrators in the natural and physical sciences who are working with new teaching technologies, multimedia, delivering courses at a distance, or exploring blended and flexible learning to complement traditional lecture settings. This would include schoolteachers, college instructors, university professors, and senior administrators.

It was our intention to include elements of both theory and applied information in an effort to set context and be of practical use. This book is not meant to be either a rigorous distance education theory book or a step-by-step "how-to" guide of educational technology. However, it does present a survey of current practices and offers a solid foundation for anyone involved in teaching science online or at a distance. We feel it also provides some ideas and guidance for related disciplines in the health sciences, computing sciences, and engineering, which share many of the same challenges.

## Opening the gate

We are taking an open approach in this book. What do we mean by open? We have certainly tried to be broad and representative in our approach in assembling the chapters. Our educational experts, the authors and reviewers of this book, are both scientist and non-scientist, they come from diverse parts of the world, and they are from various types of institutions (traditional, as well as open and distance learning). Although our selection is not exhaustive, we have also tried to find examples from different disciplines among the natural and physical sciences, and in some cases discussions within the chapters have touched slightly on other fields such as health sciences, computing sciences, and engineering. While this is arguably academically open in theory, there is also a very practical component to our interpretation of openness.

Consistent with promoting a collegial atmosphere and in the spirit of sharing knowledge, we also want to freely share our work. It is being published by an open university and we are delighted that it is an open-source licence format. We agree with many of the ideals and observations on open access set out in Athabasca University's first open book *Theory and Practice of Online Learning* (Anderson & Elloumi, 2004). We have also seen the positive results of open publications in terms of access, catalyzing ideas, and dramatically advancing research. Our hope is that this book will not only disseminate the collective efforts of its authors, but will strongly encourage further discussions and other open works to help bring about a positive change in science and science-related education.

So, knowing that an open gate can let things in as well as out, we choose to open it wide — enjoy!

## Major themes

We have organized this book into three major sections or themes, entitled simply Learning, Laboratories, and Logistics. They are the building blocks meant to address common interests and concerns in delivering science online and at a distance. It is important to remember that these three themes are not totally independent of each other. In fact, they are very much interrelated and often build on each other. However, each one represents and emphasizes an aspect worthy of serious consideration in most fundamental undergraduate science courses.

### LEARNING

It is no accident that we start here. The aim of this section is to identify, introduce, and discuss key theoretical concepts that inform teaching online and at distance. Laying the foundation for discussions in later chapters, it takes a generalist approach and is aimed primarily at scientists who are now teaching. It is not meant to be an advanced theory course in education by any means. On the contrary, the chapters under the Learning theme, which are written in the context of current issues, are intended to give the reader an appreciation of the challenges involved and the pedagogical underpinnings of the approaches used to meet them.

**Chapter 1:** *Interactions Affording Distance Science Education*

The role of the various interactions students encounter in their learning process is analyzed and the challenges of enhancing this in the distributed and mediated learning environment are explored. A good understanding of interactions is vital to any distance educator and becomes even more important when considering the science laboratory. Epistemological assumptions usually place a high value on the role of human interaction. While this can and does lead to both formal and informal learning, other forms of interaction can also lead to learning. How those interactions are ultimately supported and encouraged through strategies offered by new technologies and application of social software is of great interest and importance.

**Chapter 2:** *Learning Science at a Distance: Instructional Dialogues and Resources*

The theme of interactions is continued in this chapter from the perspective of the role of instructional dialogues and resources. A theoretical framework is provided within which questions about the factors that influence amount of dialogue or the correlation of dialogue and learning outcomes can be explored. To this end, the authors summarize a series of their own studies on chemistry and physics students to illustrate and examine the framework. One key point, emphasized throughout the chapter, is that this is a universal approach to all modes of educational delivery, where online and distance education are included.

**Chapter 3:** *Leadership Strategies for Coordinating Distance Education Instructional Development Teams*

The elements of good instructional design are introduced through a brief historical review followed up by a case study discussion on leading a DE instructional team. The lone ranger myth of the teaching professor is quickly dispelled, as one recognizes how complex components of content, design, and technology are skilfully woven together by a group of experts. One also realizes that this parallels the world of scientific research, where the shift from the lone genius to a team approach has not only become preferred, but very necessary.

**Chapter 4:** *Toward New Models of Flexible Education to Enhance Quality in Australian Higher Education*

Although presented as a case study of teaching engineering and technology at a major Australian university, many of the goals, challenges, and applications of a flexible delivery model are universal. In addition to providing an excellent review of the considerations around flexible learning, this chapter raises two important points. First, the boundaries between the traditional silos of distance, open, online, and face-to-face education are being blurred. There is gravitation to a more blended approach. Secondly, driven by external considerations, the flexible delivery model is a student-centred approach that is not limited to open universities and their ilk, but is also seriously being contemplated at more traditional institutions worldwide.

## LABORATORIES

Although this section is entitled 'laboratories,' the ideas presented are equally applicable to other forms of applied learning components such as clinical or field work. The design of any laboratory component is often undertaken to meet a variety of aims. The most general aim is the reinforcement of course concepts through illustration and making it real for the student. A number of different means have been employed by science educators to deliver an effective laboratory component at a distance. These include laboratory simulations (virtual laboratory), remote controlled laboratories, and home-study laboratory kits, as well as concentrated regional and on-campus supervised laboratory sessions or fieldwork. Without a doubt the most researched, discussed, and presented area of education among science teachers, in general, is the practical component. This is only amplified when that activity has to be delivered online or at a distance. Given the difficulty in providing effective and credible laboratory experiences, it is certainly no surprise. This section is meant to provide practical approaches used by educators around the globe.

**Chapter 5:** *Taking the Chemistry Experience Home — Home Experiments or "Kitchen Chemistry"*
The home-study laboratory enables students to carry out real experiments in the home environment offering them tremendous flexibility. However, considering (1) that there is a wide range in quality and sophistication of kits that have been employed by different institutions, (2) the popularity of science kits for children in the toy market, and (3) that the experiments carried out at home are done alone and unsupervised, there is the very real question of whether the home-study laboratory experience is equivalent to the traditional on-campus experience. This chapter summarizes the experiences of two institutions that have provided what could be best described as higher level home experiment kits for first year university chemistry. Experiences in the actual development of the higher level kit, including some student evaluation experiences, are described.

**Chapter 6:** *Acquisition of Laboratory Skills by On-Campus and Distance Education Students*
This chapter presents a study in which off-campus students in a biological sciences program complete some parts of their first year laboratory work using home-study kits. To investigate whether there

is an equivalent experience between on- and off-campus cohorts, the students' level of confidence in their laboratory skills was compared at various stages in the program. Student confidence levels have been linked to some aspects of student performance, such as grade point average and retention.

**Chapter 7:** *Low-Cost Physics Home Laboratory*
The availability of modern hand-held calculators that possess remarkable computing power has allowed the development of sophisticated, yet low-cost, home-study experiments for first year physics. The dramatic increase in student participation rates by using this more accessible mode of delivery are noted here (a more general home-study kit discussion follows later in the book in Chapter 10). The authors go on to describe the home-study kits through three concrete examples of experiments. It is important to note that while most introductory science experiments tend to be expository or recipe-style, the experiments illustrated use an Investigative Science Learning Environment, which is a more problem-based form of instruction. The authors also strongly argue that not only is this home-study kit a cost-effective way to flexibly deliver an entire first year physics laboratory experience, it also emphasizes to the student that experiments and natural phenomena can exist outside the campus laboratory.

**Chapter 8:** *Laboratories in the Earth Sciences*
Without a doubt, the earth sciences have the smallest amount of readily available literature on DE laboratory delivery amoung the natural and physical sciences. This is surprising because (1) laboratory and field work is vital in many earth science courses, and (2) there are a lot of active distance courses in this area. The author provides a broad overview of what is being done for the practical components in geology, soil science, and geomatics. The type of activity certainly varies greatly with the nature of a particular course, and there is no one correct solution in delivering laboratories for distance students.

**Chapter 9:** *Remote Control Teaching Laboratories and Practicals*

Although remote control has been with us for some time, remote control over the Internet for teaching experiments is relatively new. Remote laboratories are increasingly appearing in a variety of disciplines and quickly becoming a viable part of a science educator's teaching arsenal. This chapter provides a review of how remote laboratories are employed, the connection to learning, design considerations, and an analysis of advantages and disadvantages.

## LOGISTICS

This section addresses a very important and too often neglected aspect of teaching science online and at a distance. Most courses do not live up to their conceived potential or in some cases completely fail simply because the infrastructure is not in place to support the learning. Like the air around us, infrastructure is never given much thought unless it is taken away. We have adopted a dual approach here by providing both a big picture view and the nitty-gritty of the details that make it all work. Again, because of the challenges involved, it is no accident that substantial portions of the discussion focus on laboratory delivery.

**Chapter 10:** *Needs, Costs, and Accessibility of DE Science Lab Programs*

Most laboratory experiences require the effective and safe coordination of personnel, equipment, chemicals, samples, and biological specimens in space and time by skilled staff. It becomes an even more complex matter to offer students increased access and flexibility when the number of degrees of freedom is increased. The expression "the devil is in the details" can be all too true. The authors begin by outlining the fundamental structures that need to be in place to deliver DE science laboratories and go on to do a costing analysis in comparison with more traditional laboratory delivery. The chapter concludes with an examination of the impact on student participation of introducing home-study laboratory kits into a science course.

**Chapter 11:** *Challenges and Opportunities for Teaching Laboratory Sciences at a Distance in a Developing Country*

The wholesale importation of someone else's solution is not always the right solution. This chapter explores how laboratory and field components are delivered to large numbers of students at a mega-university in a resource-poor environment. It is noteworthy that in a very short time frame this university (founded in 1992) has scaled up its operation to over 700,000 students. The author outlines what needs to be considered in this setting and provides an analysis of the current system, identifying problems and proposing solutions to mitigate them.

**Chapter 12:** *Distance and Flexible Learning at University of the South Pacific*

Working in a resource-poor environment is reminiscent of the discussion on delivering laboratories in a developing country that we saw in Chapter 11. However, here we do not have large numbers of students at a mega-university, but rather 20,000 students spread out across the 12 founding countries of USP in the vastness of the Pacific Ocean. This case study provides both a general overview of distance and flexible delivery options within this environment and a focus on support needs for science courses. Issues of cost, lack of infrastructure, geographical isolation, technical considerations, language of instruction, and cultural differences are discussed in the context of trying to provide equal quality and service to students from all participating countries.

**Chapter 13:** *Institutional Considerations: A Vision for Distance Education*

In this final chapter we step back from the immediate particulars of delivering science online and at a distance to examine the bigger picture. The author gives us perspectives from the point of view of the institution, the academy, and even society. This chapter not only identifies larger organizational concerns, but also underscores why we are doing this in the first place. The assumption is that increased education and particularly science education, along with science literacy, are beneficial and necessary goals for the individual and society. Through a discussion of barriers and opportunities, we are ultimately taken to a vision of universal access to science education with a high level of freedom and individual choice. Along the way we see both what is already in place and what still needs to be put in place institutionally. The underlying and most pressing theme here is change — not just changes in the details of technology and teaching methodologies, but a more profound change in attitudes toward education itself.

### REFERENCES

Anderson, T., & Elloumni, F. (Eds.) (2004). Theory and Practice of Online Learning. Athabasca: Athabasca University Press. Available: http://cde.athabascau.ca/online_book

# Learning

# Chapter 1
## Interactions Affording Distance Science Education

TERRY ANDERSON
Athabasca University

### Introduction

Teaching and learning of science concepts and practice has traditionally been an interactive process. That interaction most often takes place in classrooms and includes the passive consumption of lectures, intermingled with hands-on work in laboratories or field locations. These activities are interspersed with student interaction with textbooks, computers and the completion of learning activities such as problem sets. Distance and distributed education affords new possibilities (especially related to increasing access) at the same time as it reduces capacity for traditional science instructional models and activities. In this chapter, I overview the value of interaction, briefly discuss the literature on definitions and types and conclude with implications and suggestions for creating interaction designs and mixes that together create exciting and engaging ways for science students who are distributed across time, space, and cultures.

Interaction has become synonymous with engagement, activity, and fun as illustrated by the deluge of advertising for everything from interactive toys to interactive clothing, books, music, and concerts. The adjective 'interactive' implies a degree of involvement. (National Institute for Education, 1984), mindfulness (Langer, 1997), and flow (Csikszentmihalyi, 1990). Educational researchers have linked interaction with higher levels of persistence and perceptions of better learning (Picciano, 2002).

Though often associated with widespread and multifarious use, the term interaction is plagued with conceptual misunderstanding. Educators' wide use of the term implies a need for sharper definition and meaningful qualification as to the effective use of interaction in their teaching and learning programs. Advertisements promoting "interactive toasters" make us realize that educators need to clarify and be more specific about the definition, nature, quality, and expectations of interaction in the educational process.

## Defining interaction

The education literature contains a number of definitions of interaction which I have summarized in previous work (Anderson, 2003b). At debate in discussion about definitions is the exclusiveness of the term such that it is reserved for exchanges and dialogue among people as opposed to people engaging with machines or learning objects. Perhaps the most well-known definition is that provided by Wagner (1994), who defined interaction as "reciprocal events that require at least two objects and two actions. Interactions occur when these objects and events mutually influence one another" (p. 8). Obviously, this definition includes engagement with non-humans and implies the capacity for both actors (or objects) to influence each other, thereby implying two-way control — a subject that has special interest as I discuss later in the interesting use of virtual labs.

Michael Hannafin (1989) itemized the functions that interaction purports to support in mediated educational contexts. These are:

1. **Pacing:** Interactive pacing of an educational experience operates

from both a social perspective, as in keeping an educational group together, and an individual perspective, as in prescribing the speed with which content is presented and acted upon.

**2. Elaboration:** Cognitive science informs us that interaction develops and reinforces links between new content and existing mental schema, allowing learners to build more complex, memorable, and retrievable connections between existing and new information and skills (Eklund, 1995).

**3. Confirmation:** This most behavioural function of interaction serves both to reinforce and shape the acquisition of new skills. Conformational interaction traditionally takes place between student and teacher, but is also provided generally by feedback from the environment provided through experience, and while working through content presented in computer-assisted tutorials or as "answers in the back of the book" and from peers in collaborative and problem-based learning.

**4. Navigation:** This function prescribes and guides the way in which learners interact with each other and content. Its function becomes more important as we begin to appreciate and utilize the hundreds of thousands of learning objects and experiences provided on the Net. Interaction feedback provides data necessary to channel and selectively guide learners through this maze of learning possibilities to those that are individually appropriate, accessible, and meaningful (Koper, 2005).

**5. Inquiry:** Hannafin's conception of inquiry in 1989 focused on inquiry to the computer system that was displaying content and monitoring student response. The interconnected and wildly more accessible context for inquiry now provided by the Net opens the door to much greater quantity and quality of inquiry. The interactive affordance for learners to follow individual interests and paths makes inquiry both a motivating and personalizing (though potentially distracting) function of learning.

To these I add the 'study pleasure and motivation' that Holmberg (1989, p. 43) describes as developing from interaction and relationship between teachers and students.

Thus, interaction fulfills many critical functions in the educational process. However, it is also apparent that there are many types of interaction and many actors (both human and inanimate) involved. As a result of this complexity a number of distance education theorists have broken the broad concept of interaction into component types, based largely on the roles of the human and inanimate actors involved.

## Types of interaction

Moore (1989) differentiated three types of interaction which, since they focus on student behaviour, are the most important for educational applications. These are student-teacher, student-content, and student-student interactions.

### *Student-teacher interaction*

Student-teacher interaction has been hailed by traditional educators and many students as the pinnacle and highest valued of interactive forms. This form of interaction is the basis upon which apprenticeship models of education and training are grounded (Collins, Brown, & Newman, 1989). The American President James Garfield was reported to have defined the ideal university as "Mark Hopkins [then President of Williams College] at one end of a log and a student on the other." Since then the 'log' has expanded into cyberspace and the conversation has extended talking options into multiple audio, text, and video formats. Yet there remains a sense that personal identification and other aspects of 'teacher presence' (Brady & Bedient, 2003) are important, if not critical, components of the educational process. The problem with teacher-student interaction is that there is only a limited amount of 'room on the log.' Further, the teacher often is not sitting on her 'end of the log' when their intervention is most advantageous for the learner, and finally, the student may find herself thousands of miles away from the log when instruction and support are needed. Simply put, student-teacher interaction is not scalable. Teacher-student interaction has been stretched — or perhaps stressed is a better term — to include 500-seat lecture theatres, but at a certain size interaction that does occur is mostly vicarious and certainly fails to produce the effects noted by Hannifin earlier.

Student-teacher interaction in distance education has traditionally been limited to occasional and usually student-initiated conversation mediated by the post, the telephone, or more commonly today, through Net-based interaction. The continuing increase in sophistication and complexity of computer-assisted instruction and the use of teacher agents (Yu, Brown & Ellen Billett, 2007; Feng, Shaw, Kim & Hovy, 2006; Moreno & Mayer, 2004) allow some of the student-teacher interaction to be replaced by student-content interaction, but the goal of building machine systems that can completely replace student-teacher interaction remains elusive and perhaps undesirable.

Student-teacher interaction is, however, valued by both students and teachers and has been found to be associated with positive perceptions of learning (Wu & Hiltz, 2004). Thus, provision is made for such interaction in almost all forms of formal education. Its costs, though, dictate that it must be used judicially. Interactions focused on affective concerns such as motivation, personal issues, and modelling represent perhaps the most effective use of teacher-learner interaction. Perhaps the most commonplace and effective way to "increase access to the log" has been through converting student-teacher interaction to student-content interaction, to which we next turn.

### Student-content interaction
Student-content interaction first evolved through the transcription

into text of oral stories and teachings. Historically, biblical scrolls and other sacred writings illustrate this type of interaction. Furthermore, student-content interaction still defines much learning activity today as students routinely part with hundreds of dollars annually in the university bookstore. In recent years, student-content interaction tools have become much more sophisticated and accessible. Learning games, simulations, immersive worlds, virtual labs, quizzes, podcasts and videocasts, blogs, and wikis are just a few of the new networked tools that allow students to interact with content in multiple formats enhanced by color, video, audio, animation, and the processing capabilities of powerful computers. The Net further makes this content available "anytime, anywhere."

The easiest, least expensive way to gain economy of scale is to record student-teacher interaction and convert it to student-content interaction. As noted, this model has been used for millennia to allow vicarious student-teacher interaction through texts with seers long since passed away. More recently, audio and video clips (podcasts and videocasts) have been created to record, store, and deliver this type of interaction. A hybrid form of student-teacher interaction has been developed whereby teachers create presentations on the Net (often referred to as blog postings) and students may, though typically they do not, reply or ask additional questions of these teachers. A good example of this is the Science Blog http://scienceblogs.com/ site, at which over 60 professional scientists were selected "based on their originality, insight, talent, and dedication" to post science-related reflections that can be used and commented upon by students.

Formerly, student-content interaction was a consumptive activity in which students interacted with content created by teachers and other experts. More recently the practical and pedagogical value of learners creating and sharing their own content, as celebrated in so-called Web 2.0 applications (O'Reilly, 2005), has captured public and educational attention. The construction, by all levels of students, teachers, experts, and lay people, of digital resources such as Wikipedia or the more focused creation by sets of discipline experts such as Science Environment for Ecological Knowledge (SEEK) http://seek.ecoinformatcs.org/ demonstrate the utility and cost-effectiveness of user-generated content. Pedagogically, the value of content creation instead of or in addition to content consumption has been shown to deepen commitment and quality in learning outcomes (Anderson, 2007; Collis & Moonen, 2001).

Finally, we turn to the most cost-effective and arguably the most pedagogically effective form of learning interaction — that which occurs between student and student.

## Student-student interaction

Student-student interaction is associated with academic accomplishment (Johnson, Johnson & Smith, 1998), the development of social capital (West-Burnham & Otero, 2006), and enjoyment in the learning process (Johnson, 1981). However, most of the evidence for these claims comes from face-to-face interaction that begins in the campus classroom, but often is continued elsewhere. For example, in a meta-analysis of 383 studies over 20 years Springer, Stanne and Donovan (1999) found that "students who learn in small groups generally demonstrate greater academic achievement, express more favorable attitudes toward learning and persist through science, mathematics, engineering and technology courses to a greater extent than their more traditionally taught counterparts" (p. 21).

The support for student-student interaction reveals a great and as yet unresolved tension among distance educators. For many seminal distance education theorists, including Holmberg (1989), Peters (1988), and Keegan (1990), distance education was an individual activity defined by rich and highly developed student-content interaction (professionally designed and delivered in high-quality learning packages), supplemented by irregular one-on-one student-teacher interactions. Champions of this model argued that individualized learning is an inherently superior form of higher education, because of its ability to overcome time, place, and pacing constraints, its economic scalability, the support for individualized (one-on-one) interaction between a student and a teacher and the concomitant development of a learner's capacity to be self-directed and self-motivated. The flexibility offered by this model is associated with the absence of scheduling, commuting, meetings, and other constraints and is a major reason why students choose to take courses at a distance (Poellhuber, 2005).

However, many authors have noted the lack of social interaction and the higher attrition rates associated with self-paced study and have linked this to a sense of student isolation (Morgan & McKenzie, 2003; Anderson, Annand, & Wark, 2005). One of the solutions envisioned to the lack of social interaction is to stimulate both synchronous and aysnchronous student-student interactions, thus creating a socialized form of distance education that Garrison and Shale (1990) defined as "education at a distance" rather than distance education. This distinction underscores the availability of rich (though mediated) student-student and student-teacher interaction that is celebrated (though, as noted, not always achieved) in campus-based forms of education.

To afford opportunity for student-student interaction, the majority of networked distance education or e-learning consists of groups of students, forged into cohorts, who progress through a series of learning activities while hopefully forming a supportive learning community. The Community of Inquiry (COI) model is the most widely cited theortical model for this type of paced and cohort-supported model of distance learning. This model and susbequent techniques to validate it were developed by myself and colleagues at the Univeristy of Alberta (Garrison, Anderson & Archer, 2001). The model describes the necessity of supporting three types of 'presence' if quality distance learning is to occur. These include teaching presence (largely, though not exclusively supplied through student-teacher interaction), cognitive presence (activities designed to instigate and support critical thinking skills), and social presence (the capcity to present oneself as a 'real person' and to engage in effective, integrative, and cohesive activities). This model brings the notions of social constructivism (Vygotsky, 1978; Lave, 1988; Jonassen & Carr, 2000) to distance education. Extensive applications of and studies using the COI model have shown that each of these three presences can be created at a distance. Further, the student-student interaction in paced and cohort-supported models of distance education can lead to the development of social support networks and social capital (West-Burnham & Otero, 2006; Daniel, Schwier & McCalla, 2003). In a 2004 meta-anlysis of distance programming, Bernard et al. (2004) found that distance education models that supported student-student interactions through paced and interactive activities had higher persistence rates than those based on individual study.

Unfortunately, group-paced models of distance education are associated with major restrictions of learner freedom (Paulsen, 1993), the two most critical being the time when learning can commence (enrolment dates) and the pacing or the length of time used to complete the course or program of studies. It is sometimes impossible for non-traditonal students and those with major work, family, or community obligations to synchronize their time with that of a cohort of students and the teacher. Thus, until recently they were forced to engage in educational models that required and supported only individualized learning with no student-student interaction. We are, however, seeing the dawn of a new paradigm of distance edcuation in which self-paced learners use "social software" to work co-operatively, for short time periods, in 'study buddy' or study groups, thereby gaining the benefits associated with rich student-student interaction. The key to this next generation of distance education is sophisticated social software that allows learners to find each other, schedule activities, and support the co-operative construction of learning artefacts (Anderson, 2006).

Many of the techniques developed for classroom groups have been successfully adapted to learning groups operating at a distance. However, discussions about the means, if any, to facilitate group collaboration in learner-paced education models is notably absent from the literature. While technologies exist to facilitate synchronous and asynchronous forms of group interaction, facilitating this collaboration among groups of learners — in a self-paced setting — is still problematic. This distinct divide between distance education theorists in regard to the value and means to support self-paced distance edcuation models appears to be essentially unresolved at present. Optimizing the flexibility of self-paced learning and the advantages of collaboration and social support remains an open and exciting challenge.

*Equivalency of interaction*
In 2003, I published an article (Anderson, 2003a) overviewing these three modes of interaction and claimed (somewhat tongue-in-cheek) that the value of learning is roughly equivalent among the three types of student interaction and that a high level of one form of interaction allows the other two to be reduced or even eliminated, without loss in learning effectiveness. Thus, high levels of student-teacher interaction (discussion at either end of the log!) mean that student-student and student-content interaction can be drastically reduced. Most of the implications of this "equivalency theorem" were confirmed by Bernard et al. (In Press), who found that increasing the quantity and quality of any of the three student-focused forms of interaction did increase student performance. Interestingly, increasing student-teacher interaction, despite being the most costly intervention, had the least effect on student performance as compared to student-content and student-student interaction. This equivalency theorem challenges educators to think more clearly about the advantages and limitations imposed by each form of interaction and to 'get the mix right.'

## Interaction in science-based distance education
Since the development of 'modern' forms of distance education in

the 1960s, distance science educators have struggled with the means to provide experience and training that has traditionally taken place in the science laboratory. Kirschner and Meester (1988) claim that "a university study in the natural sciences, devoid of a practical component such as laboratory work is virtually unthinkable" (p. 81). Despite this universal endorsement, the efficacy and pedagogy of lab-based education has been criticized for a number of shortcomings, including triviality, repetitive, rote 'recipe' following, inadequate supervision, and a poor return on student time invested (Kirschner & Meester, 1988). The logistical problems associated with developing and delivering lab experiences at a distance further exacerbate these challenges. However, distance educators are nothing if not inventive and persistent, and they have developed a variety of techniques and designs (see chapters in this volume) to address these problems while maintaining high levels of accessibility — the raison d'être for distance education programming. Most predominantly, distance educators have used occasional face-to-face labs sessions offered in centralized locations, the development of home- or industry-based science lab kits, and more recently, use of immersive environments and virtual and remote labs.

Rather than overview challenges, accomplishments, and examples of distance science instruction contained in later chapters, I will note that the predominant learning model, as in most traditional distance education programming, is based on high-quality learner-content interaction. As in other education, entertainment and commercial applications, the development of media, and especially Web-based tools, now support very sophisticated forms of learner-content interaction. These applications still retain high levels of accessibility through the ubiquitous Net, providing access to learners who are globally distributed.

Student-student interaction in distance science programming has often been focused on irregular face-to-face gatherings at lab sessions. Where this is logistically impossible, cohort-based models typically create spaces where students can engage in conversation, provide informal assistance to each other, and occasionally work on co-operative or collaborative projects. The nearly ubiquitous connectivity provided through text tools such as Instant Messenger and audio and video through Skype and workspace sharing via web conferencing systems such as Elluminate creates rich yet low-cost opportunities for student-student interaction in distance education. However, as always, the use of these tools must be embedded within effective learning activities that are perceived as valued by students if they are to be used at all and to result in meaningful learning outcomes. The familiar instructional designs used by distance educators in self-paced programming have often either been formally or informally designed with a sense that students are working alone. This assumption is no longer tenable and challenges instructional designers to create designs that are not only vulnerable to collaborative cheating, but that use collaborative possibility to enhance educational programming. There is a very substantial body of literature detailing the social and cognitive benefits that are afforded by well-designed collaborative and co-operative programming in both face-to-face (Johnson, Johnson & Smith, 1998) and computer-mediated distance education contexts (Koschmann, 1996). Our challenge is to integrate these techniques into programming that has a celebrated tradition of individualized learning.

The very recent development of accessible immersive environments such as SecondLife or Active Worlds heightens the sense of presence, stimulation, engagement, and enjoyment (see, for example, Harvard University's River City Project http://muve.gse.harvard.edu/rivercityproject/). Besides the capacity to support unique new forms of student-content interaction, the social nature of these environments affords development of informal and formal co-operative and collaborative science learning activities. An immersion-based introduction to learning science in the currently most popular Web-based immersive environment, SecondLife, produced by the University of Michigan at http://video.google.com/videoplay?docid=4594846425520495909, provides a fascinating overview of student-content interaction in Net-based immersive environments. These environments promise to augment student-content interaction with engaging new contexts and techniques not accessible in any environment, including the traditional science laboratory. And of course, immersive environments provide rich forms of student-student interaction that is enhanced by the social presence afforded by avatar body language, gestures, and sounds (McKerlich & Anderson, 2007).

The next frontier in distance education programming is providing rich student-student interaction in unpaced, continuous enrolment programs. At Athabasca University we are developing tools and a research program that uses the new genre of social software to allow self-paced students to meet each other and work co-operatively on short-term projects in addition to forming optional study buddy and study group relationships with other students. Social software suites such as Elgg, Ming, and FaceBook provide tools that allow students in related courses to synchronize their activities for brief periods of time and to safely introduce themselves to others through selective release of personal information.

## Conclusion

Interaction stands at the centre of the educational experience. As distance educators we are both allowed and compelled to use mediated forms of this interaction. In some cases the media is costly and gets in the way of learning. In other cases it can result in hyper-learning that easily surpasses non-mediated forms of learning. In all contexts we seek a balance of student-teacher, student-student, and student-content interaction that is cost- and learning-effective. The laboratory requirement in science-based education contexts presents unique challenges to distance educators, but the emerging Net-based information and communication tools afford many new ways in which each of these forms of interaction can be enhanced. The chapters in this book reveal ways in which innovative distance science education are meeting this challenge. Much remains to be done, especially development of robust research programs to generate and share knowledge generated from these innovations. However, the future of distributed science education seems filled with the promise of exciting new ways for learners and teachers to explore and develop their understanding of our expanding universe.

## REFERENCES

Anderson, P. (2007). *What is Web 2.0? Ideas, technologies and implications for education*. JISC Technology and Standards Watch. Retrieved February 25, 2009 from: http://www.jisc.ac.uk/media/documents/techwatch/tsw0701b.pdf

Anderson, T. (2003a). Getting the mix right again: An updated and theoretical rational for interaction. *International Review of Research in Open and Distance Learning, 4*(2). Retrieved February 25, 2009 from: http://www.irrodl.org/index.php/irrodl/article/view/149/708

Anderson, T. (2003b). Modes of interaction in distance education: Recent developments and research questions. In M.G. Moore & W.G. Anderson (Eds.), *Handbook of Distance Education* (pp. 129–144). Mahwah, NJ: Erlbaum.

Anderson, T. (2006). Higher education evolution: Individual freedom afforded by educational social software. In M. Beaudoin (Ed.), *Perspectives on the Future of Higher Education in the Digital Age* (pp. 77–90). New York: Nova Science Publishers.

Anderson, T., Annand, D., & Wark, N. (2005). The search for learning community in learner-paced distance education programming Or 'Having your cake and eating it, too!' *Australasian Journal of Educational Technology, 21*, 222–241. Retrieved February 25, 2009 from: http://www.ascilite.org.au/ajet/ajet21/res/anderson.html

Bernard, R.M., Abrami, P.C., Lou, Y., Borokhovski, E., Wade, A., Wozney, L., Wallet, P.A., Fiset, M., & Huang, B. (2004). How does distance education compare to classroom instruction? A meta-analysis of the empirical literature. *Review of Educational Research*. Retrieved February 25, 2009 from: projects.ict.usc.edu/itw/materials/clark/DE_Meta_Fin_Jan11-04.pdf

Bernard, R., Abrami, P., Borokhovski, E., Wade, A., Tamim, R., Surkes, M., et al. (In Press). A meta-analysis of three types of interaction treatments in distance education. *Review of Educational Research*.

Brady, E., & Bedient, D. (2003). The effects of teacher presence on student performance and attitudes. WebCT Impact 2003, 5th Annual WebCT User Conference. Retrieved February 25, 2009 from: http://www.ega.edu/facweb/irp/Surveysandreports/WebCTConference2003/papersfromconference/Brady.pdf

Collins, A., Brown, J.S., & Newman, S.E. (1989). Cognitive apprenticeship: Teaching the crafts of reading, writing, and mathematics. In L.B. Resnick (Ed.), *Knowing, learning, and instruction: Essays in honor of Robert Glaser* (pp. 453–494). Hillsdale, NJ: Lawrence Erlbaum Associates.

Collis, B., & Moonen, J. (2001). *Flexible learning in a digital world: Experiences and expectations*. London: Kogan Page.

Csikszentmihalyi, M. (1990). *Flow: The psychology of optimal experience*. New York: Harper & Row.

Daniel, B., Schwier, R.A., & McCalla, G. (2003). Social capital in virtual learning communities and distributed communities of practice. *Canadian Journal of Learning and Technology., 29*(3). Retrieved February 25, 2009 from: http://www.cjlt.ca/index.php/cjlt/article/view/85/79

Eklund, J. (1995). Cognitive models for structuring hypermedia and implications for learning from the world-wide web. In *Proceedings of AusWEB 95*: AusWEB. Retrieved February 25, 2009 from: http://ausweb.scu.edu.au/aw95/hypertext/eklund

Feng, D., Shaw, E., Kim, J., & Hovy, E. (2006). An intelligent discussion-bot for answering student queries in threaded discussions. *International Conference on Intelligent User Interfaces IUI-2006*. Retrieved February 25, 2009 from: http://www.isi.edu/~jihie/papers/IUI-2006.pdf

Garrison, D.R., Anderson, T., & Archer, W. (2001). Critical thinking and computer conferencing: A model and tool to assess cognitive presence. *American Journal of Distance Education, 15*, 7–23.

Garrison, D.R., & Shale, D. (1990). A new framework and perspective. In D.R. Garrison & D. Shale (Eds.), *Education at a distance: From issues to practice* (pp. 123–133). Malabar, Florida: Robert E. Krieger Publishing Company.

Hannafin, M.J. (1989). Interaction strategies and emerging instructional technologies: Psychological perspectives. *Canadian Journal of Educational Communication, 18*(3), 167–179.

Holmberg, B. (1989). *Theory and practice of distance education*. London: Routledge.

Johnson, D.W. (1981). Student-student interaction: The neglected variable in education. *Educational Researcher, 10*(1), 5–10.

Johnson, D.W., Johnson, .R.T., & Smith, K.A. (1998). *Active Learning: Cooperation in the college classroom*. (2nd ed.). Edina, MN: Interaction Book Comp.

Jonassen, D.H., & Carr, C.S. (2000). Mindtools: Affording multiple knowledge representations for learning. In S. Lajoie (Ed.), *Computers as cognitive tools: No more walls* (pp. 165–196). Mahwah, NJ: Earlbaum.

Keegan, D. (1990). *The foundations of distance education*. (2nd ed.). London: Routledge.

Kirschner, P.A., & Meester, M.A.M. (1988). The laboratory in higher science education: Problems, premises and objectives. *Higher Education, 17,* 81–98.

Koper, R. (2005). Designing learning networks for lifelong learners. In R. Koper & C. Tatterssall (Eds.), *Learning design: A handbook on modelling and delivering networked education and training*, (pp. 239–252). Berlin: Springer.

Koschmann, T. (1996). *CSCL: Theory and practice of an emerging paradigm*. Mahwah, NJ: Lawrence Erlbaum.

Langer, E.J. (1997). *The power of mindful learning*. Reading, MA: Addison-Wesley.

Lave, J. (1988). *Cognition in practice: Mind, mathematics, and culture in everyday life*. Cambridge, UK: Cambridge University Press.

McKerlich, R., & Anderson, T. (2007). Community of Inquiry and Learning in Immersive Environments. *Journal of Asynchronous Learning Networks, 11*(4), 35–52.

Moore, M. (1989). Three types of interaction. *American Journal of Distance Education, 3*(2), 1–6.

Moreno, R., & Mayer, R.E. (2004). Personalized messages that promote science learning in virtual environments. *Journal of Educational Psychology, 96,* 165–173.

Morgan, C.K., & McKenzie, A.D. (2003). Is enough too much? The dilemma for online distance learner supporters. *International Review of Open and Distance Learning, 4*(1). Retrieved February 25, 2009 from: http://www.irrodl.org/index.php/irrodl/article/view/119/598

National Institute for Education (1984). *Involvement in learning:*

*Realizing the potential of American higher education.* Washington: NIE.

O'Reilly, T. (2005). What is Web 2.0: Design patterns and business models for the next generation of software. Retrieved February 25, 2009 from: http://www.oreilly.com/go/web2

Paulsen, M.F. (1993). The hexagon of cooperative freedom: A distance education theory attuned to computer conferencing. *DEOSNEWS, 3*(2). Retrieved February 25, 2009 from: http://www.nettskolen.com/forskning/21/hexagon.html

Peters, O. (1988). Distance teaching and industrial production: A comparative interpretation in outline. In D. Sewart, D. Keegan, & B. Holmberg (Eds.), *Distance Education: International Perspectives* (pp. 95–111). London/New York: CroomHelm/St. Martin's Press.

Picciano, A.G. (2002). Beyond student perceptions: Issues of interaction, presence and performance in an online course. *Journal of Asynchronous Learning Networks, 6*(1), 21–40. Retrieved February 25, 2009 from: http://www.umdnj.edu/idsweb/idst8000/fydryszewski_article.pdf

Poellhuber, B. (2005). L'univers mouvant des formations ouvertes et à distance : quels intérêts, quels enjeux? Conference given at Laval University. Retrieved January 2009 from: http://heurepedagogique.ulaval.ca/lib_php/video.asp?idVideo=112&type=0

Springer, L., Stanne, M.E., & Donovan, S.S. (1999). Effects of small-group learning on undergraduates in science, mathematics, engineering, and technology: A meta-analysis. Review of Educational Research, 69(1), 21–51.

Vygotsky, L.S. (1978). *Mind in society: The development of higher psychological processes.* Cambridge: Harvard University Press.

Wagner, E.D. (1994). In support of a functional definition of interaction. *American Journal of Distance Education, 8*(2), 6–26.

West-Burnham, J., & Otero, G. (2006). *Leading together to build social capital.* Bedfordshire: International College for School Leadership. Retrieved February 25, 2009 from: www.ncsl.org.uk/mediastore/image2/nlg-wawla3-2-Leading-together-to-build-social-capital.pdf

Wu, D., & Hiltz, S.R. (2004). Predicting learning from asynchronous online discussions. *Journal of Asynchronous Learning Networks, 8*(2), 139–152.

Yu, J.Q., Brown, D.J., & Billett, E. (2007). Design of virtual tutoring agents for a virtual biology experiment. *European Journal of Open and Distance Learning,* Retrieved February 25, 2009 from: http://www.eurodl.org/materials/contrib/2007/Yu_Brown_Billett.htm

# Chapter 2
## Learning Science at a Distance: Instructional Dialogues and Resources

PAUL GORSKY AND AVNER CASPI
The Open University of Israel

## Introduction

Today's distance education systems include resources for individual study (intrapersonal dialogue) such as self-instruction texts, Web-based instructional systems, video recordings, etc., and resources for interpersonal dialogue such as tutorials, telephone counselling, synchronous and asynchronous conferencing, and email. Given this diversity, we analyzed some aspects of Open University students' dialogic behaviour (what they did as they studied, how, and with whom) as they studied physics and chemistry courses. In addition, we compared these findings with those obtained from campus-based college and university students studying similar courses. To carry out such an analysis, a need exists for a broad conceptual framework of instruction that recognizes the centrality of instructional dialogue.

Such a framework was initially proposed as a general theory of distance education (Gorsky & Caspi, 2005) to replace the "Theory of Transactional Distance" (Moore, 1993). The framework subsequently evolved into the "Theory of Instructional Dialogue" (Gorsky, Caspi & Chajut, 2007); the theory provides a useful working model for analyzing, designing, evaluating, and predicting outcomes in any instructional system, whether distance or campus-based.

This chapter includes three sections: (1) an overview of the "Theory of Instructional Dialogue" with emphasis placed *only* on its analytic capabilities. Prescriptive and predictive elements of the theory are *not* discussed (for an in-depth explication, see Gorsky, Caspi & Chajut, 2007); (2) a review of published empirical research findings that illustrate how Open University students and their campus-based counterparts learn science in terms of dialogues and supporting resources; and (3) current research projects and suggestions for further research.

## THE THEORY OF INSTRUCTIONAL DIALOGUE: AN OVERVIEW

The theory is based on the axiom that instruction is dialogue. Given this axiom, we assume three postulates:

> 1. Every element in an instructional system is *either* a dialogue (intrapersonal or interpersonal) *or* a resource which supports dialogue.
> 2. Certain structural and human resources, common to all instructional systems, correlate with the type, amount, and duration of dialogue that occurs, or may occur.
> 3. Specific, situated dialogues correlate with learning outcomes.

For the purposes of this chapter, only the first postulate is discussed.

### Intrapersonal dialogue

Intrapersonal dialogue *mediates* learning (Gorsky, Caspi & Chajut, 2007). It is defined as the interaction between a human resource (the learner) and a structural resource (any subject matter material, such as texts or instructional web sites, provided within any given course). This approach enables us to quantify students' study/learning behaviours in terms of media choice (which resources were utilized, when, and where), utilization rates, "time on task," instructional outcomes and efficiencies. Students, of course, may utilize subject matter materials other than those offered by the course. Such materials are not "structural resources" since they are not specifically designated by the teacher.

The type, extent, and quality of intrapersonal dialogue that occurs in any given course or instructional system is related to variables that characterize learners (age, prior knowledge, motivation, learning styles, perceived course difficulty, and other possible variables that define the student's predisposition toward learning) and variables that characterize structural resources, especially their usability and quality.

We note that the mental processes assumed to occur during intrapersonal dialogue have been described in many ways: "assimilation" and "accommodation" (Piaget, 1970), "accretion," "structuring," and "tuning" (Rumelhart & Norman, 1978), "intra-psychological processes" (Vygotsky, 1978) or an "an internal didactic conversation" (Holmberg, 1989). We reiterate that the Theory of Instructional Dialogue deals only with quantifiable instructional events, not with learning processes that occur or not.

## Interpersonal dialogue

Interpersonal dialogue *facilitates* learning. This is supported historically by leading philosophers and educationists of the previous century (Dewey, 1916; Buber, 1965; Bruner, 1966; Rogers, 1965, 1969; Vygotsky, 1978). More up-to-date findings also support this claim (Wells, 1999; Laurillard, 2002; Garrison & Anderson, 2003). To summarize, Rogers (1965) wrote: "We cannot teach another person directly; we can only facilitate his learning" (p. 389). Interpersonal dialogue is defined as the interaction between two or more human resources (instructors and/or students). Interaction is an observable message loop: Instructor-Student-Instructor *or* Student-Instructor-Student *or* Student A-Student B-Student A. Such dialogues may be face-to-face or mediated; if mediated, synchronous or asynchronous. Students, of course, may engage in dialogues with significant others such as family, friends, or employers. These human resources, however, are not within the domain of instructional systems. Interpersonal dialogue has two distinct classes of outputs: subject-matter oriented and non-subject-matter oriented. One or both types may characterize a message.

Earlier studies have found that the extent of interpersonal dialogue is affected to a very large degree by three structural variables:

1. instructional design (Clark, 1983, 1994, 2004; Clark & Choi, 2005; Gorsky, Caspi & Trumper, 2004);
2. group size (Chen & Willits, 1998; Vrasidas & McIsaac, 1999; Caspi, Gorsky & Chajut, 2003); and
3. student and instructor availability (Chen, 2001a, b; Gorsky, Caspi & Tuvi-Arad, 2004; Gorsky, Caspi & Trumper, 2004)

and by two variables associated with human resources (i.e., individual learners):

1. prior acquaintance with fellow students (Caspi & Gorsky, 2006); and
2. autonomy (Moore, 1993; Caspi & Gorsky, 2006).

Instructors' personality traits and facilitation skills play a critical role in creating and maintaining dialogue with students, be it online or on-site. A teacher-centred, content-oriented approach decreases opportunities for interpersonal dialogue while a student-centred, learning-oriented approach may increase such opportunities.

The following two examples describe interpersonal dialogues in terms of human and structural resources:

1. Student A phones Student B to discuss the concept of angular momentum, which he doesn't understand. The availability of students' telephone numbers is a structural resource for interpersonal dialogue. Students are human resources for interpersonal dialogue. A subject-matter oriented dialogue between them occurs.

2. Student J wants the answer to an assigned exercise and posts a message in an asynchronous discussion group. Student K responds and provides an answer. The discussion group is a structural resource that enables interpersonal dialogue. A subject-matter oriented dialogue occurs between Students J and K; both students are human resources for interpersonal dialogue.

The final two examples, cited from Gorsky, Caspi & Chajut (2007), illustrate instructional processes in terms of dialogue types and their associated human and structural resources:

1. A face-to-face tutorial session is led by an instructor who encourages discussion. The tutorial is a structural resource for *both* intrapersonal and interpersonal dialogue. Instructor and students are human resources for dialogue.
· Student X attended and listened attentively, but did not actively participate. This student utilized the resource for intrapersonal dialogue only; he did not utilize the human resources, instructor, and fellow students for direct interpersonal dialogue.
· Student Y attended the same tutorial and, in addition to listening attentively, also asked the instructor several questions that were answered to her satisfaction. This student utilized the resource for *both* intrapersonal and interpersonal dialogue.

2. An instructor distributes exercises to her students. A student solves the assigned exercises and submits them

to the instructor, who then corrects, grades, and returns them to the student. The student reads the corrected exercises and understands the source of his mistakes.

The assigned exercise is a structural resource for *both* intrapersonal and interpersonal dialogue. The dialogue is intrapersonal as the student solves the exercises. It becomes interpersonal when the student submits the completed exercise to the instructor, thereby closing the loop — instructor to student, student to instructor. An additional interpersonal link occurs when the instructor returns the corrected exercise to the student. A further *intra*personal dialogue occurs when the student reads the corrected exercises with the intent to learn from them.

This brief overview should enable the reader to understand and to evaluate the following research findings and conclusions within the paradigm of the "Theory of Instructional Dialogue."

## LEARNING SCIENCE AT A DISTANCE: RESEARCH FINDINGS, CONCLUSIONS, AND IMPLICATIONS

### Findings from empirical studies

To date, a total of five studies that map students' dialogic behaviour as they learn science at a distance have been published. Findings and conclusions from these studies are reported below.

Two small-scale qualitative studies investigated the dialogic behaviour of distance education students as they studied introductory level courses in chemistry and physics at the Open University of Israel. In the first (Gorsky, Caspi & Tuvi-Arad, 2004), 10 out of a total of 128 students who completed the course "Pathways in Chemistry" participated in the study. In the second (Gorsky, Caspi & Trumper, 2004), 8 students out of 41 who had completed the course "Foundations of Physics II" participated. All participating students met the following two criteria: they had successfully completed at least two science courses in previous semesters and they expressed a willingness to explore their own learning processes. The first criterion ensured that students were experienced in distance learning so that their study behaviour would be the result of conscious decision making and not the result of random trial and error.

Data were gathered from semi-structured interviews lasting about 40–60 minutes. Each student was interviewed once, toward the end of the course. Participants were asked neutral and open-ended questions which also probed for particular, idiosyncratic aspects of experience. The following examples are cited from Gorsky, Caspi, and Tuvi-Arad (2004):

- How did you learn? (continuously or by "cramming"?)
- Did you personally communicate with the instructor or with other students?
- Did you post messages on the website?
- What did you do when you couldn't solve a problem?
- How did your study practices in chemistry compare with how you studied in other courses?
- Were these other courses simpler or more difficult than the chemistry course?

Five major findings were reported:

1. *All* activities engaged in by students as they studied/learned introductory level undergraduate chemistry and physics courses could be categorized as dialogues enabled by a given resource.
2. A general approach to the use of dialogue was discerned. All students cited a clear preference for intrapersonal dialogue. This finding is supported by several other research studies (Rourke et al., 1999; Rourke & Anderson, 2002). At the start of the courses, intrapersonal dialogue, mediated through self-instruction texts and tutorials, was the primary dialogue

type utilized by students. This general course of action, individual study through self-instruction materials, is indeed the paradigm of distance education at the Open University of Israel.

3. Students opted for interpersonal dialogue only when they couldn't solve assigned problems.

4. The predominant first-partner choice for interpersonal dialogue was peers. Instructor-student dialogues were generally used as a last resort. Students reported that instructors offered concept explication as opposed to giving them the desired answer. Therefore, most students preferred collaborating with peers rather than with the instructor.

5. The preferred communication mode was synchronous, mediated first by telephone and second by face-to-face meetings. Asynchronous communication, offered by the website, was utilized to a limited extent. These preferences reflect student desire for immediate answers.

In a third small-scale study, Gorsky, Caspi, and Trumper (2006) investigated the dialogic behaviour of campus-based college and university students learning physics and chemistry in large and small classes. This study was carried out in order to compare the dialogic behaviours of campus-based students with distance education students. A total of 14 students participated in the study: 4 physics majors and 4 chemistry majors from a large university alongside 6 physics majors from a small college. As in the previous two qualitative studies, data were gathered from semi-structured interviews. Findings follow:

1. For most university students participating in large introductory level lecture-based courses (about 175 students), interpersonal dialogue was not a significant dialogue mode engaged in while learning physics and chemistry in the classroom. At any given lecture, more

than 90% of the students did not engage in interpersonal instructor-student dialogue. Even though tutorials were more interactive than lectures, they constituted only 20% of total instruction time.

2. For college students participating in small introductory level courses (about 12 students), interpersonal dialogue was a significant dialogue mode for learning in the classroom.

3. For both college and university students, interpersonal student-student dialogue was the primary dialogue mode engaged in for the purpose of solving problems. In other words, students predominantly turned to one another for help in problem solving, not to instructors.

Gorsky, Caspi, and Trumper (2006) noted that the first two findings illustrate clearly the impact of group size and instructional strategy on dialogue. The small group size at the college (a structural resource) afforded the *potential* for discussion-based class sessions while faculty (human resources) *chose* to implement this instructional strategy. Furthermore, the first finding highlights discrepancies between instructional theories on the one hand and actual practices engaged in by campus-based students participating in large lecture-oriented courses, on the other. Classical theories, such as those advanced by Bruner (1966) and Rogers (1969), as well as more recent ones (Garrison & Anderson, 2003), often assign an importance to interpersonal dialogue, especially instructor-student interactions, that may not be realized in practice. This finding was also reported by Beyth-Marom, Saporta, and Caspi (2005). Indeed, instructor-student dialogue in large lecture courses was very limited in scope. The third finding, highlighting the importance of peer dialogue for campus-based students, replicated findings from the first two studies.

Based on these preliminary findings, we developed a "Tactical Approaches to Study" questionnaire (see Appendix) appropriate for large-scale studies. In our fourth study (Caspi & Gorsky, 2006), this questionnaire was distributed via e-mail to 3,512 students at the Open University of Israel, and 521 completed questionnaires were returned. Here, participating students represented all faculties and disciplines, not just physics and chemistry. Findings from the smaller-scale qualitative studies were replicated. In other words, the dialogic behaviour of distance education students from all disciplines, not just the exact sciences, was similar.

In addition, several correlations between students' self-reported characteristics and their corresponding dialogic behaviour were found.

> 1. Students having prior acquaintances with peers generally turned to peers for help while students without prior acquaintances generally turned to the website or asked questions at the tutorial sessions.
> 2. Students who reported a preference for working alone (high autonomy) generally posted questions on the website or asked questions at the face-to-face tutorials. Less autonomous students generally turned to peers.

In the fifth study (Gorsky, Caspi & Smidt, 2007), the dialogic behaviour of 121 Open University UK students was investigated as a function of perceived course difficulty. Here, all 355 students studying an advanced level quantum mechanics course were sent written questionnaires. Of the 123 students who returned the questionnaires, 121 perceived the course as difficult or very difficult. Again, previous findings were replicated, namely, students tend to study and learn alone until confronted with an insurmountable obstacle, either a concept not understood or, most commonly, a problem that can't be solved. One finding, however, was quite different. We found that a very large majority of students turned to instructors for help, not to their peers. This finding differed from previous ones wherein Israeli students turned overwhelmingly to peers for help, not to instructors.

## Conclusions and implications

The findings from these five studies are straightforward and not surprising, *at least in retrospect*. What we believe important, however, is that these anecdotal and unrelated truisms are now grounded and linked in a unified framework or theory of instruction. We have suggested (Gorsky, Caspi & Chajut, 2007) that the widespread use of the theory will enable researchers to work from a common frame of reference with a common set of variables toward a common goal.

*Implications for distance education and online science courses*
First, we contend that the unified theory relates to online instructional design in precisely the same manner that it relates to any and all instructional systems. The structural resources for intra- and interpersonal dialogue (instructional materials, group size, instructional strategy, and instructor/peer accessibility) are the same. The only difference lies in the amount and type of resources, not in the instructional dialogues that occur or not. In addition, the human resources for interpersonal dialogue (instructors' facilitation skills, students' autonomy, and their need to overcome conceptual difficulty or to solve an insoluble problem) are also the same.

Furthermore, we contend that the mere existence of additional online resources has no significant effect on the learning process itself, although it may change students' satisfaction or attitudes toward learning. For example, in terms of achievement, an on-ground lecture and an online recorded copy of the lecture have essentially the same impact on learners (Beyth-Marom, Saporta & Caspi, 2005). Similar findings were noted when comparing students participating in remote videoconferencing with students attending on-ground lectures (Lou, Bernard & Abrami, 2006). The fact that all instructional resources are available for online and on-ground learners implies that there is nothing unique about online instruction *per se* and the subsequent learning that occurs or not.

Second, some initial and tentative practical implications vis-à-vis the relationship between perceived course difficulty and dialogic behaviour have emerged. To summarize the findings:

1. In courses perceived as difficult, (UK) students turned primarily to instructors for help when confronted with difficulty.
2. In courses perceived as moderately difficult or easy, (Israeli) students turned primarily to peers for help when confronted with difficulty.

These phenomena may be culturally biased. Further research will provide answers. In practical terms, however, these findings can help us optimize class size as a function of perceived course difficulty. On the one hand, if instructor-student dialogues are limited in "easy" or "moderately difficult" courses, then a large class size may be feasible and justifiable, both from economic and pedagogical points of view. On the other hand, if levels of instructor-student dialogue are high in "difficult" courses (as we have found), then a small class size may be feasible and justifiable, both from economic and pedagogical points of view (a higher rate of student success along with a reduction in dropout rates may be attained given a higher level of instructor presence).

Third, the correlation between "prior acquaintance with peers" and dialogic behaviour seems straightforward and meaningful: students who know other students speak with them. If so, and if such relationships help students learn as several educational theories contend and research findings have supported (Anderson, 2004; Ashwin, 2003; Garrison & Anderson, 2003), then organizational steps may be taken by both campus-based and distance education universities to help students become acquainted with each other prior to, or at the start of a course or program. Instructors might actively encourage students to participate in study groups, be they face-to-face or virtual. Furthermore, virtual forums, both synchronous and asynchronous, should be set up and their use encouraged.

## CURRENT AND FURTHER RESEARCH

1. The dialogic behaviour of diverse populations. We are currently exploring on a large scale (N>3,000) the dialogic behaviour of K-12 students as they learn in the classroom and as they learn at home by dealing with homework assignments. We hope to map students' dialogic behaviour as a function of age, gender, academic discipline, socio-economic background, etc.

2. The cross-cultural aspects of dialogic behaviour. We have found that western students, both distance and campus-based, tend to study and learn alone. Students turned to interpersonal dialogue in order to resolve some specific difficulty. From informal meetings with colleagues, it seems that eastern cultures adhere to group learning. We suggest comparing the dialogic behaviour of students from diverse cultures and backgrounds in order to discover, what, if any, aspects of learning are universal.

3. To expand the theory's second postulate, namely, that certain structural and human resources, common to all instructional systems, correlate with the type, amount, and duration of dialogue that occurs, or may occur, both in-class and out. Some typical research questions might be:
· Students' dialogic behaviour may be correlated with a changing rate of instructor accessibility.
· What are the optimal limits for instructor accessibility, especially for courses perceived as difficult by students?
· To what extent, if any, should expensive communications media (structural resources) be made available?
· What kinds of intrapersonal structural resources (hyper-text, simulations, etc.) best support constructivist pedagogy and under what circumstances?

· To investigate the relationship, if any, between students' strategic approaches to study (deep/shallow) and the tactics they adopt to implement their strategies (dialogic behaviour). The importance of the research lies in the possibility that a relationship does indeed exist between students' strategic and tactical approaches to learning. For example, students' adoption of deep or surface-level approaches may be investigated as a function of the structural resources (e.g., course websites, videotaped lectures, or synchronous and asynchronous communication tools, etc.) available in an instructional system. Certain structural resources may enhance the use of deep-level approaches by students.

4. To investigate the theory's third postulate, namely, that specific, situated dialogues correlate with learning outcomes. Some typical research questions:
· What kinds of interpersonal dialogue types (inquiry, conversation, instruction, and debate) facilitate or retard students' abilities to make conceptual changes?
· Assuming a relation between "communities of inquiry" (Garrison & Anderson, 2003) and learning outcomes, what is an effective ratio between non-subject-matter (social presence) and subject-matter oriented dialogues (cognitive resence)?

These research questions are all interrelated in a single unified theory that assumes instruction is dialogue. To conclude, we're talking about building working models for *all* instructional systems in the cognitive domain based on dialogues and resources. We believe that such an endeavour, based on valid qualitative and quantitative research, will advance our field to new levels.

## REFERENCES

Anderson, T. (2004). Teaching in an online learning context. In T. Anderson & F. Elloumni (Eds.) *Theory and practice of online learning* (pp. 271-294). Athabasca: Athabasca University Press. Retrieved February 26, 2009, from: http://cde.athabascau.ca/online_book

Ashwin, P. (2003). Peer support: Relations between the context, process and outcomes for the students who are supported. *Instructional Science, 31,* 159-173.

Beyth-Marom, R., Saporta, K., & Caspi, A. (2005). Synchronous vs. asynchronous tutorials: Factors affecting students' preferences and choices. *Journal of Research on Technology in Education, 37,* 245-262.

Bruner, J.S. (1966). *Toward a theory of instruction.* Cambridge, MA: Harvard University Press.

Buber, M. (1965). *Between man and man* (R.G. Smith, Trans.). New York: Macmillan.

Caspi, A., Gorsky, P., & Chajut, E. (2003). The influence of group size on non-mandatory asynchronous instructional discussion groups. *The Internet and Higher Education, 6,* 227-240.

Caspi, A., & Gorsky, P. (2006). The dialogic behavior of Open University students. *Studies in Higher Education, 31,* 735-752.

Chen, Y.-J., & Willits, F.K. (1998). A path analysis of the concepts in Moore's theory of transactional distance in a videoconferencing learning environment. *The Journal of Distance Education, 13*(2), 51-65.

Chen, Y.-J. (2001a). Transactional distance in World Wide Web learning environments. *Innovations in Education and Teaching International, 38,* 327-338.

Chen, Y.-J. (2001b). Dimensions of transactional distance in World Wide Web learning environment: A factor analysis. *British Journal of Educational Technology, 32,* 459-470.

Clark, R.E. (1983). Reconsidering research on learning from media. *Review of Educational Research, 53,* 445-459.

Clark, R.E. (1994). Media will never influence learning. *Educational Technology Research and Development, 42*(2), 21-29.

Clark, R.E. (2004). What works in distance learning: Instructional strategies. In H. O'Neil (Ed.) *What works in distance learning: Guidelines.* Greenwich, CT: Information Age Publishers.

Clark, R.E., & Choi, S. (2005). Five design principles for experiments on the effects of animated pedagogical agents. *Journal of Educational Computing Research, 32,* 209–223.

Dewey, J. (1916). *Democracy and education.* Toronto: The Macmillan Co.

Garrison, D.R., & Anderson, T. (2003). *E-Learning in the 21$^{st}$ century: A framework for research and practice.* London: Routledge.

Gorsky, P., & Caspi, A. (2005a). Dialogue: A theoretical framework for distance education instructional systems. *British Journal of Educational Technology, 36,* 137–144.

Gorsky, P., Caspi, A., & Chajut, E. (2007). The Theory of Instructional Dialogue: Toward a Unified Theory of Instructional Design. In Zheng, R. & Ferris, S.P. (Eds.) *Understanding Online Instructional Modeling: Theories and Practices.* Hershey, PA: Idea Group Inc.

Gorsky, P., Caspi, A., & Smidt, S. (2007). Use of instructional dialogue by university students in a difficult distance education physics course. *Journal of Distance Education,* 21(3), 1–22.

Gorsky, P., Caspi, A., & Trumper, R. (2004). Dialogue in a distance education physics course. *Open Learning, 19,* 265–277.

Gorsky, P., Caspi, A., & Trumper, R. (2006). Campus-based university students' use of dialogue. *Studies in Higher Education. 31,* 71–87.

Gorsky, P., Caspi, A., & Tuvi-Arad, I. (2004). Use of instructional dialogue by university students in a distance education chemistry course. *Journal of Distance Education,* 19(1), 1–19.

Holmberg, B. (1989). *Theory and practice of distance education.* Routledge, London.

Laurillard, D. (2002). *Rethinking university teaching. A conversational framework for the effective use of learning technologies.* London: Routledge.

Lou, Y., Bernard, R.M., & Abrami, P.C. (2006). Media and pedagogy in undergraduate distance education: A theory-based meta-analysis of empirical literature. *Educational Technology Research and Development, 54,* 141–176.

Moore, M.G. (1993). Theory of transactional distance. In D. Keegan (Ed.), *Theoretical principles of distance education* (pp. 22–38). New York: Routledge.

Piaget, J. (1970). *The science of education and the psychology of the child.* NY: Grossman.

Rogers, C. (1965). *Client-centered therapy.* London: Constable.

Rogers, C. (1969). *Freedom to learn.* Columbus: Merrill Publishing Co.

Rourke, L., Anderson, T., Garrison, D., & Archer, W. (1999). Assessing social presence in asynchronous text-based computer conferencing. *Journal of Distance Education, 14*(2), 50–71.

Rourke, L., & Anderson, T. (2002). Exploring social presence in computer conferencing. *Journal of Interactive Learning Research, 13*, 259–275.

Rumelhart, D., & Norman, D. (1978). Accretion, tuning and restructuring: Three modes of learning. In J.W. Cotton & R. Klatzky (Eds.) *Semantic Factors in Cognition.* Hillsdale, NJ: Erlbaum.

Vygotsky, L.S. (1978). *Mind in society: The Development of Higher Psychological Processes.* Cambridge, MA: Harvard University Press.

Vrasidas, C., & McIsaac, S.M. (1999). Factors influencing interaction in an online course. *The American Journal of Distance Education, 13*(3), 22–36.

Wells, G. (1999). Reconceptualizing education as dialogue. *Annual Review of Applied Linguistics, 19*, 135–155.

## APPENDIX

Tactical Approaches to Study Questionnaire
(for distance education students)

1. Age: ____
2. Gender: M / F
3. How do you rate your motivation to achieve a high grade? very high, high, moderate, low or very low
4. How difficult do you consider the course to be? very difficult, difficult, moderate, easy or very easy
5. How do you prefer to learn? independently or with others
6. Did you know at least one other student in the course before you started? Y / N

How did you typically address conceptual difficulties that occurred while reading the course materials? Mark *all* actions undertaken:

a. reread the text(s) Y / N
b. found alternative texts or instructional materials Y / N
c. <u>without</u> participating, browsed the (asynchronous) course forum Y / N
d. contacted another student from the course Y / N

- if yes, then typically how (circle the appropriate response):
    1. face-to-face meeting
    2. telephone
    3. email
    4. asynchronous course forum
    5. other _____

e. contacted your tutor Y / N
- if yes, then typically how (circle the appropriate response):
    1. face-to-face meeting
    2. telephone
    3. email
    4. course forum
    5. other _____

f. contacted someone from outside the course (parent, friend, employer, etc.) Y / N

g. asked a question at the next tutorial Y / N

h. gave up Y / N

i. enter any other additional actions taken: _____

7. List the order in which your <u>first four actions</u> were carried out (enter the appropriate letter) and estimate the relative contribution made by each (Total 100%).
    1$^{st}$ action: ____ ; relative contribution: ____%
    2$^{nd}$ action: ____ ; relative contribution: ____%
    3$^{rd}$ action: ____ ; relative contribution: ____%
    4$^{th}$ action: ____ ; relative contribution: ____%

{Questions 9 and 10 are identical to questions 7 and 8 except that they refer to solving difficult problems or exercises}

# Chapter 3
## Leadership Strategies for Coordinating Distance Education Instructional Development Teams

GALE PARCHOMA
Lancaster University

### Introduction
Boundaries between classroom-based, blended, and distance education are blurring. Contemporary classroom-based courses typically have a course website. Instructors' editions of textbooks include PowerPoint lectures that can be either presented in a classroom or licensed for distance distribution. Students' editions include e-tutorials and quizzes for independent learning. Classroom 'contact' hours are being reduced via the introduction of Web-based video lectures, online tutorials, discussions, virtual laboratories, simulations, and more recently, academic computer gaming (Naylor, 2005; Parchoma et al., 2007). Social software applications, Second Life, MySpace, and Facebook, along with blogs, wikis, podcasts, and e-portfolios, are commonly incorporated into learning designs across delivery modes (Wasson, 2006). Key administrative services, such as Web-based registration, assignment 'drop-boxes', grade reports, and transcript orders have been moved online. This "fusion of face-to-face and technology mediated learning experiences" (Garrison & Vaughan, 2008, p. 5) is making it increasingly difficult to define distance education (DE) and delineate

DE-specific practices from common practices in contemporary higher education.

However, only distance educators deal with the unique challenges of motivating, teaching, and evaluating the work of learners whom they never meet in a face-to-face setting. This lack of same-time, same-place contact expands the transactional distance between educators and learners. Transactional distance is pedagogical, rather than geographic; overcoming it requires specialized instructional structures and dialogic teaching approaches (Moore, 1991). Developing DE teaching and learning activities involves applying learning theory and design, communication theory, organizational theory, human-computer interaction theory, media expertise, and project management skills to create appropriate instructional structures and pedagogical approaches to meet the needs of DE learners (Bates, 2000). For scientists, acquiring and maintaining current, in-depth understanding of these disparate fields, in addition to specialized scientific knowledge, is not always possible. Therefore, most scientists need to work collaboratively with teams of specialists occupying emergent educational and technical roles in higher education (Bates, 2000; Hanley, 2001; Hanna, 2000). Thus, DE project leadership requires a shift from perceiving teaching as fulfilling a traditional, independent role to "one where teaching and learning are the products of an integrated group of individuals" (Hanley, 2001, p. 59).

## Overview of the chapter

This chapter is intentionally practical and purpose-driven. The first section provides a brief history of DE for the purpose of providing new project leaders with a backdrop of existing perspectives and practices. The ensuing development team section describes roles of team members and outlines typical processes development team leaders need to manage. The social negotiation section addresses the 'soft skills' side of leadership through a research-based model of stages of DE development team formation. The chapter concludes with suggestions for sources of support for leadership activities.

## Dichotomy of voice

Two voices are juxtaposed in this chapter. The historical section is based on a review of distance education literature, and it is written in an expository voice. The remainder of the work is written in a narrative voice because it is based on my personal experiences as a distance education student, an instructional designer, a faculty leader for DE development teams, and finally, as an educational researcher.

## Distance education: perspectives and practices

Multiple definitions of DE are scattered across disciplinary literatures. Over time—within discipline-specific literatures—commonplace DE terms have been subject to diverse interpretations. As DE development teams are made up of individuals from a variety of disciplinary backgrounds, and who have varying degrees of experience and a range of philosophical and theoretical perspectives on instructional development, effective communication can be problematic. I have included a brief history of DE in order to provide project leaders with practical insights into a range of DE perspectives and their associated terminologies, as well as approaches to constructing a shared project vision among team members.

## Five generations of distance education

Over the approximately 150 years of DE history, the field has evolved to include five "generations" of practice (Taylor, 2001). Each of the generations has been distinguished from the others by the technologies used for communication and content distribution. While the term 'generations' suggests a progression from one set of technologies and practices to another, in the field of DE, each new generation has most often added new technologies and practices, rather than replacing existing ones.

*First generation, Correspondence-based* DE consisted of print-based course content distribution and infrequent post-based communications between the instructor and the learner, as well as between the learner and institution administrators (Anderson & Elloumi, 2004). Predominant theories of learning were undergoing a process of change in this early era of DE. Behavioural psychology and educational measurement were beginning to displace a long-held view:

> That the mind, like the body, could be developed with exercise. That the study of certain disciplines would improve the mind just like callisthenics could improve certain muscles. (McNeil, 2007, ¶ 4)

About a hundred years later, *second generation, Multi-media* DE added audio and video tapes, along with early computer-based programmed learning, to content delivery models, and telephone service to communications options (Taylor, 2001). However, print packages of readings, delivered by mail, remained a mainstay of these two generations.

In both first and second generation models, communications tended to be limited to learner-to-institution and institution-to-learner communications to accomplish administrative tasks, and infrequent learner-to-instructor and instructor-to-learner communications for the purpose of accomplishing academic tasks. For the most part, learners were passive recipients of packaged instructional materials. As a result, a common criticism of first and second generation DE was that learners were left to learn in isolation, and as a result, attrition rates were often high (Potashnik & Capper, 1998).

Throughout the first two generations of DE, educational theory and practice focused on expanding and refining applications of research from behavioural psychology to the processes of teaching and learning. Task analysis, learning objectives, and programmed instruction came to the fore. Programmed instruction was characterized by behavioural objectives, small chunks of instruction, independent learning and self-pacing, required learner responses to periodic questions, and immediate feedback on the quality of responses (McNeil, 2007).

Glaser (1962) introduced the idea of instruction as a system, made up of discrete components in carefully pre-defined sequences designed to complete a learning process. Over time, applications of strictly sequenced, highly structured approaches to developing instruction for independent learning proved somewhat effective in supporting rote learning of factual material, but it did not well support critical thinking or problem solving in higher education. Better communication tools were needed to support interactions among learners and with instructors in order to allow for discourse and debate in DE.

*Third generation, Telelearning* DE added broadcast media, such as television and radio to content delivery. Teleconferencing and videoconferencing introduced opportunities for synchronous instructor-to-cohort and learner-to-learner communications (Anderson & Elloumi, 2004).

In concert with advances in third generation media — for which larger production teams were required — the need to better understand instructional development teams emerged. The *British Journal of Educational Technology* was launched:

> To meet that need for an informed dialogue, to provide links between research workers and teachers, educational planners and administrators, and between public educational systems and the broadcasting, publishing and other information agencies involved in the production and dissemination of learning materials. [The journal was, from the outset designed to be] interdisciplinary in character because the improvement of learning is by its nature an inter-disciplinary and co-

> operative process; and because there is no formal discipline which encompasses the extensive repertoire of theories and practices with which educational technology is concerned. (Black, 1970)

During the 1970s and 1980s, Robert Gagne introduced a professional model for instructional designers. Gagne's model blended behaviouralist learning theories and cognitivist learning theories to designing conditions for and events of instruction. This work underpinned the development of instructional systems design and human performance technology schools of thought (Merrill, 2002).

In the closing decade of the twentieth century, Internet- and Web-based access to hypertext content, computer-mediated synchronous and asynchronous communication, along with software to support collaborative student projects as well as instructional administration tasks, marked the transition to *fourth generation, Flexible Learning* DE (Taylor, 2001). Developments in electronic access to library catalogues, databases, journals, and books provided the necessary resources to support graduate students in DE. Concurrent expansion of the knowledge economy rapidly increased demand from knowledge workers for DE access to both undergraduate and graduate higher education (Bates, 2000; Mohan & Daniel, 2004; Hanna, 2000). For-profit 'virtual' universities emerged to meet these demands, and for the first time, higher education had corporate competitors (Archer, Garrison & Anderson, 1999).

Traditional universities responded by expanding DE access and adopting selected DE practices into campus-based teaching. The combination of the availability of sophisticated ICT tools and the need to use these tools to provide DE access to all levels and modes of higher education made large-scale use DE tools desirable because they were perceived as necessary and practical solutions to emergent challenges (Rogers, 1995). However, uneven effectiveness in applications of DE tools in new contexts, as evidenced by the failure of many for-profit higher education ventures (DiPaolo,

2003), as well as persistent concerns about attrition rates in traditional universities' online course offerings (Carr, 2000), sparked new areas of research and practices in DE.

Communications and organizational theories currently rival psychological theories in the study of learning. Logan and Stokes (2003) synthesize ideas from each of these fields in their analysis of how the Internet is influencing contemporary life. They argue that there are five collaborative messages of the Internet: (1) two-way flow of information, (2) ease and speed of access to information, (3) continuous learning, (4) alignment and integration of common objectives, and (5) creation of community (Logan & Stokes, 2003). Interest in collaboration (Daniel, Schwier & McCalla, 2003), continuous learning (Ghosh, 2004), and the creation of networked learning communities (Hodgson & Reynolds, 2005; McConnell, 2006; Schwier, 2001) have come to the fore.

The nature of knowledge itself came under re-examination in the *fourth generation* DE era. Proponents of constructivism have rejected conceptual models of learning that claim objective knowledge that can be transmitted from instructors to learners (West & Graham, 2007). Constructivism is neither a learning theory nor a design method (Jonassen, 2006); rather it is an epistemological stance on collaborative knowledge creation on which design innovations, such as problem-based learning, microworlds (gaming), and simulations, have been based (Jonassen, 2006).

*Fourth generation* technologies include learning management systems (LMS), such as *WebCT*, *BlackBoard* and *Moodle*. Social negotiation tools, including blogs, wikis, podcasts, and e-portfolios have also been applied to supporting learners in collaborative knowledge construction in fourth generation e-learning environments.

*Fifth generation, Intelligent Flexible Learning* DE has expanded e-learning to include e-commerce applications for administrative functions, such as registration, fee payment, access to campus-based services, and transcripts (Taylor, 2001). However, what really distinguishes fifth generation DE from earlier generations is the addition of automated response systems (Taylor, 2001), which are based on intelligent agent (IA) technologies capable of real-time individualization and customization of e-learning environments (Zaïane, 2002).

While the implications of fifth generation DE for research and practice are still unfolding, initial indicators include an expansion of interdisciplinary research into teaching and learning across more and more diverse settings (e.g., Daniel, Schwier & McCalla, 2003; Durham & Arrell, 2007; Giddings, Campbell & Maclaren, 2006; McCalla, 2004; Parchoma, et al., 2007). As fifth generation DE projects increasingly involve international institutional partnerships, inter-culturality and identity in e-learning spaces are also emerging as fields of interest and debate (Durham & Arrell, 2007; Hung & Chen, 2007; Rogers, Graham & Mayes, 2007).

While a great deal is changing at an almost alarming pace, much remains the same. Modified versions of each of the first four generations of DE technologies and pedagogies persist. There are substantive and pragmatic reasons for continuing to offer this range of 'low-tech' DE options. Early generation DE technologies and practices still provide access to higher education for groups of learners whose geographic, economic, demographic, political, and cultural contexts preclude access via more current modes.

## Your development team

Prior to the formation of a development team, faculty leaders often work within departments or colleges, and perhaps, with external institutions, funding agencies, or publishing houses to define the scope of a DE project. This process can include extensive program, curriculum, and course planning. Typically, the plan undergoes peer review and approval processes. When a plan is finally approved, it typically identifies potential students, defines topics for instruction and required readings, outlines major learning goals and assessment strategies, predicts technologies and modes of instruction, and includes a timeline and a budget. As a leader of a DE development team, by the time you have guided a project plan through these lengthy processes, you will rightfully feel a strong sense of ownership of the project. Paradoxically, this is often when the DE team is formed. If you are new to DE development projects, it may be a bit difficult to suddenly make the shift from the independence and personal initiative needed to get the project approved to the interdependence required to lead a team project through to completion. Understanding team members' expertise sets and potential project roles can assist you in meeting those challenges.

DE development team membership varies across institutions, as well as among individual projects. Institutional e-learning strategies, organizational structures, and unit functions, as well as funding levels for individual projects, all influence the number of specialized educational and technical staff available to support you. While development teams are made up various numbers of individuals, typically teams are comprised of members who provide three general kinds of expertise: subject matter expertise, educational expertise, and media-information technology expertise.

*Team leaders* are often referred to as subject matter experts. As well as specialized scientific subject matter expertise, you have valuable specialized knowledge in the teaching of science. Your comfort levels with using the educational technologies and implementing new teaching practices will be crucial measures for your leadership decisions. No matter what team members tell you can be done, no matter how sophisticated or flashy the result, you are the person who will be guiding students through the completed learning environment, and you must be comfortable with both the technologies and pedagogy of your project.

*Educational specialists* hold a variety of titles across institutional settings, such as instructional designer, instructional developer, course designer, or educational technologist. As this variety of titles suggests, individuals in these roles tend to have a range of academic backgrounds. Typically, they have discipline-based undergraduate or graduate degrees followed by a graduate degree in learning theory or instructional technology. In addition, some individuals will have project management training and experience. Therefore, individual educational specialists will have varying theoretical and practical expertise sets to contribute to your project. The primary remit of an educational specialist is to advise the project leader on structures, functions, pedagogies, and assessment strategies that align well with technological options and media choices.

*Media specialists and information technologists* may have educational backgrounds that include applications of learning theory to developing DE learning resources and learning environments, as well as media production, computer programming, and/or human-computer interaction expertise. The primary remit of a media specialist is to provide high-quality media that support teaching and learning goals. Informational technologists typically build and refine learning environments, integrate media resources into those environments, and provide support for their use.

While the expertise sets required to construct effective electronic learning environments are disparate, it is important to note that there are frequently distinctions to be made between roles and individuals. Getting to know your team members prior to making firm decisions about individual roles and responsibilities will afford you the opportunity to have your project benefit from the full range of expertise sets available to support your efforts.

## Leading a DE development team through the development process

Developing a clear view of the scope and sequence of the work your project team is undertaking will afford you a time management guide and support your efforts to coordinate team activities. There have been a number of theoretical models developed to guide this process, and I have worked with most of them. My recommendation is strongly underpinned by a personal preference for practical approaches to complex tasks.

I have not found any model as useful or as comprehensive as the "tried and true" ADDIE model (Laks, 2005, ¶ 4) for project development. There are five basic phases in the ADDIE model for project development: (1) Analysis, (2) Design, (3) Development, (4) Implementation, and (5) Evaluation. While these phases appear sequential, that is rarely the case (Parchoma, 2003). Expect your team to periodically go a back a step or two, revisit earlier decisions, and make modifications. Progress will be incremental and the process often cyclical.

*Analysis*

There are four general areas for analysis: (1) learner analysis, (2) task analysis, (3) team analysis, and (4) project analysis. In preparing a project plan, you have most likely initiated several important learner and task analyses. You may feel that the analysis stage is already complete.

Team members may not share your sense of completion. Each team member will want to read the project plan, consider where he or she can add value to the project, and prepare suggestions for revisions or refinement. You will need considerable time to negotiate individual team members' roles and responsibilities during this phase. Part of the process of negotiating roles and responsibilities is establishing working definitions for key terms. Dissimilar definitions for common terms can result in contested roles and pervasive delays. While it may not seem as though much progress is accomplished in opening meetings, if you take the time to define a shared project vocabulary, to establish clear working relationships among team members, and to form a shared project vision, you will accelerate all subsequent work.

As it is not possible to predict how applications of team members' expertise sets may influence the development of a project over time, it is good to consider your comfort level with change and with distributed decision making. No doubt, at points throughout the project, team members will ask you to consider unforeseen possibilities, and occasionally, to defer judgments. Leave room for change.

*Design*

The design phase of a DE development project is the creative phase. Design activities include aligning instructional goals, course or program content, required and supplemental resources, teaching strategies, assessment of learner achievement, and course or program evaluation. Typically, the team's educational specialist(s) will review the initial project plan, and in close consultation with the leader, begin to develop a design blueprint. Initial drafts are 'living documents.' A draft begins as an extended syllabus, expands to outline one or more prototypes for review, and evolves into a detailed project blueprint. All team members use the design blueprint to guide their contributions and monitor their progress.

In DE projects where media production, CD ROM development, website programming, electronic simulation, or gaming is planned, the educational specialist(s) and media-IT producers, again in close consultation with you, use the design blueprint to develop storyboards. The term 'storyboard' is borrowed from the film industry. A storyboard is like a cartoon strip. Storyboards are frame-by-frame illustrations of each 'page' or 'place' in the learning environment, accompanied by production notes for still images, audio and video files, animation, hyperlinks, navigation pathways, interactivity options, and feedback. In fifth generation DE projects, user-tracing and intelligent agent specifications are added. Completed storyboards become development blueprints.

Unchecked, creative thinking and innovation can become out-of-control, time- and budget-consuming experiences. Curtailing brainstorming and experimentation activities in the design phase is often difficult and always necessary. Balancing the potential value of suggested innovations against the quality of the end result and the ability to ensure a project is completed on time and within budget will be one of your most daunting leadership tasks.

*Development*
The development phase includes the production of all learning materials, resources, assessment tools, and the learning environment in which they are hosed. Generally, production begins with a prototype, which is piloted, reviewed, and revised in order to create a model for subsequent work.

In projects where third-party learning materials are used, copyright clearance for the use of those materials needs to be secured. In projects where electronic learning resources are produced, media and IT-producers will delegate portions of the production work to members of their staff with appropriate technical skills. In addition, content editors, graphic artists, and other specialty roles may be required.

Three leadership challenges mark the development stage of a DE project: (1) coordinating and monitoring the quality of individual contributions from an expanding project team, (2) ensuring that all contributions fit the vision for the completed project, and (3) maintaining timelines within budget limitations. This is a really good time for you to consider delegating project management and quality control responsibilities to the educational specialist(s) and IT-media producers. Your most important role in this phase is to periodically review progress to ensure that the final production meets your expectations.

*Implementation*
Implementation begins when a DE course or program is offered to students for the first time. Many institutions support continued team involvement for the initial offering of a new DE project. The Media-IT producers who developed the learning environment are often much better equipped than are Help Desk personnel to resolve unexpected technical problems. The team's educational specialist(s) can provide support and advice in responding to student queries, managing the learning environment, and supporting you in becoming proficient in using the environment's features and tools. If

you take full advantage of the benefits of team members' support to make the transition from interdependent development to independent teaching, you will be better able to focus on teaching and leave extraneous concerns to those best equipped to manage them.

*Evaluation*

The first student and/or peer evaluation of a DE course or program will provide you with valuable feedback on what is working well and where improvements can be made. In an ideal world, you and key members of your development team will be able to review the feedback and full team support will be available to refine the DE project. However, universities rarely provide sufficient funding for a full evaluation and revision cycle. Leaders typically need to prioritize revisions and oversee the implementation of as many as is possible. At a minimum, it is important to distribute whatever feedback you receive to your team members to inform their future practice.

## Project leadership as a process of social negotiation

Creating the conditions for a newly formed development team to gel into an effective and creative integrated group of individuals who are highly committed to you and your project, involves negotiating a shared project vision and a sense of trust — based on mutual respect for each individual's expertise set — among team members. An established sense of trust among team members provides a basis for strong commitment to quality work and timely completion.

## A study of project leadership

The following section reports the results of a two-year study I undertook to examine the experiences of faculty team leaders, educational specialists, and media-IT producers involved in DE development projects. I conducted a series of interviews and focus groups with eight project leaders and eight media-IT producers and educational specialists. A purpose for the study was to investigate relationships among team members in order to gain insight into development team dynamics.

The leadership participants in this study were situated in eight of the thirteen colleges (faculties) at a medium-sized, traditional, research-oriented university. The eight media-IT producer and educational specialist were situated in three separate organizational units. Educational and media specialists had a range of academic and experiential backgrounds. All participants reflected on their involvement in technology-enhanced DE development projects over a period of five years: 2000 to 2005.

## Data collection and analysis

My research design included four stages. First, I conducted focus groups with a group of eight media-IT specialists and instructional designers. Data collected from this first stage were analyzed for themes. Participants reviewed and critiqued the findings. Revisions were made.

An outcome of Stage 1 was the identification of fifteen potential leadership participants who had been involved in information-rich projects. Information-rich projects include "critical," "typical," and "politically sensitive" cases (Patton, 1990, pp. 102–103). Critical cases included those projects with exceptionally high or exceptionally low expectations for success. Typical cases were broadly considered "run-of-the-mill" (Patton, p. 102) projects. Politically sensitive cases were those projects where exceptions were made to institutional policies in order to accommodate specialized research or teaching agendas.

Nine of the fifteen potential leadership participants agreed to take part in the subsequent stages of the study. One participant was involved in Stage 2, piloting the study questions. Eight participants engaged in Stage 3, a series of interviews on leadership issues. Data from the first three stages were analyzed for the purpose of developing a leadership model. Study participants reviewed and critiqued the model.

Stage 4 involved soliciting model critiques from project leaders in other settings and examining evidence from other studies to refine the model. The result is a depiction of the life cycle of a successful DE project, based on a three-stage process of negotiated team building and task sharing within a social field.

A social field is an "ecological setting" in which "coexisting social entities, such as groups, subgroups, members, barriers, [and] channels of communication" undergo periods of relative constancy and change (Lewin, 1951, p. 200). The "relative positions of the entities" within the social field illustrate their roles as either driving or restraining forces (Lewin, 1951, p. 200). Driving forces initiate and sustain change; restraining forces resist change. In order to successfully facilitate change, leaders can undertake a three-step process within a social field: *unfreezing, moving,* and *refreezing*. *Unfreezing* involves destabilizing the status quo. *Moving* includes identifying and evaluating the relative strengths of social field forces, considering available options and initiating incremental change. *Refreezing* is the process of supporting a return to a sense of stability in the changed environment. The distillation of reported experiences of participants in this study of DE development teams paralleled Lewin's (1951) leadership model for affecting change.

## Stage 1

At the outset, team members usually have a sense of low social capital. Social capital is here defined as "the stock of active connections among people: the trust, mutual understanding, and shared values and behaviours that bind E members E and make cooperative action possible" (Cohen & Prusak, 2001). In the early stages of team formation, members are typically unsure of their status, roles, and personal responsibilities to project goals, and therefore, often experience strong senses of ambiguity and anxiety. As a result, members' abilities to make decisions and formulate plans tend to be *frozen*.

Building social capital among team members begins with gaining an understanding of members' motivations for involvement and perceptions of their own and others' roles, responsibilities, and status within the team. Delegated roles, responsibilities, and status tend to erode trust. Negotiated roles and responsibilities tap personal talents and expertise sets, and provide the basis for establishing social capital. Project leaders can facilitate the creation of social capital and team loyalty through facilitating role and responsibility negotiations. Rather than being linked to any particular role, status within the team tends to be earned through the value of individual contributions to the project and sustained commitment to completion. See *Figure 1* for an illustration of a naturally *frozen* beginning point for a DE development project.

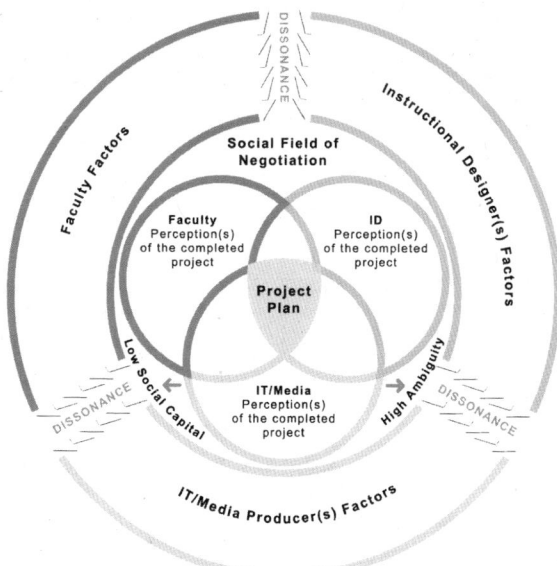

**Figure 1.** Illustration of a DE development project beginning point, where activity and planning processes are **frozen**.

## Stage 2

When negotiations go well, team members gain insight into each other's expertise sets and professional concerns. At this point, the project leader can facilitate *unfreezing*. Initial project plans are collaboratively analyzed to determined scope and goals, learner needs and intended learning outcomes, instructional strategies, and evaluation techniques. Potential media-IT solutions are analyzed for their ability to support over-arching project goals. The range of potential media-IT options is narrowed to a manageable subset. Team members' roles and responsibilities become increasingly well defined. A shared team vision for the project begins to emerge.

Shared work leads to a deeper understanding of and appreciation for each team member's expertise and contributions. Individuals' status in decision-making processes can be established. When team members more clearly understand how their contributions support broader project goals, dissonance and ambiguity decrease and social capital increases.

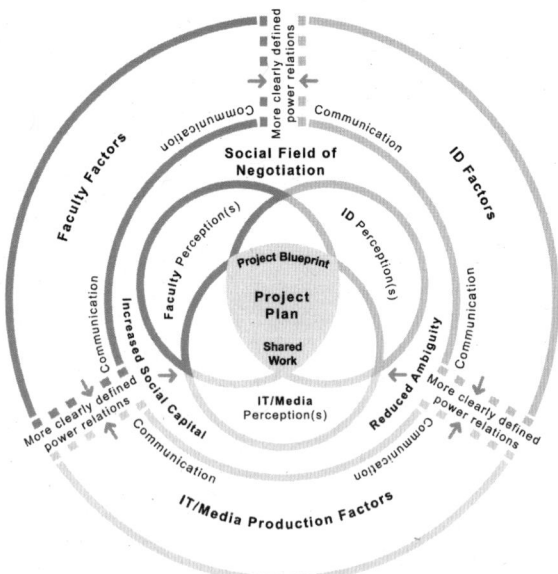

**Figure 2.** Illustration of a project maturing during the negotiation process, where team members are **moving** toward collaborative progress.

As team members move from sharing broadly defined goals to consensus on finer details of the completed project, a collaboratively constructed project blueprint can be completed. The project blueprint becomes an acknowledgement of the value each team member has contributed to refining the project vision. The project team can move on to defining clear specifications for the production phase. See *Figure 2* for an illustration of a project *moving* toward maturity in the negotiation process.

## Stage 3

Affirmation of individual contributions deepens individuals' commitments, increases awareness of all members' needs and perspectives, and promotes willingness to defer individual preferences to maintain harmony across the team effort. With a design blueprint in place, detailed production planning can be undertaken with assurance that timelines and budgets can be mapped to project

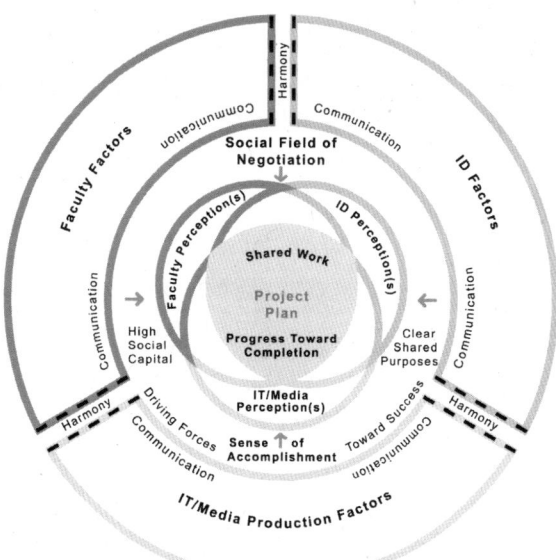

**Figure 3.** Illustration of a project moving toward successful completion, where team members are **refreezing** or stabilizing collaborative efforts of an integrated team.

LEARNING · Chapter Three · 55

specifications. A shared sense of accomplishment and confidence buoys continued collaboration directed toward successful project completion. See *Figure 3* for an illustration of a project *stabilizing* as it moves toward completion.

## Conclusion

This model of project progression is based on successfully completed DE projects. Leaders of every successfully completed DE project in this study encountered some measure of difficulty, disruption, and delay. Scientists are, by definition, expert problem solvers. Expect to meet daunting challenges and be confident that you can lead your team through them.

Your DE development team members will be familiar with the kinds of problems that typically occur in your institutional context. Ask for their advice and trust them to provide insight into solutions. Network with other project leaders within and beyond your disciplinary field. Commiserate on current challenges. Share descriptions of complex problems — the broader your network, the more likely you are to meet a peer who has resolved even the most pervasive problem you will encounter.

Most of all, plan to enjoy the process. One of the participants in this study summarized a common experience among DE project leaders. At the outset, he was enthusiastic. His enthusiasm waned significantly under the pressures of problem solving, negotiating, and a seemingly endless time commitment. He considered abandoning the endeavour. Team members' commitments to project completion helped stay that decision. When the project ended he reflected on the challenges he faced and on the result: "It widened my horizons about how I think about teaching and the whole education process."

# REFERENCES

Anderson, T., & Elloumni, F. (Eds.) (2004). Theory and Practice of Online Learning. Athabasca: Athabasca University Press. Available: http://cde.athabascau.ca/online_book

Archer, W., Garrison, R. & Anderson, T. (1999). Adopting disruptive technologies in traditional universities: Continuing education as an incubator for innovation. *Canadian Journal of University Continuing Education*, 25(1), 13–44.

Archer, W. & Wright, K. (1999). Back to the future: Adjusting university continuing education research to an emerging trend. *Canadian Journal of University Continuing Education*, 25(2), 61–84.

Bates, A.W. (2000). *Managing technological change: Strategies for college and university leaders*. San Francisco, CA: Jossey-Bass.

Black, J. (1970). Editorial. *British Journal of Educational Technology*, 1, 7–8.

Burnes, B. (2004). Kurt Lewin and the planned approach to change: A re-appraisal. *Journal of Management Studies*, 41, 977–1002.

Carr, S. (2000). As distance education comes of age, the challenge is keeping the students. *The Chronicle of Higher Education*. February 11.

Cohen, D. & Prusak, L. (2001). *In good company: How social capital makes organizations work*. Massachusetts: Harvard Business School Press.

Daniel, B., Schwier, R.A. & McCalla, G.I. (2003) Social capital in virtual learning communities and distributed communities of practice. *Canadian Journal of Learning and Technology*, 29(3). Retrieved Febrauary 25, 2009 from: http://www.cjlt.ca/index.php/cjlt/article/view/85/79

DiPaolo, A. (2003). Choices and challenges: Lessons learned in the evolution of online education. *Presentation to the Association of Pacific Rim Universities' 2003 Distance Learning and the Internet conference*. Retrieved February 4, 2009 from: the National University of Singapore's Web site: http://www.cit.nus.edu.sg/dli2003/Presentation/Andy_DiPaolo.pdf

Durham, H. & Arrell, K. (2007). Introducing new cultural and technological approaches into institutional practice: An experience from geography. *British Journal of Educational Technology*, 38, 795–804.

Garrison, D.R. & Vaughan, N.D. (2008). *Blended learning in higher education: Framework, principles, and guidelines*. San

Francisco, CA: John Wiley & Sons.

Ghosh, A. (2004). Learning in strategic alliances: A Vygotskian perspective [Electronic version]. *The Learning Organization: An International Journal, 11*, 302–311. Retrieved February 4, 2009 from: Emerald Full Text.

Giddings, L.S., Campbell, S. & Maclaren, P. (2006). Going online to learn health sciences research methods: The student experience. *Australasian Journal of Educational Technology, 22*, 251–267.

Glaser, R. (1962). Programmed instruction: A behavioral view. *American Behavioral Scientist, 6*(3), 46–51.

Guba, E.G. (1984). The effect of definitions of policy on the nature and outcomes of policy analysis. *Educational Leadership, 42*(2), 63–70.

Hanley, G.L. (2001). Designing and delivering instructional technology: A team approach. In C.A. Barone & P.R. Hagner (Vol. Eds.), *Educause leadership strategies: Vol.5. Technology-enhanced teaching and learning: Leading and supporting transformation on your campus* (pp. 57–64). San Francisco, CA: Jossey Bass.

Hanna, D.E. (2000). Emerging organizational models: The extended traditional university. In D.E. Hanna & Associates (Eds.), *Higher education in an era of digital competition: Choices and challenges* (pp. 93–116). Madison, WI: Atwood.

Hodgson, V. & Reynolds, M. (2005). Consensus, difference and 'multiple communities' in networked learning. *Studies in Higher Education, 30*, 11–24.

Hung, D. & Chen, D.-T.V. (2007). Context-process authenticity in learning: Implications for identity enculturation and boundary crossing. *Educational Technology, Research and Development, 55*, 147–167.

Jonassen, D.H. (2006). A constructivist's perspective on functional contextualism. *Educational Technology, Research and Development, 54*, 43–47.

Laks, A. (2005). Focusing on learners. Retrieved February 4, 2009 from: http://www.epsilonlearning.com/learners.htm

Lewin, K. (1951). *Field theory in social science: Selected theoretical papers* (D. Cartwright, Ed.). New York: Harper & Brothers.

Logan, R.K. & Stokes, L.W. (2003). *Collaborate to compete: Driving profitability in the knowledge economy.* Wiley: Mississauga, ON.

McCalla, G. (2004). The ecological approach to the design of e-learning environments: Purpose-based capture and use of information about learners [Electronic version]. *Journal of Interactive Media in Education. 7*, 1–23. Retrieved February 4, 2009 from: www-jime.open.ac.uk/2004/7

McConnell, D. (2006). *E-Learning groups and communities.* Maidenhead, UK: Open University Press.

McNeil, S. (2007). A hypertext history of instructional design. Retrieved February 4, 2009 from the University of Houston Website: http://www.coe.uh.edu/courses/cuin6373/idhistory/before1920.html

Merrill, M.D. (2002). A pebble-in-the-pond model for instructional design. *Performance Improvement, 41*(7), 39–44.

Mohan, P., & Daniel, B. (2004). The learning object's approach: Challenges and opportunities. In Richards (Ed.), Proceeding of World Conference on E-Learning in Corporate, Government, Healthcare, and Higher Education 2004 (pp. 2512–2520). Cheasapeake, VA: AACE.

Moore, M.G. (1991). Editorial: Distance education theory. *The American Journal of Distance Education, 5*(3), 1–6.

Motidyang, B.K.D. (2007). A Bayesian belief network computational model of social capital in virtual communities. (Doctoral dissertation, University of Saskatchewan). Retrieved February 4, 2009, from: http://library2.usask.ca/theses/available/etd-07132007-141903/unrestricted/ben_m.pdf

Naylor, J.M. (2005). Learning in the information age: Electronic resources for veterinarians. In G. Parchoma (Ed.), *Large Animal Veterinary Rounds, 5*(5), 1–6.

Parchoma, G. (2003). Learner-centered instructional design and development: Two examples of success. *Journal of Distance Education, 18*(2), 35–60.

Parchoma, G., Taylor, S.M., Naylor, J.M., Abutarbush, S.M., Lohmann, K., Schwarz, K., Waldner, C., Porterfield, S., Shmon, C.L., Polley, L. & Clark, C. (2007). Integrating human-computer interaction in veterinary medicine curricula. In E. MacKay (Ed.). *Enhancing learning through human-computer interaction* (pp. 204–221). Idea Group: Hershey, PA.

Patton, M.Q. (1990). *Qualitative evaluation methods.* (2nd ed.) Thousand Oaks: CA: Sage.

Potashnik, M. & Capper, J. (1998). Distance education: Growth and diversity. *Finance & Development, 35*(1), 42–45. [Electronic version]. Retrieved February 4, 2009 from: http://www.worldbank.org/fandd/english/0398/articles/0110398.htm

Rogers, E.M. (1995). *Diffusion of innovations* (4th ed.). New York: The Free Press.

Rogers, P.C., Graham, C.R. & Mayes, C.T. (2007). Cultural competence and instructional design: Exploration research into the delivery of online instruction cross-culturally. *Educational Technology, Research and Development, 55,* 197–217.

Schwier, R.A. (2001). Catalysts, emphases and elements of virtual learning communities: Implications for research and practice. *Quarterly Review of Distance Education, 16*(3), 5–18.

Taylor, J.C. (2001). The future of learning —learning for the future: Shaping the transition. *Proceedings of the 20th ICDE World Congress.* Retrieved February 4, 2009 from: http://www.fernuni-hagen.de/ICDE/D-2001/final/keynote_speeches/wednesday/taylor_keynote.pdf

Wasson, B. (2006, October). From ARIES to iTELL: Technology enhanced lifetime learning. Paper presented at the *2006 P.G. Sorenson Distinguished Graduate Lecture,* University of Saskatchewan, Canada.

West, R.E. & Graham, C.R. (2007). Communities of networked expertise: Professional and educational perspectives. *Educational Technology, Research and Development, 55,* 391–393.

Zaïane, O.R. (2002). Building a recommender agent for e-learning systems. In the *Proceedings of the 7th International Conference on Computers in Education,* 55–59. Auckland, New Zealand: December 3–6.

# Chapter 4
## Toward New Models of Flexible Education to Enhance Quality in Australian Higher Education

STUART PALMER, DALE HOLT, AND ALAN FARLEY
Deakin University

## Introduction

In this chapter we focus on models of flexible education as related to Australian higher education (with an argument that this is typical of developments worldwide). Moreover, Deakin University's long-standing experience in flexible, online, and distance education, as a case study of changes in Australian higher education, will be highlighted, with a particular emphasis on developments in teaching engineering and technology flexibly. To begin, we provide coverage of contemporary developments in quality enhancements in teaching and learning in Australian higher education, arguing that flexible education is a key institutional response to external demands. The meanings of flexible education and blended learning are then considered and a contingency-based framework for designing flexible education outlined. The framework will consider models of flexible education design in the light of goals, the roles, needs, and circumstances of teaching staff and learners, the changing technological environment, and the requirements of various external stakeholders. The focus will then move to course and unit concerns relating to flexible educational models of course design and operation as illustrated through the case of engineering and technology at Deakin. The final section will give some consideration to future directions in flexible education.

## Enhancing quality in teaching and learning in Australian higher education

Since 1993, Australia has surveyed all completing undergraduate students (on- and off-campus) using an instrument known as the Course Experience Questionnaire (CEQ) (Graduate Careers Australia, 2007). The CEQ has a long history of development and research that confirms that it is a reliable and valid measure of students' perception of their learning environment, and is based on earlier work which shows there is a strong link between this and quality of student learning (Wilson, Lissio & Ramsden, 1997). A large analysis of open-ended comments made by university graduates on their studies as part of the CEQ has recently been completed (Scott, 2006). Apart from highlighting the complex and multi-faceted nature of quality that arises from such a diverse group of users, graduates indicated that it is the total university experience that counts. This finding confirms the idea from total quality management that all areas of an organization contribute to the final quality of the services and products (Juran, 1988). There is a system-wide 'quality function' that exists and impacts on quality. In a flexible and distance education context, this implies that the student perception of quality is likely to be influenced just as much by the late delivery of materials, the amount of network downtime, the promptness of replies from student services, and the availability of titles for borrowing from the library as it is to be influenced by currency of course material. Increasingly, with the services traditionally offered to distance education students now being made available to their on-campus counterparts through electronic means (and vice versa in the case of recorded lectures delivered over the Web to distance students), quality failures can adversely affect all types of students' learning experiences in the system. Equally, quality improvements can benefit the full range of students' learning experiences as well. A unifying philosophy is therefore required to enhance the quality of teaching and learning across all student cohorts serviced by a university committed to distance education.

With a focus on pedagogy, excellence in teaching involves:
- placing learning at the centre of interactions with students, with optimal use of learning time and available resources;
- creating rich learning environments that give varied opportunities for active learning that lead to the development of appropriate knowledge, technical skills, and competencies required in many disciplines;
- knowing curriculum content well and using it creatively, as well as knowing the gaps in relevant current disciplinary bases and how both students and staff might contribute to development in the field of knowledge;
- preparing well for teaching — including establishing challenging but clear expectations as well as developing efficient and well-structured course materials and active and engaging pedagogical activities;
- having highly developed skills for working in teaching teams (sometimes cross-disciplinary) and for supporting teaching colleagues;
- maximizing uses of diverse learning environments, both traditional and leading-edge tools, and a variety of modes of communication, learning, and teaching;
- recognizing the integration of, and connections between, teaching, learning, and research;
- having high levels of skills suitable for a variety of teaching roles; and
- attending to the need for teaching staff to liaise with sections of the university that provide support for teaching and learning.

With a focus on learners, excellence in teaching involves:
- recognizing and building on the knowledge, skills, and experiences that learners bring to teaching contexts;
- identifying and catering for the varying needs, expectations, requirements, characteristics, and the idiosyncratic learning styles and circumstances of learners;
- aiming to develop skilled, mature learners who are responsible for their own learning; and
- allowing for the fact that tertiary students are generally well motivated but need quality information about the subject matter and intellectual property attached to the unit of study in which they are enrolled, the applicability of new ideas to practical contexts, and the gaps in current knowledge.

With a focus on assessment and evaluation, excellence in teaching involves:
- giving students timely, constructive, and informative feedback about their work;
- using consistent and transparent methods of assessing and rewarding achievement;
- using varied, timely evaluation of teaching and learning to inform ongoing improvement of course materials and pedagogical practices; and
- having a self-evaluative approach and openness to critique of teaching and its products.

## Flexible education as response to quality concerns

A study commissioned by the then Federal Government Department of Education, Training and Youth Affairs (DETYA), identified seven domains of flexibility where it was possible to offer guided choice to the learners (Ling et al., 2001). These are as follows:

1. the time at which study occurs;
2. the pace at which the learning proceeds;
3. the place in which study is conducted;
4. the content that is studied, which includes the concept of flexible entry and exit points to a program;
5. the learning style adopted by the learner;
6. the form(s) of assessment employed; and
7. the option to collaborate with others or to learn independently.

It is not asserted that all forms of flexibility at all times will be beneficial for the quality of teaching and learning. There are both the possibilities and limits of designing flexible environments for enhancing the quality, satisfaction, efficiency, and accessibility of learning and teaching. Choosing these possibilities and recognizing the limits of flexibility is dependent on considering carefully teacher and learner needs, preferences, and circumstances (see further below). It clearly must relate to attributes of excellent teaching enabling quality learning for targeted student groups. A related concept to flexible education is that of blended learning, which brings more explicitly to the fore the role of information and communications technologies (ICT) in enabling flexible teaching and learning environments. Graham (2006) defines

> [blended learning (BL) systems as a combination of] face-to-face instruction with computer-mediated instruction.... BL is part of the ongoing convergence of two archetypal learning environments. On the one hand, we have the traditional face-to-face learning environment that has been around for centuries. On the other hand, we have distributed learning environments that have begun to grow and expand in exponential ways as new technologies have expanded the possibilities for distributed communication and interaction. (Graham, 2006, p. 5)

Increasingly, universities are designing a range of blended learning environments with various degrees of face-to-face and ICT supported learning, using an increasing range of e-learning technologies, to afford opportunities for various educational benefits as related to the seven domains of flexibility outlined above. What is blended and how it is blended, associated with what is made flexible and how it is made flexible, requires professional judgement making at the institutional and individual levels.

## Institutional context

From its inception as a single campus university, Deakin was conceived as a 'dual-mode' institution, servicing both traditional on-campus students and students studying by distance education (Jevons, 1982). Despite being formed from a number of antecedent institutions, Deakin is not a federated university — all principal academic and administrative functions are centralized and standardized, with the same programs of study and services being available to all students and staff, regardless of location (Calvert, 2001). The multi-campus-but-identical-program nature of Deakin's academic programs means that it has a tradition of unit development by teams and a common presentation of the unit to all students that is also similar to distance-only institutions. Generally, off-campus students study the same syllabus, complete the same assessment, and sit the same examinations as on-campus students. In 2006, the total student enrolment at Deakin was 32,374 students, of which 35% (11,264) were off-campus students.

Over time, the nature of off-campus study has changed. Initially, Deakin's off-campus students were predominantly distance students, who received study materials and studied primarily by themselves remotely. The introduction of computer/multimedia technology meant that greater levels of student interaction were possible with learning materials. The wide-scale availability of computer communication technology meant that off-campus students could take part in computer-mediated communication forums open to all students. In fact, making educational technologies equally available to off-campus and on-campus students to use has helped to justify ever-expanding investments in online systems to this very day. The growth in part-time study, by both on- and off-campus students, and Deakin's partnering with other institutions internationally to deliver its programs 'off-shore,' led to the conception of 'flexible learning,' which is based on equivalency of syllabus and learning outcomes. Flexible learning emerged strongly in the mid-1990s as organizational vision, but delivered in the combination of modes best suited to the circumstances of the student. The pervasive growth in online systems has meant that in many areas 'distance education' has become synonymous with 'online learning' (Calvert, 2005). In 2003, Deakin sought to formalize and give even greater strategic direction to its growing use of online teaching and learning under a project entitled 'Deakin Online' (Corbitt, Holt & Segrave, 2006).

While elements of online delivery and interaction are now central to most Deakin off-campus programs, and all Deakin undergraduate students must complete at least one unit in their programs that is delivered wholly online, the postal delivery of print and other study materials still remains an essential element of most off-campus study at Deakin. The intermingling of online, on-campus, and off-campus education should not be seen as unique to Deakin in the Australian higher education system. However, the shift, nonetheless, has been pronounced in the case of the development of our own university. The move, therefore, to such an all-encompassing approach to flexible education can be seen in the context of four fundamental forces in the university's historical development, namely: (1) geographical expansion of operations; (2) growth of ICTs of benefit to all students; (3) increasing diversity of students; and (4) growing development and recognition of attributes of excellent teaching and what constitutes quality learning in higher education.

## Contingency-based approach to designing flexible education

Clearly, teaching and learning happens in a wider context (e.g., internationalization and demands for lifelong learning), not in isolation. Approaches to teaching and learning need to be considered within some sort of framework if the design, development, and delivery of educational services are to be fully effective. Universities like Deakin are dedicated to exploring the meaning of teaching and learning. Academic and administrative staff members, both individually and in functional groups, are now expected to participate in defining and enacting Deakin's distinctive style as a quality, flexible education provider for undergraduate and postgraduate students, as well as those seeking professional development and advanced training. New challenges need to be met with reflective evaluations that may lead to new ways of doing things. A university is a complex institution. The design and conduct of teaching and learning needs to be responsive to the changing complex realities (i.e., it needs to be contingency-based).

Figure 1 takes these complexities and creates a contingency-based framework that places the practice of teaching and learning at its centre, surrounded by increasingly wider spheres of influence. Teaching and learning are contingent upon the core values to which the university is committed. These in turn are contingent upon a multitude of internal educational and organizational factors. The framework depicts a complex 'web' of interactions between factors and people which are useful to recognize and understand in relation to conceiving and enacting effective teaching and learning in particular settings. These factors go beyond immediate interconnected educational concerns relating to such elements as curriculum, pedagogy, assessment, student profiles, and teaching and learning contexts — complex enough in themselves — to encompass broader factors in the organizational and external environments. The contingency-based framework prompts us to recognize the range and levels of such factors operating in our design, development, and teaching environments.

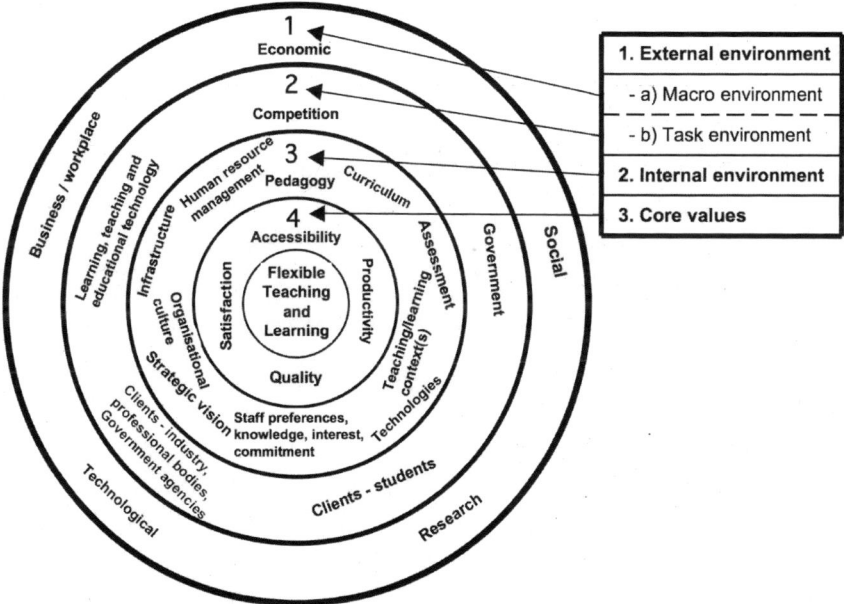

**Figure 1.** A Contingency-based framework for flexible teaching and learning.

## Case study of flexible education in action at Deakin from engineering and technology

The possibilities, limits, and potential problems in designing flexible programs are best illustrated through a case study of flexible education in action in engineering and technology at Deakin. Flexible delivery of engineering and technology education is now an essential component of the engineering education scene, catering to significant numbers of students who cannot attend traditional, full-time, on-campus studies. In Australia the standard entry into professional engineering practice is via the completion of a four-year Bachelor of Engineering (BE) undergraduate course. The Deakin School of Engineering and Information Technology offers BE, Masters, and Doctoral engineering programs in flexible delivery mode. The undergraduate programs are delivered on-campus, full-time for conventional entry students. Mature-age students may study the programs off-campus and/or part-time. The programs are designed to articulate with a range of national and international vocational, technical, and diploma-level engineering study programs. A formalized system of granting advanced standing into the course based on recognition of prior learning (RPL) and workplace experience has been developed that permits block credit of up to half of a Bachelor of Engineering degree (Lloyd, Baker & Briggs, 1996). While the Deakin Engineering programs are labelled as 'flexible,' the flexibility is principally in the place of study; because the course units are all available in off-campus mode, students can study at the place of their choosing, including interstate and internationally. The following sections explore some of main issues relating to 'flexibility' observed in the engineering program at Deakin.

*Modular curriculum*

Most flexible learning systems employ some form of modular curriculum, where the entire program, year level, semester or even unit/subject are organized into discrete, separable sections of content. Modularization offers the advantage of being able to customize a study program based on individual student needs and rearrange combinations of content into alternate units of study or new programs/courses, and it divides the content development task into smaller, more manageable chunks (Briggs, 1995).

Engineering accreditation bodies around the world are moving toward systems based on demonstrated graduate attributes and competencies, and away from systems based on rigidly prescribed course contents. This is likely to increase course flexibility and student choice in all study areas. Modularization does challenge the assumption about the importance of year-long integrated study programs, and it can lead to the compartmentalization of knowledge, rather than integration across the full curriculum.

As many engineering schools move toward an integrated curriculum and/or problem based learning strategies, there is a challenge to flexible, modular engineering programs to provide a high level of integration across their many, potentially isolated course components. In an environment of modular study the hierarchy of unit prerequisites needs to be carefully designed and tested. At Deakin it is possible to find students enrolled in units from three year levels during the same semester. In such an environment, student cohorts fragment, with many students undertaking what is effectively an individual study program.

*Recognition of prior learning*
Recognition of prior learning (RPL) plays a central role in flexible teaching and learning. In engineering education it is an essential part of creating pathways for engineering associates and para-professionals to articulate to higher occupational categories. Where either block or unit-by-unit credit for prior learning may be granted, similar considerations to modularization regarding the student's study path and prerequisites need to be taken into account. Where advanced standing is granted, academic staff must be confident that the student possesses the required prerequisite knowledge for the balance of their study program, and that students will attain all the required attributes and skills by the completion of their studies. Under RPL schemes, it is common for mature-age students to be routinely exempted from a number of units (particularly those in the early years of the program) as advanced standing. 'Essential' course content should not be placed in units that are subject to exemption under RPL.

Flexible learning programs with RPL mean a significant proportion of students may be mature-age and may have many years of experience working in the engineering workforce, including extensive practical experience. It is not uncommon for mature-age students to possess more knowledge and practical experience than their academic counterpart in particular subject areas. Engineering students with practical experience of the 'real world' are more than happy to highlight deficiencies, simplifications, and other shortcomings in study materials. The maturity and practical experience of mature-age students need to be acknowledged and catered for; they are looking for knowledge and skills that will underpin their current practice with theory, and that they can apply in their workplace. One approach to contextualizing the content of the course is to include assessable assignment tasks that require the student to use their own workplace as a case study for the analysis and application of the course content. For example, it is possible to ask students to identify the approaches/methodologies used by their organization in addressing issues and processes covered in the course. For on-campus students and those without workplace experience, an exercise in locating a relevant case study from the literature can provide the context for the analysis, as well as developing investigation and research skills.

*Learning resources*
The traditional distance learning resources are print-based study guides. Flexible learning materials take advantage of all available media, including face-to-face lectures for on-campus students and those off-campus students who can attend, print-based materials, video and audio recordings, home experimental kits, static and streamed electronic materials, residential sessions, computer programs and simulations, teleconferencing, synchronous and asynchronous electronic communication, and the Internet as an information source and material delivery medium. Flexible learning employs many new and traditional teaching technologies, and the pre-eminent consideration in the selection of a teaching technology must be its appropriateness for the task required. For instance, simply placing existing print-based study materials onto the Web 'because you can,' to 'save money on printing notes,' or because 'someone else is doing it' is not an effective use of the teaching potential of the Web. There are many advantages in converting course material to print, electronic, or other media. The course can be delivered to remote students who can study at the time of their choosing. Through the appropriate selection of a range of media, a range of learning experiences can be offered that replace, supplement, or enhance traditional on-campus teaching.

*Two-way communication*

The addition of flexible-study mode students to the class can pose difficulties and bring benefits. Many flexible study students are mature-age, with experience of the engineering workforce; this can be a valuable asset and a real-world contribution to class discussion. Many flexible mode students will study off-campus. Therefore, to avoid isolation ways must be found to bring them into the 'learning community' of the class (Rovai, 2002). One-way communication can occur with printed or electronic study materials, but more effective learning can occur where there are means for student—teacher and student—student communication. Telephone, fax, and e-mail communication can be very effective for point-to-point communication, and multi-point teleconferencing is possible. Developments in Internet-based, computer-mediated communication (CMC) have opened up new and rich opportunities for collaboration and communication at a distance (Davies & Graff, 2005). The general availability of Internet communications technology has seen the development of both asynchronous conferencing systems (such as newsgroups and bulletin boards) and synchronous conferencing systems (such as Internet Relay Chat and Web-based equivalents).

While it is desirable to have timely communication with off-campus students generally, it is very important that assignments are assessed and returned with meaningful feedback in the shortest time-frame possible. The issues of delay in returning assignments and brevity of written feedback are perhaps the two most common complaints of off-campus students. If the university has a central off-campus operations department that handles hardcopy assignment submissions and returns, then this may add several days to the turnaround time for assignments. As more university programs include online elements, it is not surprising that assessment, and in particular assignment submission and return, are to be found moving online. In addition to being part of the general move toward online delivery of education, a key reason cited for adopting online submission and return of assignments is the decrease in the assessment turnaround time leading to the more timely provision of feedback to students (Palmer, 2005).

Another important form of two-way communication is reflective dialogue, with oneself and others. Effective use of reflection is an important element of the ongoing professional development of engineers. The use of a reflective learning journal (due to the requirement to transfer thought processes into words) is thought to be a valuable tool in developing 'reflexivity.' For the practising professional, the use of a work journal offers additional benefits — it may be an admissible legal document in the case of a dispute about the conduct of work, and it may be a valuable record of the conduct of project work. Collaborative reflective activity and the ability to compare one's own thinking with that of other learners may yield positive results and better facilitated learning than individual reflection alone. Online journals are one method for all students to participate in social reflective activities (Palmer, Holt & Bray, 2008).

*Laboratory work*
Engineering, by its nature, contains a significant practical element. The provision of satisfactory laboratory/practical experiences for off-campus engineering students requires novel solutions (Abdel-Salam, Kauffman & Crossman, 2006; Hall, Jones & Palmer, 2006; Lang et al., 2007; Weller & Hopgood, 1997). The flexible approach to laboratory work requirements at Deakin encompasses: exemption if the student can provide satisfactory evidence of relevant prior experience; development of home experimental kits for appropriate units, such as electronics and basic materials experiments; use of computer-based simulations in appropriate discipline areas, such as digital electronics and control theory; remotely controlled/Internet-based practicals that allow students to interact with real experimental equipment in real-time, often at a time of their choosing; provision of intensive, on-campus practical sessions for

several units at a time, delivered by the same staff/demonstrators who present practical sessions for on-campus students, normally timetabled on weekends, so off-campus students may travel, attend the university, and complete their practical requirements; and individual arrangements where the student negotiates to conduct the required laboratory work using the facilities of their workplace or another educational institution closer to them.

*Accreditation*

As with many professions, the institutions (professional and educational) that control the education of engineers are inherently conservative. For public safety and international mobility, there is an essential need to maintain the standard, and ensure equivalence of educational outcomes. However, institutional conservatism can lead to inflexibility in the face of social and societal change. The face and background of the 'typical' engineering student has changed dramatically. In many countries, interest from traditional secondary school students in engineering as a study and career option has waned, while demand from mature-age lifelong learners seeking to upgrade their trade, technical, or other qualifications and enter the professional sphere of the engineering workforce has increased. The increased diversity of engineering undergraduates challenges accepted models of professional formation premised on a uniform and particular type of preparation of candidates for engineering undergraduate studies.

## Toward new flexible education models and practices

There is now a need to recognize that Deakin is not just an educational provider for one age/generation of learner studying predominantly in one particular context, but for many ages/generations of students, each with their own particular learning requirements. We now educate not just for the off-campus, mature-age student or the on-campus, school leaver group, but for a broad base of students representing the new ages of learning across the life-span. The strategic positioning of Deakin University's quality teaching and learning agenda requires the re-integration of traditional classroom teaching, distance education, and online education in ways most appropriate to the needs of these different student cohorts. This now requires a renewed conception and set of practices around educational choice: choices available for staff and choices available for our students. In the wake of the massification of education and in the context of increasing technology options, a new emphasis on integration and choice while maintaining diversity will be achieved through new teaching/learning models, strategies, and behaviours. We see these models, strategies, and behaviours as constituting an institution-wide Learner Experience Design Framework focusing on diverse learning experiences and shaped by strong academic teaching agency. Educational choice needs to be situated in the context of Deakin's commitment to open and productive engagements: within and across its campuses; with its local, rural, regional, and international communities; and with its professional, governmental, and industry partnerships. It needs to be informed by a renewed commitment to the investigation and development of valued graduate attributes to the rapidly changing world of workplace and professional practice, and informed citizenship.

There can be no single model of quality teaching and learning for all student cohorts, and a response of merely adding the online model to conservative models of traditional classroom and distance education forestalls genuine renewal. A new, coherent teaching and learning framework is needed to achieve a set of defined benefits for defined student cohorts, so that their course experience is one of learning environments and teaching strategies that are relevant, innovative, and responsive. The defined benefits lie in the areas of creating more open, enriched, and active customized and personalized learning environments. A strategic frame of reference for creating differentiated, rich learning environments should guide and empower academic staff at the local level to deal with their realities — the disciplines, levels, ages, locations, etc. of their known target market segments. It is the responsibility of academic authority empowered 'locally' to select the appropriate teaching strategies for different student cohorts — different education strategies to meet the needs of the market segments. This can be at all levels — Programs, Courses, Units — when evaluated, reviewed, revised, and re-accredited. Using appropriate learning experience design, the aim is to achieve fitness of purpose so that students realize the benefits. Policy must impact on students' learning experiences of quality teaching and learning environment design at the grassroots level (the unit level, peer level / students' individual 'felt' career trajectory level). Massification of education need not lead to a 'sameness' of teaching strategies.

## Conclusion

Like many universities, Deakin needs to define, develop, and brand a new strategic niche for itself, building on the many strands of its past accomplishments in ways which will allow productive alignments with a broader range of organizations in pursuit of its mission and goals. In the Australian context, flexible education is seen as a key institutional response to the many expectations placed on the modern higher educational institution. The contingency-based framework (Figure 1) visually illustrates these various spheres of influence on flexible teaching and learning designs. Flexible education simply offers the opportunity to give students an individually tailored quality learning environment, while still allowing the institution to scale up its delivery. How this is successfully realized in practice is very much dependent on an intimate understanding of the program and its students. The particulars considered in the case study of teaching engineering and technology at Deakin demonstrate such a grassroots approach to designing a flexible program.

What is the future direction for flexible education? Deakin's distinctive profile and achievements relating to progressive forms of distance, open, online, and face-to-face education will need to merge with its myriad external relationships as supported by new technologies. The renewed commitment to educational choice, and the response to the diversity of learning needs and circumstances of its students, along with the university's various communities of engagement, will represent a new nexus between teaching and research within the university for the benefit of new age learning for all stakeholders. It will reflect a development path in common with other similar universities in Australian higher education. The full potentials and limits of flexibility in educational provision will be explored in the next stage of its historical evolution.

REFERENCES

Abdel-Salam, T., Kauffman, P.J., & Crossman, G. (2006). Does the lack of hands-on experience in a remotely delivered laboratory course affect student learning? European Journal of Engineering Education, 31, 747–756.

Briggs, H. (1995). Towards student-centred engineering education at Deakin University. Paper presented at the 12th Biennial Forum of the Open and Distance Learning Association of Australia, Vanuatu.

Calvert, J. (2001). Deakin University: Going online at a dual mode university. International Review of Research in Open and Distance Learning, 1(2). Retrieved February 25, 2009 from: http://www.irrodl.org/index.php/irrodl/article/view/20/52.

Calvert, J. (2005). Distance education at the crossroads. Distance Education, 26, 227–238.

Corbitt, B., Holt, D., & Segrave, S. (2006). Strategic design for web-based teaching and learning: Making corporate technology systems work for the learning organisation. International Journal of Web-Based Learning and Teaching Technologies, 1(4), 15–35.

Davies, J., & Graff, M. (2005). Performance in e-learning: Online participation and student grades. British Journal of Educational Technology, 36, 657–663.

Graduate Careers Australia. (2007). Graduate course experience 2006 — The report of the course experience questionnaire. Melbourne: Graduate Careers Australia and Australian Council for Academic Research. Retrieved February 25, 2009 from: http://www.educ.utas.edu.au/TandL/TaskGroups/files/CEQ_2006Final272007.pdf

Graham, C.R. (2006). Blended learning systems: Definition, current trends, and future directions. In C.J. Bonk & C.R. Graham (Eds.), The handbook of blended learning global perspectives, local designs (pp. 3–21). San Francisco: John Wiley & Sons.

Hall, W., Jones, J.T., & Palmer, S. (2006). Providing a practical education for off-campus engineering students. British Journal of Engineering Education, 5, 49–57.

Jevons, F.R. (1982). How different is the distance student? In J.S. Daniel & M.A. Stroud (Eds.), Learning at a distance: A world perspective (pp. 126–128). Edmonton: Athabasca University.

Juran, J.M. (1988). The quality function. In J.M. Juran & F.M. Gryna (Eds.), Juran's quality control handbook (4th ed., pp. 2.1–2.13). New York: McGraw-Hill.

Lang, D., Mengelkamp, C., Jäger, R.S., Geoffroy, D., Billaud, M., & Zimmer, T. (2007). Pedagogical evaluation of remote laboratories in eMerge project. European Journal of Engineering Education, 32, 57–72.

Ling, P., Arger, G., Smallwood, H., Toomey, R., Kirkpatrick, D., & Barnard, I. (2001). The effectiveness of models of flexible provision of higher education — 01/9. Canberra: Department of Education, Training and Youth Affairs. Retrieved February 25, 2009 from: http://www.dest.gov.au/archive/highered/eippubs/eip01_9/eip01_9.pdf

Lloyd, B., Baker, L., & Briggs, H. (1996). Off-campus articulated education in engineering at Deakin University for mature students. Paper presented at the 8th Annual Convention and Conference of the Australasian Association for Engineering Education, Sydney.

Palmer, S. (2005). An evaluation of the use of on-line submission and return of assignments. Journal of Educational Technology Systems, 34, 57–67.

Palmer, S., Holt, D., & Bray, S. (2008). The learning outcomes of an online reflective journal in engineering. Paper presented at the 25th Annual Conference of the Australasian Society for

Computers in Learning in Tertiary Education, Melbourne. Retrieved February 25, 2009 from: http://www.ascilite.org.au/conferences/melbourne08/procs/palmer.pdf

Rovai, A. (2002). Building Sense of Community at a Distance. International Review of Research in Open and Distance Learning, 3(1). Retrieved February 25, 2009 from: http://www.irrodl.org/index.php/irrodl/article/view/79/153.

Scott, G. (2006). Accessing the student voice — Using CEQuery to identify what retains students and promotes engagement in productive learning in Australian higher education. Barton, Australian Capital Territory: Department of Education, Science and Training. Retrieved February 2009 http://www.dest.gov.au/NR/rdonlyres/9196224F-FEEA-4CF8-AEC/-4DB4AFFD41E5/10605/HEIPCEQueryFinalv21stFeb06.pdf

Weller, M.J., & Hopgood, A.A. (1997). Implementing a learning model for a practical subject in distance education. European Journal of Engineering Education, 22, 377–387.

Wilson, K.L., Lissio, A., & Ramsden, P. (1997). The development, validation and application of the Course Experience Questionnaire. Studies in Higher Education, 22, 33–53.

# Laboratories

# Chapter 5
## Taking the Chemistry Experience Home — Home Experiments or "Kitchen Chemistry"

**ROBERT LYALL AND ANTONIO (TONY) F. PATTI**
Monash University

## Introduction

Chemistry is a practical science, and practical experiments are regarded as an essential part of the chemistry curriculum at all levels, so much so that many professional bodies for chemists specify a minimum number of hours to be spent on practical experimental work before a course will be accredited by them.

It is difficult to provide the distance education student with experience of laboratory equipment, expensive instruments, or hazardous chemicals in a safe and controlled environment except through on-campus attendance. This has generally been achieved through weekend attendance or residential laboratory schools. For organizational reasons, and for the learner, financial reasons or practical reasons (e.g, distance of travel), the laboratory schools and/or weekend attendances are usually restricted to four or five days per semester. Even so, it can provide the full "laboratory experience" for the distance student in much the same way as for the on-campus student.

In a study of Australian distance education students who were required to attend a residential activity, Warner and Wilkinson

(1992) claimed that a significant number found the experience neither useful nor important. Surveys of students attending laboratory schools at the authors' university over several years do not support these claims. The majority of students surveyed found the contact with staff and peers beneficial, with the main problem being in the concentration of 30 hours of experimental work into these few days and many of them reporting they felt confused at the time.

However, for many students, attending a laboratory school is a considerable burden, or in some cases impossible, and may be a disincentive to study laboratory-based science courses. Often the problem is the cost of travel and accommodation, since many of our students live hundreds, and sometimes thousands, of kilometres from the campus. Other reasons are the difficulty in getting time off from their employment and family commitments. For these students it is essential to find an alternative to the laboratory school, particularly in the first year of their course, when they are still considering their options for studying.

"Virtual laboratories" and computer simulations of expensive and/or complex instruments have been used (Kennepohl, 2001; Martinez-Jiménez et al., 2003; Baran, Currie & Kennepohl, 2004) to enable learners to gain experience in the use and control of chemical apparatus and instruments without the necessity of having the equipment available. Provided he or she has a suitable computer, these can be readily made available to the distance learner and provide a "doing" experience which, although less direct than actual hands-on experiments, still gives the student a measure of control over the experiment and may be as educationally valuable as using the real instrument. Although virtual laboratories are a valuable educational tool, they do not provide hands-on manipulation of laboratory equipment and techniques, and Forinash and Wisman (2001) cautioned that they should not replace practical laboratory experimentation entirely.

Home experiments using common household materials and equipment (so-called kitchen chemistry) have been suggested as an alternative to laboratory experiments (Kennepohl, 2000). This may be a suitable approach in introductory chemistry courses and for students who just require a basic knowledge of chemistry. However, in the authors' opinion, "kitchen chemistry experiments" are clearly not adequate for those who intend to make a career in chemistry, biochemistry, or other disciplines that require a high degree of chemical experimentation. These students need a solid practical base of experimental chemical techniques early in their studies so that they can ultimately proceed to the more complex and demanding procedures in later years. The prior learning experiences of the student also need to be considered, as distance education students are also more likely to have some background in chemistry and/or have worked or may be working in a laboratory in their employment, and kitchen chemistry is unlikely to give them the experience they want.

Another way of providing the students with hands-on experience is by a "home experimental kit" using actual laboratory apparatus and essentially the same experiments that would be conducted in a conventional laboratory class. Thus, the practical experiments can be done at a place convenient for the individual student. This would appear to provide an opportunity for the student to learn by "direct, purposeful experience" (Dale, 1969). In practice, however, it has some disadvantages for the distance education learner. The major problem is that the teacher is unable to observe and guide the learner as would be done in the laboratory and therefore is unable to ensure that the experience is the required one — for instance, that the learner was using apparatus in the correct way. Other problems are that the experiments have to be modified for safety reasons and are therefore less valuable as an experience, and comments from some students indicated that they often spent more time in setting up the experiment (because it was a non-laboratory environment) than actually doing it.

Nevertheless, the home laboratory kit remains an essential component and useful option in the delivery of first level chemistry courses to distance education students at some universities that provide distance education studies in chemistry (Patti, Mayes & Lyall, 1991; Patti, 1991; Kennepohl, 2007). This chapter summarizes the experiences in two institutions (Monash University, Australia, and Athabasca University, Canada) that have provided what could be best described as higher level home experiment kits for first year university chemistry. Experiences in the actual development of the higher level kit including some student evaluation experience are described.

## Development of the experimental program and kit

It is generally accepted that experimental work is essential to any chemistry program. Beginning from this premise, in developing the experiments for the chemistry kit there were several fundamental questions to be answered:
- Who is the target audience?
- What is the purpose of the experiments?
- What are the expected outcomes?

The role of practical work in the chemistry curriculum has been extensively discussed by numerous educators, including Kember (1982), Lagowski (1989), and Bennett and O'Neale, (1998). Bennett and O'Neale (1998) have pointed out that many students studying chemistry at first level have no intention of going on to graduate in chemistry and even of those who do many will never make use of their skills in their work.

This is also true at our university, where only a small number of first level chemistry students will go on to major in chemistry and many need only a basic knowledge of the theory of chemistry and will not use their practical laboratory skills at all.

This has major ramifications for the second question: what is the laboratory work for, and the corollary, what skills should we be developing in the students? In a literature review of this subject

Johnstone and Al-Shuaili (2001) compiled a set of principal aims for practical work which can be summed up as:
- Manipulation
- Observation and recording
- Processing and interpretation of data
- Ability to plan experiments

Other skills which were judged as being important were to reinforce the theoretical work, to demonstrate principles already taught, to show by observation the connection between macro- and micro-elements of chemistry, and to stimulate an interest in chemistry. These are, of course, skills for any laboratory course and were developed with the premise that students would be working in a purpose-built school or university laboratory. The challenge here was to translate these into a home experiment kit. Many of the processes of scientific enquiry can take place outside the laboratory; however, it is important that students gain a realistic view of what the practical side of chemistry is all about, regardless of whether they will continue further studies in the discipline. A laboratory program based around home experiments might be viewed as too trivial. This issue can be addressed by incorporating a compulsory 2–3 day residential school, requiring students to experience a real laboratory environment.

However, there were several other important criteria that had to be kept in mind. These were to keep the experiments as similar as possible to those being done on campus, to keep the cost of the kit as low as possible, to make sure the kit was reasonably transportable, and last, but not least, to make the kit as safe as possible.

Of the four aims suggested above, the most difficult would be developing manipulative skills, given the limitations of providing apparatus and instruments that could be transported and used in a home environment. The number of exercises that can be safely performed without supervision is limited. If this aim could be achieved the others could be built into the experiments, as is done in laboratory-based experiments.

Reid and Shah (2007) have also summarized the purpose for laboratory work in chemistry under four headings:
- *Providing skills,* relating to learning chemistry.
- *Practical skills,* including handling equipment and chemicals, learning safety, mastering techniques, accurate measurement, and careful observation.
- *Scientific skills.*
- *General skills,* which include team work, oral and written communication, time management, and problem solving.

They stressed the notion that if university chemistry laboratory activities are to be useful, they need to have clear aims with effectively designed experiences for the students.

## Contents of the kit

Given that the majority of the students using the kit would be non-chemistry majors and would have little need for advanced chemical techniques, there was little point in training them to use complex instruments such as spectrophotometers. Also, as Johnstone and Al-Shuaili (2001) have pointed out, manipulative skills for instrumentation often depend on the brand of instrument being used, and should students encounter a different type then, in all probability, they will need to relearn their manipulative skills. Thus a kit would contain only common apparatus such as might be used in a high school or first-year chemistry laboratory, and use of complex (and expensive) instruments could be left to advanced levels where the students were more likely to be dedicated chemists.

General manipulative skills such as using correct glassware, weighing, making up solutions, titrating, and measuring pH were considered essential, and there were already developed experiments to accommodate these. Packaging apparatus such as burette stands and clamps was of little concern, as was glassware such as beakers, burettes, and pipettes, provided they were properly protected. Some of this apparatus (e.g., burettes) is available in plastic and is suitable for use with appropriately chosen experiments and certainly for handling aqueous solutions. As far as possible, the procedures were modified (usually amounts of reagents) so that the same item of equipment could be used between several experiments, thus limiting the number of pieces of apparatus in the kit.

One of the major challenges was in finding a suitable balance for weighing. Providing students with a laboratory balance, or requiring them to access one of their own, was not feasible because of the cost. Common household electronic scales were not accurate enough. Most would weigh down to only two grams, whereas an accuracy of at least 0.1 g was considered necessary in order to weigh yields and also to make up solutions, which was a key strategy. The suggestion that students could make up more concentrated and/or larger quantities of solutions was considered to be wasteful and there were some difficulties with solubility. In the end a simple two-pan balance was selected because it was robust, easily packed and could weigh to 0.1 g (Figure 1). Its only downside was that it is slow to use.

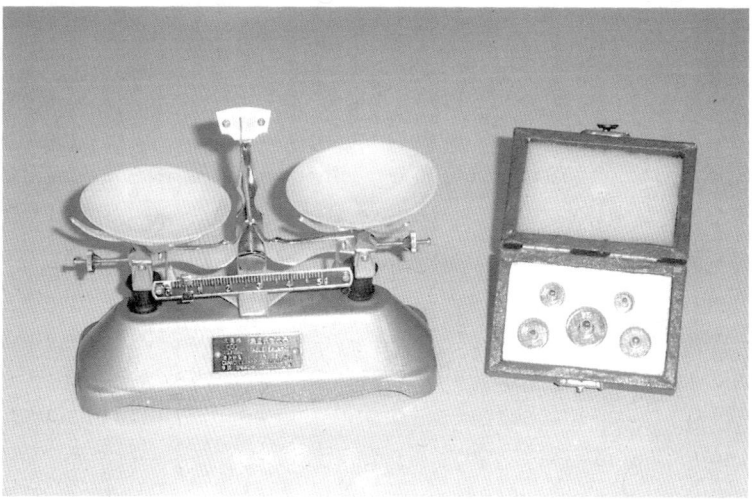

**Figure 1.** Pan Balance (Monash University)

Since pH is an important concept for chemists and other scientists, a reliable and relatively accurate instrument for measuring pH was considered to be essential. It was out of the question to provide students with a laboratory quality pH meter because of cost and difficulties in transporting and setting up such fragile instruments. Ultimately a simple hand-held meter was sourced. This instrument was inexpensive, compact, its electrodes well protected, and it could be calibrated using buffer solutions and a small screwdriver. It was claimed to measure pH to two decimal places, and whereas there was some skepticism about this claim, particularly with regard to the environment it was used in, it proved to be sufficiently accurate for this program.

The kits also contained equipment that allowed the determination of melting and boiling points, reaction end points, specific heat, enthalpy of formation, reaction rate constants, and electrochemical cell potentials. The inclusion of the various pieces of equipment listed allows for quantitative experiments to be included in the home exercises. This is an important feature of these kits, extending the complexity of possible laboratory exercises that can be included.

The chemicals required for the experiments needed to be appropriately packaged, and compliance with health and safety requirements was central in designing the packaging. This is further discussed under the section on Occupational Health and Safety issues.

The kit developed in Canada by Athabasca University costs approximately $800 CAN ($680 US, euro 500, £350 GB), whereas the Australian development by Monash University costs approximately $A750 ($US670, €460, £340). These kits both provided the essential chemicals and equipment for all the experiments. The Canadian kit dimensions are 41×46×47 cm and it weighs 5.4 kg. The Australian kit is somewhat larger, with dimensions 60×40×23 cm, and weighs 10 kg. This difference reflects the fact that the Australian kit covers more experiments (Figure 2).

The kits are shipped cost-free to the students and the university also covers the return shipping costs. In Canada, no kit deposit is required, but grades are withheld until the kits are returned. The Australian practice is to require a deposit of A$300 which is refunded when the intact kit has been returned.

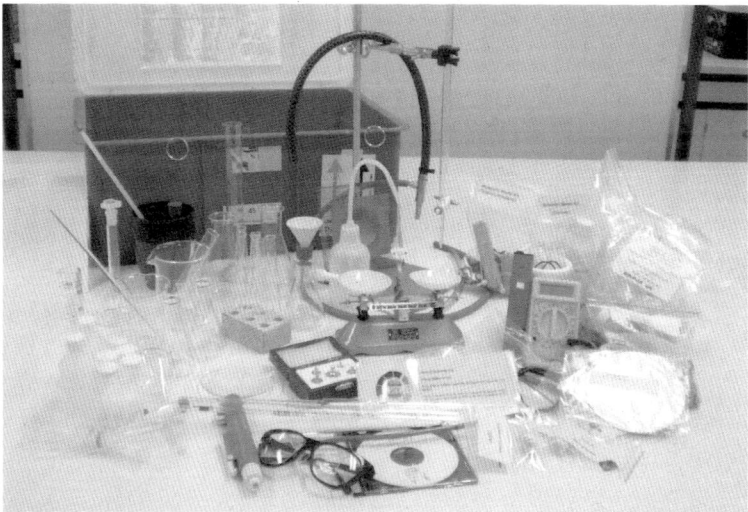

**Figure 2.** A complete Monash University Home Experiment Kit

## Instructional media that accompany the kit

The specific instructional media that accompany a kit can be primarily based around printed materials accompanied by video footage. The printed materials need to include:

> 1. Diagrams and brief descriptions of glassware, equipment, and how the equipment should be assembled, if deemed necessary. Safety issues should be constantly repeated and explained. All this information should be referenced to the relevant sections of the video, which is also supplied with the kit (see next section).
> 2. Detailed descriptions of the laboratory exercises which include the theoretical background, illustrations of experimental design, interactive questions and examples that assist the student's understanding, detailed

instructions for undertaking the experimental program, safety instructions, and guidance regarding how the data and observations should be recorded, analyzed and subsequently written up.

3. Information on the correct disposal procedures for any chemical residues after completing the experiments.

These printed materials need to be well-designed and appealing to the student. It is advisable to include the input of instructional designers to achieve this aim. Hard copy text still plays a central role as a learning medium for the off-campus student. Bennett and O'Neale (1998) have emphasized the importance of providing a linear study program, particularly when the learner is required to interact with a range of learning materials. In this context, clear directions, including a timetable, are needed, as the laboratory exercises themselves constitute learning experiences that need to be linked to other parts of the course.

## Development of and rationale for a video

A video that can effectively be used to illustrate techniques, describe equipment, and illustrate the experimental setup is strongly recommended as an essential part of the home experiment kit. There is likely to be obvious repetition of information provided in the printed material, but this is generally necessary and important to ensure the student has an alternative mode of presentation of the principles that need to be understood and/or learned.

This can be supplied in the form of a digital video disk (DVD) included in the kit. Current technologies allow DVDs to be readily viewed through dedicated DVD players and home computers.

The video fulfils the role of the demonstrator, and in order to be used effectively the video should be viewed prior to attempting any experiments in the kit. The video provides familiarization with the equipment and illustrates experimental techniques and can also reinforce the theory content of the subject. Hence, based on the content of the kit and the rationale previously discussed for this content, the video needs to effectively act in place of the demonstrator.

The preparation of the video, based on prior experience, can be approached in the following manner:

1. Determine the visual content one wishes to include.
2. Distinguish between techniques that are to be illustrated and any related theory.
3. Safety considerations are of paramount importance and can be strongly reinforced in the vision supplied.

These have been separately addressed in the next section.

The inclusion of an instructional video through a DVD also provides the opportunity to enrich the experimental program. This can be done by the inclusion of interactive instrument simulations (that can also be related to particular exercises), supplementary images, and "correct" data that may guide the student regarding what to expect from their own experimentation.

## Occupational health and safety issues

There were two aspects of Occupational Health and Safety (OH&S). The first was that the chemicals and apparatus in the kit must be safe to use in the home environment, keeping in mind that many distance education students would have children. The second was the safe transport of the kit to the home of the students.

As is always done, all the experiments were subject to a comprehensive risk assessment, but in this case more emphasis was given to reducing the risks to a low or very low rating. For the apparatus, most was regarded as being safe to use in the home. Some thought was given to replacing glassware with plastic, and this was done in some cases. However, only the most expensive plastic can withstand heating on a hotplate, and glassware is still the material of choice for most laboratories. As glassware is also commonly used in the home it was considered that most people would be aware of the dangers and so it was decided to use glass beakers, flasks, etc. with appropriate warning being given about its use.

Chemicals were more problematic. The properties considered to be the most important were corrosiveness, flammability, and toxicity. Corrosive chemicals were not commonly used in the first year laboratory anyway, solutions of sodium hydroxide and the mineral acids being the main exceptions. In most cases only dilute solutions of these were used. One experiment (chemical reactions) did use a small amount of concentrated sulphuric acid, but even this was considered to be too dangerous and so this part of the experiment was eliminated. Even dilute solutions of sodium hydroxide are dangerous to the eyes, but it was difficult to eliminate these completely so specific warnings in the laboratory manual were given about the dangers and students were instructed to wear safety glasses at all times (as is done in the laboratory).

Flammability was of particular concern, as a domestic stove was the usual method of heating in the home. Highly flammable solvents such as acetone and ethers were eliminated from the kit. Wherever possible, common industrial solvents such as methylated spirits and mineral turpentine were used. Warnings were given in the laboratory manual.

Toxicity was perhaps of the most concern and, using the risk assessments, toxic chemicals were replaced with those of lower toxicity. This did cause some problems, as often the less toxic compounds were not as effective and in some cases a reasonable substitute could not be found. In these cases the experiments were eliminated from the program. A case in point was the use of potassium dichromate as an oxidizing agent. Due to the toxicity of Cr(VI) this compound could not be included in the kit. Potassium permanganate is less toxic and can be substituted in some reactions but can cause side reactions in some organic reactions.

Transport of chemicals was the other OH&S issue. In our home state of Victoria, as in most Australian states, there are very strict regulations for the storage and transport of chemicals. The same situation applies in Canada. The kit had to be delivered by courier, and these firms were very conscious of the regulations since fines for non-compliance are very severe and could result in their licence for transport of dangerous goods being withdrawn. Originally the regulations were drawn up for large quantities of dangerous substances, which led to the ludicrous situation of a courier refusing to transport the kit because it contained 0.5 g of potassium permanganate, an oxidizing compound which had to be packed and transported separately. Fortunately the regulations have been amended to take quantities into consideration, and this has made compliance easier to obtain. In large countries like Australia and Canada, consideration should be given to compliance with air transport regulations, which may often provide limitations as to what can be included in a home experiment kit.

Even so, dangerous substances must be separately packaged according to their dangerous goods classification. These chemicals were packed in tightly sealed plastic containers which were then placed in secondary plastic bags. For liquid chemicals the secondary bags contained absorbent material in case the primary container ruptured (Figure 3).

**Figure 3.** Packaged Chemicals including Vermiculite Adsorbent (Monash University)

There were several layers of safety information given to the students. The kits contained Material Safety Data Sheets (MSDS) for all chemicals contained in the kit. Further information was given in the laboratory manual. Firstly, there were several pages, printed on brightly coloured paper, containing general information called "Safety Aspects for Home Experiments." At the beginning of each experiment specific safety instructions, also printed on the same coloured paper, were provided. For procedures considered more hazardous, warnings were given in the Experimental Procedure section of the manual.

To make safety a proactive part of the laboratory program, all chemistry students (both on campus and distance education) are required to complete their own safety audits for each experiment before beginning any experimental work. This audit must be submitted with the laboratory report and contributes to their grade.

Finally the video on Chemical Experimentation discussed previously contains, among other things, additional safety information, which is supplied with the kit.

## Design of the experiments

First level chemistry experiments can be divided into two groups, depending on the desired outcomes. First were the experiments which would train the students in technique and manipulative skills. Second were those experiments which were designed to reinforce the concepts taught in the theory component and/or to demonstrate the macroscopic effects of microscopic phenomena. Of course many experiments will have both elements designed into them.

In both cases one of the main problems in designing the experiments is the diverse background of the students. This varies from those who have no background in chemistry through to those who have studied chemistry at a basic high school level or have studied chemistry some years previously to those who have recently passed chemistry at the final level of their secondary schooling. The challenge is to design experiments that inexperienced students can reasonably be expected to satisfactorily complete without making them too easy and uninteresting for the experienced students who may then quickly become bored with the course.

In our experiences, this was particularly difficult for the first few experiments, since the inexperienced students would probably not be familiar with common apparatus and techniques of even the most basic chemistry procedures. Therefore it was essential that in the first few weeks these students be trained in these techniques before tackling more complex experiments. Fortunately the first few topics in the theory course were the basic concepts such as atomic structure, bonding, structure of compounds, and writing equations, which are largely abstract concepts for which there are no simple hands-on experiments available to reinforce the theory. A further reason for delaying the theory-reinforcement type experiments was that there was no guarantee that the students would be up to date in their studies and anecdotal evidence based on many years of experience suggests that new students spend proportionally more time on the first few topics to the detriment of later topics. For these reasons the first two experiments were completely technique-driven with little direct relevance to the theory component.

In the first experiment in the Australian kit, students were taught to recognize common glassware. They were required to draw the apparatus and then nominate in what circumstances they would use particular items of apparatus. To make the exercise more challenging, questions were posed asking them to explain why a particular piece of apparatus would be used — questions such as "why do you use a round bottom flask for distillation" and "in what circumstance would you use a conical flask rather than a beaker when heating solutions." Whereas these questions may seem simple to the experienced chemist, it was surprising that many of the relatively experienced students had given little thought to why they would use different pieces of apparatus. Students were then introduced to the principles of preparation of analytical solutions and titration, which were two techniques originally identified as being key to the practice of chemistry. These concentrated on the actual manipulation of the apparatus, including using a balance, volumetric flasks, pipettes, and burettes. They did not include a calculation of molarity or stoichiometric principles, since these had not been covered in the theory program. Calculations such as the ratio of titrant to analyte were used to introduce the concepts of accuracy and precision. This experiment was easy to develop as it only required the use of the common apparatus supplied with the kit. In the first experiment of the Canadian kit, quantitative technique was also emphasized whereby the students learnt how to calibrate and use a general pan balance and subsequently determine the density of water.

Continuing this theme, in the second experiment (Australia), students had to purify a sample of water which had been contaminated with a variety of solid and soluble material. In this way they were introduced to common separation and purification techniques, including gravity filtration, extraction using a separating funnel, adsorption using activated carbon (which involved filtering a hot solution), vacuum filtration, and distillation. A simple recrystallization exercise where water is used as a solvent can also be presented. Salicylic acid or acetylsalicylic acid provides a good substrate for purification, and a "dirty" sample can easily be contrived! This exercise and many others are illustrated in detail in the video provided with the kit. To avoid OH&S issues and packaging of flammable solvents the students were required to purchase the common solvent mineral turpentine themselves to use in the extraction procedure. As in the previous experiment the first few techniques used only common apparatus. One difficulty with vacuum filtration was providing a vacuum. This proved more problematic than expected because, although a water aspirator was included in the kit, students found it difficult to attach to a domestic tap. Several adaptors had to be included in the kit to solve this problem. Distillation also proved to be a difficult technique for the kit students since, for similar reasons, it was difficult to connect a Liebig condenser to a domestic tap. Instead an air-cooled copper coil was used as a condenser. This contradicted the stated aim of providing apparatus that was used in the laboratory, but it was considered important that the students use distillation as a technique and end up with a sample (albeit very small) of pure water as the ultimate outcome of the experiment.

The remaining experiments for the first semester were related to the theory program, which included gases, solutions, chemical reactions, acids and bases, and the chemistry of carbon.

For gases, several simple quantitative experiments could be used. The Australian kit featured an adaptation of the well-known Boyle's Law apparatus, using a large syringe and weights to measure volume under different "pressures" and hence enable the determination of the pressure-volume relationship. This simple apparatus had no safety implications. In this case books were used as weights and these could be weighed using domestic scales. The Canadian kit provided an exercise to determine the universal gas constant (R). Nitrogen gas was chemically generated, trapped over water, and the student calculated R and compared the value obtained with the literature value.

For the Chemical Reactions topic a simple kinetics experiment was developed where speed of reaction could be measured by observing the relative number of bubbles of hydrogen gas evolved when zinc granules were placed in a sulphuric acid solution. Reaction conditions were changed to demonstrate the effects of concentration, temperature, surface area, and the addition of a catalyst. Experiments to show the different types of reactions such as precipitation, decomposition, single replacement, and redox were not difficult, with established reactions being used.

Likewise, experiments to demonstrate acid-base properties were not difficult to design and were included in both the Australian and Canadian design. Students were able to measure the pH of various common liquids and solutions using pH paper. They were then required to prepare curves for strong acid/strong base, weak acid/strong base and strong acid/weak base titrations using the simple pH meter provided in the kit. An alternative experiment (Canada) involved the hydrolysis of a commercial acetylsalicylic acid tablet with a known amount of NaOH and titration of the excess NaOH with standard HCl. The calculated amount of acetylsalicylic acid present was compared with the value obtained spectrophotometrically in a separate experiment. Acetylsalicylic acid also provides an excellent substrate for a recrystallization exercise, where water can be used as the solvent.

A relevant organic experiment proved more difficult, mainly due to OH&S issues. Many chemicals used in the kit could not be easily transported, and there was the concern about using flammable and toxic chemicals in the home environment where experienced supervision was absent. For these reasons the kit experiment on properties of simple organic compounds differed considerably from that done in the laboratory. Students were asked to source out common organic compounds such as hydrocarbons, methylated spirits, aspirin, and paracetamol and perform simple tests such as solubility and some limited reactions. In addition, the traditional organic molecular modelling type activities were presented, although these can now be presented in a more sophisticated manner through the numerous computer software packages that are now available.

Experiments in the Australian kit for the second semester were somewhat easier to design as the students had all completed the first unit and so were familiar with the kit and chemical apparatus.

An experiment in thermochemistry (determination of specific heat and enthalpy of formation) was designed using a simple "insulated coffee cup" calorimeter. A kinetics experiment determining the rate constant of a reaction and Arrhenius constant used a well-known titration method. An electrochemistry experiment measuring cell potentials and determining half-cell reduction potentials was designed using an inexpensive multimeter (part of the kit) and a variety of metal rods and solutions. This required the use of a salt bridge, but the common design of using a glass U-tube filled with conducting gel was thought to be too fragile. This problem was overcome by using a short piece of cord which the students soaked in a concentrated solution of potassium chloride. When dried, the saturated cord proved to be a very effective salt bridge.

Other experiments made available in such kits have included alternative titrations, such as the empirical determination of the stoichiometry of a reaction using a redox titration, and the preparation of several organic chemicals and coordination complexes, which can be readily done using the laboratory glassware and chemicals supplied.

## Outcomes and evaluation of chemistry home experiment kits

Evaluations of home experiment programs that have substantially or wholly replaced laboratory programs at first year level chemistry are scarce in the literature. Canadian survey data of students enrolled by distance at Athabasca University is shown in Table 1. This data compares responses from students taking the full home-study laboratories, previous students taking half the laboratories at home and half by campus attendance, and those only doing one kitchen chemistry experiment at home.

The actual student performance of the Athabasca University students is summarized in Table 2. This data covers the period January 1990 to July 2006. Major course revisions to the theory component of the course were undertaken over this period and have been identified as version 1 through to 6.

**Table 1:** Summary of CHEM 217 student surveys of the Home-Study Experiments — Athabasca University, Canada.

|  | Full Home Lab | Half Home Lab [†] | Kitchen Chemistry [†] |
|---|---|---|---|
| Female | 65% | 41% | 48% |
| Male | 35% | 59% | 52% |
| Average Age | 30 years | 28 years | 29 years |
| University degree | 39% | 50% | 48% |
| College diploma | 22% | 45% | 45% |
| No post-secondary experience | 7% | 5% | 6% |
| Average time since last chemistry laboratory experience | 6.7 years | Not available | Not available |
| Average time since last science laboratory experience | 4.7 years | 5.7 years | 6.3 years |
| University quality achieved | 83% | 85% | No (anecdotal) |
| Want home-study option for other science labs | 78% | 83% | 85% |
| Instructions easy to follow* | 3.9 | 4.5 | 4.3 |
| Easy to obtain all equipment* | 4.5 | 4.1 | 4.0 |
| Experiments interesting* | 4.2 | 4.0 | 3.1 |
| Course material reinforced* | 4.1 | 4.0 | 3.0 |
| Number of responses | 182 | 218 | 59 |

\* students were asked to rate on a five-point Likert scale.
[†] Previously reported data (Kennepohl 2000)
Table 1 taken from Kennepohl (2007) with permission.

**Table 2:** CHEM 217 Student Performance (1990 to 2006).

| Course version | 1 | 2 | 3 | 4 | 5 | 6 |
|---|---|---|---|---|---|---|
| Home-study laboratory component | None | | | Half | | Full |
| Number of students | 52 | 49 | 19 | 15 | 124 | 222 | 60 | 194 |
| Assignments (%)[†] | 85.8 | 85.7 | 80.5 | 84.0 | 86.5 | 85.2 | 87.5 | 88.9 |
| Midterm exam (%)[†] | 74.7 | 80.6 | 84.4 | 78.0 | 83.6 | 71.4 | 75.3 | 74.4 |
| Final exam (%)[†] | 68.2 | 76.0 | 75.5 | 73.9 | 74.9 | 67.5 | 71.9 | 68.8 |
| Laboratories (%)[†] | 78.8 | 81.6 | 80.7 | 80.4 | 82.5 | 83.5 | 87.5 | 87.8 |
| Composite (%)*[†] | 75.8 | 80.1 | 79.6 | 78.4 | 80.4 | 74.7 | 77.7 | 76.6 |

\* Composite grade is a weighted average equal to 20% assignments plus 20% midterm exam plus 20% lab plus 40% final exam from original values.
† Percent values truncated to one decimal place.
Table 2 taken from Kennepohl (2007) with permission.

The first chemistry home experiment kit designed for first year chemistry, by Monash University, was released for student use in the early 1990s. The design of the kit itself has not changed significantly, although some of the exercises have been replaced and updated. In the first year of release, 34 students completed the first semester chemistry subject and 28 successfully passed the first semester subject. Two of the students who failed did not submit at least two-thirds of the required laboratory reports, even though they had successfully passed the theory exams.

In Australia, the same kit was also used for the subsequent second semester subject, although not all laboratory exercises were completed through home experiments, since a compulsory residential school was incorporated into semester two. The residential school attendance satisfied a number of aims, including provision of a real laboratory experience for the student, which included a reinforcement of safety issues; providing access and exposure to analytical equipment, checking and reinforcing the acquisition of correct techniques, and providing an opportunity for social interaction between the students. One innovation attempted in the second semester was to require the students to commence an exercise at home, using the home experiment kit, and then complete the activity at the residential school. For example, the esterification of 1-butanol with acetic acid to give n-butyl acetate could be verified by bringing the sample prepared at home to the lab, where an infrared (IR) spectrum was recorded and compared with an authentic sample. While the home-prepared sample may not have been pure, the IR spectrum provided some evidence of ester formation and a discussion point to explain and reinforce the theory behind this reaction.

A questionnaire was sent to all the first cohort of students who were still enrolled at the end of semester one, 1991, and although this information may be considered somewhat dated, it is consistent with the more recent evaluations previously described in the Canadian experience. A 70% response rate was achieved. About 80% of respondents to the survey found the experiments interesting and stimulating and claimed that the exercises helped their understanding of the theory components of the course. Significantly, 70% also claimed that they enjoyed carrying out the experiments on their own, while only 12% were undecided on this point. This was not a surprising response, if one considers that off-campus students are accustomed to being independent and having to work alone. A number of respondents commented on the value of being able to self-pace themselves through the exercises. By choice, distance learners who are successful with their studies are likely to want a fair degree of freedom and tend to be self-motivated. The disadvantage that distance learners have is the lack of peer interaction and guidance from an instructor when unsure about what to do or how to interpret a result.

Moore and Paulsen argue that a high level of freedom and individual choice is crucial in distance education (Moore, 1983; Paulsen, 1993). The absence of peer interaction may adversely affect the laboratory learning experience (Kennepohl, 2007).

The video demonstrations and details associated with the home experiment kit were generally very favourably received. Numerous students expressed the view that the video material was particularly helpful where they had experienced difficulty in understanding written instructions. Off-campus students will view video demonstrations with enthusiasm, and they certainly fulfil part of the role of a "live" demonstrator.

Generally, the quality of laboratory reports was very good and often better than those submitted by on-campus students. Off-campus students showed evidence of thorough research into interactive questions posed for their reports, and a good understanding of the chemistry involved was demonstrated through the interpretation of results provided in their reports. The quality of samples required for submission with some lab reports (e.g., the recrystallization exercise) indicated that students had executed the techniques successfully.

In a more recent study, student performances in the three modes of laboratory work (home experiment kit, residential school, and on campus) were compared over three years from 2005 to 2007 for both first level chemistry units. CHM1731 was the first semester unit and CHM1742 was the second semester unit. Students were required to pass CHM1731 (or an equivalent subject) before attempting CHM1742. This data is summarized in Table 3. Students who did not complete the practical course or did not sit the final examination have been excluded from the data.

**Table 3:** CHM1731 Student Performance (2005 to 2007).

|  | Home kit | Residential | On-campus |
|---|---|---|---|
| Number of students | 19 | 39 | 120 |
| Average laboratory mark (%) | 76.1 | 75.0 | 73.4 |
| Average overall mark (%) | 70.0 | 61.7 | 63.7 |

**Table 4:** CHM1742 Student Performance (2005 to 2007).

|  | Home kit | Residential | On-campus |
|---|---|---|---|
| Number of students | 7 | 16 | 102 |
| Average laboratory mark (%) | 78.6 | 75.1 | 71.6 |
| Average overall mark (%) | 74.6 | 65.7 | 61.0 |

Student performance outcomes from data gathered from the Athabasca study indicate that there is little difference between student performance when using home-experiment kits versus traditional supervised laboratories (Kennepohl, 2007). However, the data from the Monash University study indicates that the students using the home kit consistently gain slightly higher marks for the practical work and significantly higher final grades than on-campus students and those attending the residential school. This is consistent with studies carried out by Boschmann (2003) and Casanova et al. (2006) suggesting that student performance, when comparing home experiments with on-campus laboratories in general chemistry, is better in the home-experiment kit students.

Whereas it is perhaps not surprising that distance education students achieve higher grades than on-campus students, since they are generally more mature and more highly motivated (Lyall & McNamara, 2000), the difference between the home kit and residential school distance education groups is more difficult to explain. This could be due to the fact that the home kit students need to spend a considerable time in setting up the experiments. They will therefore be more familiar with the experiment and probably more determined to see that it is done properly.

## Conclusion

Our experiences in developing a chemistry home experiment kit for first level university students have shown it is possible to design an experience similar to that of regular on-campus laboratories. In particular students are able to gain familiarity with common laboratory apparatus without having to compromise the development of manipulative skills so important to a practical chemistry course.

The second objective of a practical course is to reinforce the theoretical knowledge, and the consistently better-than-average grades of the home experiment students show that this has been achieved.

## REFERENCES

Baran, J., Currie, R., & Kennepohl, D. (2004). Remote instrumentation for the teaching laboratory. *Journal of Chemical Education, 81,* 1814–1816.

Bennett, S.W., & O'Neale, K. (1998). Skills development and practical work in chemistry. *University Chemistry Education, 2,* 58–62. Retrieved February 25, 2009 from: http://www.rsc.org/pdf/uchemed/papers/1998/22_bennett.pdf

Black, P.J., & Ogborn, J. (1979). Laboratory work in undergraduate teaching. In McNally, D. (Ed.) *Learning strategies in university science.* University College Cardiff Press.

Boschmann, E. (2003). Teaching chemistry via distance education. *Journal of Chemical Education, 80,* 704–708.

Casanova, R.S., Civelli, J.L., Kimbrough, D.R., Heath, B.P., & Reeves, J.H. (2006). Distance learning: A viable alternative to the conventional lecture—lab format in general chemistry. *Journal of Chemical Education, 83,* 501–507.

Dale, E. (1969). *Audiovisual methods in teaching* (3rd ed.), New York: Holt, Rinehart and Winston, Inc.

Forinash, K., & Wisman, R. (2001). The viability of distance education science laboratories. *T.H.E. Journal, 29*(2), 38–45. Retrieved February 25, 2009 from: http://www.thejournal.com/articles/15590

Johnstone, A.H., & Al-Shuaili, A. (2001). Learning in the laboratory; some thoughts from the literature. *University Chemistry Education, 5,* 42–51.

Kember, D. (1982). External science courses: The practicals problem. *Distance Education, 3,* 207–225.

Kennepohl, D. (1996). Home-study microlabs. *Journal of Chemical Education, 73,* 938–939.

Kennepohl, D. (2000). Microscaled Laboratories for home study: A Canadian solution. *Chemeda: The Australian Journal of Chemical Education*, 54/55/56, 25–31.

Kennepohl, D. (2001). Using computer simulations to supplement teaching laboratories in chemistry for distance delivery. *Journal of Distance Education*, 16(2), 58–65.

Kennepohl, D. (2007). Using home-laboratory kits to teach general chemistry. *Chemistry Education Research and Practice*, 8, 337–346.

Lagowski, J.J. (1989). The FIPSE Lectures: Reformatting the laboratory. *Journal of Chemical Education*, 66, 12–14.

Lyall, R., & McNamara, S. (2000). Influences on the orientations to learning of distance education students in Australia. *Open Learning*, 15, 107–121.

Moore, M.G. (1983). . In D. Sewart, D. Keegan & B. Holmberg (Eds.) 68–94). Croom Helm/St. Martin's Press: London/New York.

Martinez-Jiménez, P., Pontes-Pedrajas, A., Polo, J., & Climent-Bellido, M.S. (2003). Learning in chemistry with virtual laboratories. *Journal of Chemical Education*, 80, 346–352.

Patti, A.F., Mayes, R.E., & Lyall, R. (1991). First year university chemistry by distance learning. *Proceedings of the 11th International Conference on Chemical Education*, York, UK.

Patti, A.F. (1991). Laboratory sciences by distance education: The Australian experience. *Proceedings of the Invitational Conference on Teaching Laboratory Sciences by Distance Education, USA National Science Foundation*, Indianapolis, USA.

Paulsen, M.F. (1993). The hexagon of cooperative freedom: A distance education theory attuned to computer conferencing. *DEOSNEWS*, 3(2). Retrieved February 25, 2009 from: http://www.nettskolen.com/forskning/21/hexagon.html

Reid, N., & Shah, I. (2007). The role of laboratory work in university chemistry. *Chemistry Education Research and Practice*, 8, 172–185. Retrieved February 25, 2009 from: http://www.rsc.org/images/Issue%208-2_tcm18-85055.pdf#page=76

Warner, L., & Wilkinson, J. (1992). Evaluation of on-campus activities in disciplines necessitating compulsory attendance. *Research in Distance Education*, 4(3), 2–5.

# Chapter 6
## Acquisition of Laboratory Skills by On-Campus and Distance Education Students

JENNY MOSSE AND WENDY WRIGHT
Monash University

## Introduction
*Teaching biological sciences by distance*
Teaching experimental sciences by distance education is acknowledged to be difficult (Dalgarno, Bishop & Bedgood, 2003). Although computer simulations can be used to illustrate scientific concepts and to introduce students to experimental techniques, only "hands-on" sessions can ensure that students acquire appropriate laboratory skills. For this reason, many distance education providers avoid experimental sciences (for a discussion see Trindade, Carmo & Bidarra, 2000). Remote, online, access to instrumentation can provide a real experience in areas such as chromatography and spectrometry, where instruments are often computer-controlled (Kennepohl et al., 2005), but there is evidence that many distant students lack relevant expertise, so the requirement to work in an online environment can be a major barrier (Galusha, 1997; Hara & Kling, 2000).

Studying by distance education is challenging; it is important that first year studies stimulate students and maintain their interest. Practical work engages and enthuses students (Handelsman et al.,

2004; Ford, Prudente & Newton, 2008) and has been shown to significantly improve retention of first year students (Hoit & Ohland, 1998; Aziz, 2003). However, a compulsory on-campus laboratory program can be problematic for those distant students who have chosen to study in distance education mode because of difficulties associated with university attendance. A recent study considered factors leading to students' decisions to withdraw from a Bachelor of Science program at Indira Gandhi National Open University, where students are required to attend full-time lab sessions of at least seven days' duration. The dropout rate in this program is very high, with approximately 50% of students failing to move on to second year and 63% of students failing to complete their degree program. In this study, 53% of students cited "difficulty in attending lab sessions" as a reason for withdrawal (Fozdar, Kumar & Kannan, 2006).

At the School of Applied Sciences and Engineering (SASE), Monash University (Gippsland campus), it is certainly our experience that the first year of distance education is a difficult one, as students make the transition to university study. Laboratory kits, which allow experiments to be conducted at home, enable first year students to become involved with unit material and to develop technical skills, yet postpones the requirement for on-campus attendance until the second year of the program. By this time, students are well committed to their degree studies and more prepared to accommodate this requirement, as are their families and/or employers.

Teaching staff at SASE have extensive experience in delivering experimental science programs by distance education. During the 1970s and 1980s, the school was part of the Gippsland Institute of Advanced Education (GIAE) and the student population comprised students in local regional areas and students from metropolitan Melbourne studying for diplomas and degrees in the applied sciences. Courses were first made available by distance education to students who were employed in local industries and therefore unable to attend classes during business hours. While the basis of the theory course was delivered in print form, supplementary tutorials and laboratory classes were held on weekends. Students attended what came to be known as "Weekend Schools" three to four times per semester.

In the late 1980s, the GIAE became part of Monash University. Distance education courses became attractive to people further afield, and gradually the geographical range of the student population expanded. It became clear that the weekend school model was unsuitable for many of the students, since the costs associated with travel to the campus (from interstate and sometimes overseas) were considerable. It was at this time that laboratory kits for first year units were introduced. Second and third year laboratory programs were also blocked into concentrated residential schools, held once per semester, so that travel to the campus was minimized.

Given the strong focus on applied sciences, all courses emphasize hands-on, practical work. We feel that this training is essential from the beginning of the course, as it has a dual role: allowing students to develop skills and competencies, and encouraging them to apply their theoretical knowledge to practical situations, which enhances their understanding and facilitates learning. Learning objectives for laboratory classes, which are provided to the students in written form, relate to the development of both generic laboratory skills and skills which are discipline-specific.

While the student demographic varies from year to year, the on campus cohort is comprised mainly of students who have taken up university studies directly after completing their secondary school education, so this cohort consists predominantly of full-time students in their late teens or early twenties. Distance education students are typically older than students in the on-campus cohort and their personal circumstances are extremely varied. Many work full-time (in science-related jobs or in other fields), some are parents who are caring for young children at home, and some travel frequently, for example elite athletes and members of the defence forces.

## Programs in biological sciences at SASE
*First year units*

Two first-year biology units, Human Biology and Cell Biology, are available in both on-campus and distance education study modes. Students complete their laboratory requirements in weekly laboratory sessions (on campus) or by distance education using portable experimental kits.

The Human Biology laboratory program includes practical exercises in which students investigate various aspects of human physiology from a systems-based approach. Distance education students receive a laboratory kit containing glassware; basic chemicals; histological specimens; equipment including a spirometer, sphygmomanometer, and a dissection kit; and a preserved rat. There is an option to request either a "full" or a "half" kit. The "half" kit contains equipment for only three of the five practical exercises, and students who choose half kits must complete the other two exercises at a single weekend school; approximately 50% of students choose this option. Students who do not attend may live interstate (typically 20% of the distance education cohort) or have work or family commitments.

The practical exercises in the Cell Biology program are arguably more complex, particularly for distance education students. Again, the laboratory kit contains glassware and chemicals, but there is also a significant requirement for students to source their own materials, such as fresh plant materials and chicken hearts. There is no weekend school option for this unit.

The first year distance education and on campus programs are similar, but not identical; however, they are designed to provide an equivalent educational experience for both groups of students. Certainly, the time commitment required by distant students is greater, as they have to prepare many reagents and source experimental materials. However, this is outweighed by the flexibility provided by the kits, which enables distant students to choose where and when they complete their experimental work.

*Second and third year units*

The first year biology program provides a background for students who may then extend their studies into the ecology and/or biotechnology discipline areas.

About two thirds of the first year biology cohort proceed to second and third year biotechnology units, primarily biochemistry and microbiology. In these units, laboratory work is performed in concentrated periods (residential laboratory schools) of four or five days per unit per semester. During this time, students are trained in specialized skills and the use of instrumentation appropriate to the discipline; the practical work undertaken by on-campus and distance education students is identical. In many ways the residential school mimics the workplace, providing opportunities for students to dovetail activities and perform experiments that are not easily accommodated in weekly lab sessions. As a consequence, this concentrated "block laboratory" model has been extended to many on-campus biotechnology units at third year.

**Table 1:** Summary of laboratory programs for on campus and distance education students in biological sciences at SASE, Monash University (Gippsland campus).

| Year level | On campus | Distance education |
|---|---|---|
| First year | Practical exercises conducted throughout the semester. | Practical exercises using home-based experimental kit; option to complete some labs at weekend school for the first semester unit |
| Second year | Weekly practical exercises (3–4 hrs) conducted throughout semester. | Practical exercises conducted at compulsory residential schools (4–5 day block) |
| Third year | Practical exercises conducted either weekly (~4 hrs) throughout semester or in a block (~5 days) | Practical exercises conducted at compulsory residential schools (~5 day block) |

## Comparing the student experience

The diversity of the on- and off-campus student populations, and the variety of modes in which the laboratory components of the units are delivered, raise the question of parity of experience for students in the distance education and on-campus cohorts. It is essential that both on- and off-campus students acquire the skills and competencies required in the workplace or for higher level studies. It is difficult to assess student competence, particularly prior to their participation in laboratory classes. In this study, students were asked to rate their confidence in performing particular tasks related to the unit learning objectives.

While the link between confidence and competence is tenuous (Haun et al., 2000; Morgan & Cleave-Hogg, 2002), there is some evidence for a link between confidence and performance as measured by grade point average (GPA) (Lotkowski, Robbins & Noeth, 2004), and there is significant evidence supporting a link between student confidence and subsequent student retention (Felder, Felder & Dietz, 1998; Irizarry, 2002; Lotkowski, Robbins & Noeth, 2004; Rickinson & Rutherford, 1995). Therefore, we contend that confidence is a meaningful parameter to measure, especially for practical skills, since students' confidence is reflected in how they approach a task and how, as graduates, they make career choices (Betz & Borgen, 2000) and present themselves to potential employers.

## Methods

### Surveys

While it would have been ideal to track students throughout their studies, the extended time frame of off-campus studies (most distance education students study part-time, so take six years or more to complete their degree) was prohibitive. This study involved two 'snapshots' of students' perceptions about their laboratory skills: On-campus and distance education students enrolled in first year biology units, and in second and third year biotechnology units, were surveyed at the beginning and end of a single teaching semester.

Questionnaires were distributed to 95 on-campus students during first, second and third year laboratory classes; 72% of these surveys were returned. Eighty-three questionnaires were also distributed by mail to first year distance education students; 40% of these questionnaires were returned. Fifty-six distance education students received questionnaires during second and third year residential schools; 52% of these were returned. In total, 234 questionnaires were distributed and the overall response rate was 57%.

Students enrolled in first, second and third year units received different questionnaires, but all survey questions related to students' confidence in their laboratory skills. Questions were of two types: general questions and questions specific to each year level. General questions were common to all questionnaires and related to generic laboratory skills. For example, some of these general questions asked students to rate their confidence in:

- Handling biological samples safely
- Coordinating work with that of other students
- Managing several experimental tasks concurrently
- Drawing a reasonable conclusion from experimental data
- Writing a scientific report

Questions specific to each year level related directly to skills described by one or more learning objectives for the unit in which they were enrolled. For each question, students were asked to rate their confidence level for a particular laboratory skill on a 5-point scale, where 1 represented "lacking in confidence," 3 represented "confident," and 5 represented "very confident." Full questions from each of the questionnaires are provided in Table 2.

It is important to stress that these surveys assessed *confidence* rather than *competence*, and that the students reported their own confidence levels.

*Analyses*

Survey results were analysed according to mode of offering (distance education versus on campus) and year level (first, second, third year). An average confidence ranking was determined for each question by taking the mean of all student responses to that question. The standard error (a measure of the variance of the mean) was also calculated for each mean. Results that differed by at least two standard errors were considered to be significantly different (95% CI).

---

**Table 2:** See pages 117–118. Mean confidence rankings (with standard errors in brackets) for on-campus and distance education students at four time points: start of semester 1, year 1 (new students); end of semester 1, year 1; end of semester 1, year 2; and end of semester 1, year 3. Questions 1–8 were common to multiple year levels. Questions 11–15, 21–25 and 31–35 were restricted to students in year levels 1, 2 and 3 respectively. Results that differ by two standard errors are indicated as follows:

Means in bold represent significant differences between students at the beginning and end of first year studies.

Means underlined represent significant differences between on campus and distance education cohorts at the same year level.

Significant differences between students at different year levels within a single cohort are indicated by superscripts († #).

| Indicate your ability to perform the following tasks | On campus cohort | | | | Distance education cohort | | | |
|---|---|---|---|---|---|---|---|---|
| | New students | Sem 1, Year 1 | Sem 1, Year 2 | Sem 1, Year 3 | New students | Sem 1, Year 1 | Sem 1, Year 2 | Sem 1, Year 3 |
| 1  Handle Biological samples safely | 3.2 (0.2) | 4.4 (0.3) | 3.9 (0.4) | 4.1 (0.4) | 4.1 (0.4) | 4.6 (0.3) | 4.5 (0.3) | 4.1 (0.3) |
| 2  Draw a reasonable conclusion from experimental data | 2.6 (0.2) | 3.4 (0.3) | 3.5 (0.4) | 3.9 (0.4) | 2.8 (0.4) | 3.8 (0.4) | 3.8 (0.4) | 3.8 (0.4) |
| 3  Write a scientific report | 2.6 (0.2) | 3.5 (0.3) | 3.4 (0.3) | 3.4 (0.3) | 2.8 (0.4) | 3.5 (0.5) | 3.6 (0.4) | 3.6 (0.4) |
| 4  Working independently, perform an experiment using written instructions, such as those provided in a lab manual | 3.0 (0.3) | 3.6 (0.4) | 3.5# (0.4) | 4.3# (0.4) | 3.3 (0.5) | 3.6 (0.4) | 3.4# (0.4) | 4.1# (0.3) |
| 5  Coordinate your work with that of other students working in the laboratory | 3.5 (0.2) | 4.3† (0.2) | 3.9†# (0.4) | 4.8# (0.3) | 3.0 (0.4) | 3.3† (0.5) | 3.8 (0.3) | 4.1† (0.4) |
| 6  Manage several experimental tasks concurrently | | | 3.0# (0.3) | 4.2# (0.3) | | | 3.3# (0.4) | 4.2# (0.3) |
| 7  Accurately measure pH | 3.1 (0.2) | 4.0 (0.3) | 3.5 (0.3) | | 3.5 (0.3) | 3.7 (0.3) | 4.1 (0.3) | |
| 8  Calculate the rate of an enzyme catalysed reaction | 1.8 (0.2) | 2.9 (0.4) | 2.4 (0.3) | | 2.0 (0.3) | 2.5 (0.3) | 3.1 (0.4) | |
| 11 Accurately measure 20mL of liquid | 4.5 (0.2) | 4.5 (0.3) | | | 4.8 (0.2) | 4.9 (0.2) | | |
| 12 Accurately pipette a 1mL sample of liquid | 3.6 (0.3) | 4.4 (0.2) | | | 3.8 (0.4) | 4.7 (0.2) | | |
| 13 Use a microscope to identify features in a tissue section | 2.6 (0.2) | 2.9 (0.4) | | | 3.1 (0.4) | 3.9 (0.3) | | |
| 14 Prepare biological samples (e.g., enzymes or chloroplasts) from raw materials | 1.7 (0.2) | 2.2 (0.3) | | | 2.3 (0.3) | 3.4 (0.3) | | |

|  |  | On campus cohort | | | | Distance education cohort | | | |
| --- | --- | --- | --- | --- | --- | --- | --- | --- | --- |
|  |  | New students | Sem 1, Year 1 | Sem 1, Year 2 | Sem 1, Year 3 | New students | Sem 1, Year 1 | Sem 1, Year 2 | Sem 1, Year 3 |
| 15 | Monitor a biological process, such as photosynthesis | **1.8** (0.2) | **3.1** (0.3) |  |  | **2.3** (0.3) | **3.3** (0.3) |  |  |
| 21 | Accurately measure 0.35mL of liquid |  |  | 4.0 (0.4) |  |  |  | 4.4 (0.3) |  |
| 22 | Accurately pipette a 220µL sample of liquid |  |  | 3.5 (0.4) |  |  |  | **4.3** (0.4) |  |
| 23 | Accurately measure the absorbance of a solution using a spectrophotometer |  |  | 3.9 (0.3) |  |  |  | 4.0 (0.3) |  |
| 24 | Determine the concentration of a specific metabolite in a solution using a standard curve |  |  | 3.9 (0.3) |  |  |  | 3.9 (0.3) |  |
| 25 | Perform an electrophoretic separation |  |  | 3.1 (0.3) |  |  |  | 2.8 (0.4) |  |
| 31 | Use an oil immersion lens to distinguish stained micro-organisms |  |  |  | **4.9** (0.1) |  |  |  | **4.2** (0.4) |
| 32 | Successfully isolate a pure culture from a mixed microbial population |  |  |  | 4.4 (0.3) |  |  |  | 3.9 (0.4) |
| 33 | Accurately identify a pure bacterial culture using a rapid test kit |  |  |  | 3.8 (0.4) |  |  |  | 3.7 (0.4) |
| 34 | Working independently, prepare microbiological media |  |  |  | 2.9 (0.4) |  |  |  | 3.0 (0.4) |
| 35 | Perform your experimental work in a totally aseptic manner |  |  |  | 4.3 (0.3) |  |  |  | 4.3 (0.3) |

# Results

*Comparisons across year levels*

Data was collected at the beginning and end of a single semester. For each time point and each year level, mean responses for on-campus students, distance education students and all students were calculated. Table 2 shows mean responses for on-campus and distance education students at four time points: start of semester 1, year 1 (new students); end of semester 1, year 1; end of semester 1, year 2; and end of semester 1, year 3.

Combined data for all students (data not shown) show that confidence levels generally increase across year levels. Whilst differences in the mean response for individual questions are not always significant between students in consecutive years, there is a significant increase between first and third year students in all cases. This combined data also shows that students beginning semester 1, year 1 (new students) are much less confident than any other group, all of which are much more similar to one another than to the new student cohort.

New **on-campus students** (beginning semester 1, year 1) have significantly lower mean levels of confidence for many questions (Table 2) compared to students completing semester 1, year 1. Interestingly, first year on-campus students tend to be more confident than students beginning years 2 and 3 (data not shown), although these differences are significant only for the question regarding co-ordinating their work with others in the lab (Q5). In general, confidence levels are similar or increase for on-campus students between years 2 and 3. There are significant increases in confidence between second and third year on-campus students for questions 4, 5 and 6. These questions relate to: working independently (Q4); the co-ordination of work with that of other students (Q5); and managing several tasks concurrently (Q6)

The tendency for new students (beginning semester 1, year 1) to be less confident than other groups of students is also apparent for some questions in the **distance education cohort** (Table 2), although the difference is not as great as that seen in the on-campus cohort for many of the questions. Questions 4 and 5 also show clear increases in confidence from first to third year level for this cohort. Third year distance education students also had higher confidence rankings for question 6 compared to second year students from the distance education cohort.

## Comparisons between on-campus and distance education cohorts

Responses from **new students** (beginning their first semester) differed significantly between on-campus and distance education students for three of the twelve questions (Table 2). Distance education students are more confident than on-campus students about handling biological materials safely (Q1), preparing biological samples from raw materials (Q14), and monitoring biological processes (Q15).

First year on-campus and distance education students surveyed at the **end of their first semester** generally have similar perceptions of their abilities. However, significant differences occur in the mean rankings for questions 5, 13, and 14 (Table 2). The on-campus cohort is more confident about their ability to coordinate their work with that of other students (Q5). The distance education students are more confident about using a microscope (Q13) and preparing biological samples (Q14).

**Second year students** studying in on-campus and distance education modes have similar perceptions about their laboratory skills (Table 2). Distance education students appear more confident than on-campus students; differences are significant for questions 7, 8 and 22 (Table 2). These questions relate to the accurate measurement of pH (Q7), the calculation of the rate of an enzyme catalysed reaction (Q8), and the accurate use of a pipette at the scale of microlitres (Q22).

On-campus and distance education students surveyed at the end of first semester in their **third year** generally have similar perceptions of their abilities. Significant differences occur in the rankings for questions 5 and 31 (Table 2). On-campus students are more confident in their ability to coordinate their work with that of other students (Q5) and in using an oil immersion lens (Q31).

## Discussion

In general, we found that confidence levels of on-campus and distance education students are similar, although on- campus students were generally more confident about coordinating their work with others in the laboratory (Q5). Some differences related to specific skills, rather than to generic skills, were also noted.

*First year*
The higher confidence levels reported by first year distance education students, especially those reported at the beginning of first semester, may reflect the hands-on experience that some distance education students have obtained in the workplace. Some of these differences persist until the end of the first semester. For example, distance education students remain more confident about preparing biological samples (Q14).

At the end of first semester, first year distance education students report lower levels of confidence in their ability to coordinate their work with others. During first year, distance education students have been working at home, alone, during the semester, while on-campus students have been part of a team, and well supported by demonstrators, in their class-based laboratories. This difference is important, and it is interesting that experiences in second year, where students attend residential schools at second and third year level, increase student confidence in this area. By contrast, the distance education students are significantly more confident in the use of the microscope (Q13). Distance education students must organize access to a microscope, usually though a local school or hospital, and generally learn to use this apparatus independently. They are, therefore, more self-reliant and more confident with respect to this particular skill.

*Second year*

Distance education students entering the second year subject have completed their first year laboratory requirements using home experiment kits, or have gained a credit for their first year studies from another institution. Some of these students work either part- or full-time in a related field and have significant workplace laboratory experience; others may have completed laboratory requirements elsewhere, up to ten years previously.

Distance education students surveyed at the beginning of their second year (data not shown) are less confident with respect to coordinating their work with that of others, working independently following written instructions, and performing electrophoretic separations. Distance education students completed their first year laboratory requirements on their own with limited feedback from their classmates and instructors. Their lack of confidence in their ability to follow written instructions may be related to a lack of feedback about their performance during experimental work. Depending on their work environment, they may have had minimal experience working with others in a laboratory situation. The educational laboratory differs in many ways from the professional laboratory; those distance education students with workplace experience perhaps have had laboratory space, equipment, and other resources allocated to them and may be more familiar with oral rather than written instructions.

The lower confidence of distance education students about performing a specialized experimental task (electrophoretic separations) may reflect their lack of knowledge about, and their understanding of, this task. In contrast, first year on-campus students, due to their interactions with later year students and opportunity to watch others working in the laboratories, gain some familiarity with such experiments. They may be more relaxed about their capabilities because they have had an informal induction into the "mysteries" of this particular technique.

The second year distance education laboratory program requires on-campus attendance; distance education students complete their laboratory requirements at residential schools. By the end of semester, all second year students (on-campus *and* distance education) will have attended some laboratory classes. It seems that this experience is enough to reduce the differences in confidence levels between on-campus and distance education students, although confidence regarding accurate execution of common laboratory tasks and calculations is a little higher for distance education students. Attendance at residential school classes seems to address the problem of distance education students' perceived abilities to work as a part of a team.

*Third year*
At the beginning (data not shown) and end (Table 2) of semester 1, year 3, confidence levels are generally high for both on-campus and distance education cohorts. At the beginning of semester, on-campus students feel more confident in coordinating their work with that of others and in their ability to isolate pure cultures of microorganism. At the end of semester their confidence in working with others, and in another specific technique (use of an oil immersion lens), is higher than that of the distance education students (Table 2). Both groups, however, rate themselves as higher than "3" for these skills, i.e., more than "confident," so the differences may simply reflect a tendency toward conservatism in the distance education population and/or youthful exuberance in the on campus population!

*Comments from graduates*
Twenty-five recent graduates who had completed a Bachelor of

Science majoring in experimental sciences by distance education were also invited to comment on their experiences. Students who had acquired laboratory skills from sources outside the university were also asked to indicate whether they would have applied for an exemption from laboratory classes if that option had been available.

Twelve responses were received and eight of these graduates indicated that they had been employed in a scientific area while completing their distance education studies. Seven of these eight graduates had developed some laboratory skills in their workplace, but the majority indicated that they would not have applied for a laboratory exemption. Student comments indicated that the majority of their laboratory skill development occurred in residential laboratory programs. Graduates felt that residential programs had an important role in helping them, as students, to develop the "big picture," as workplace training was often narrowly focused. Student responses indicated that residential laboratory programs provided access to modern equipment and new techniques and exposure to a wider range of techniques than those encountered in the workplace. The opportunity to apply practical skills to a variety of experimental situations was also welcomed.

All students appreciated the networking opportunities provided by residential schools:

*"I had various skills but they needed updating as the workplace did, to keep up to date with changes"*

*"There is often more than one way to perform any task, even laboratory skills"*

*"There are more to labs than just having laboratory skills — we learnt how and why things worked (or didn't) ..."*

*"It was also a great way to meet other DE students and form friendships under pressure."*

"Residential lab blocks were a great reinforcement for centering on my goal (i.e. passing) and touching base with teachers and others in a similar position. Lab classes help develop other skills than just techniques. At the end of the day this gave me a degree of confidence I would otherwise have lacked."

## Conclusion

We contend that our on- and off-campus laboratory programs provide students with a different, but equivalent, experience that facilitates the development of laboratory skills in both student cohorts. Further, we advocate a mix of independent, off-campus laboratory exercises (with some necessary equipment supplied) and on-campus 'residential school' laboratory classes to allow distance education students to develop basic laboratory skills without the need for on campus attendance. This is especially important for students who are new to off-campus study and are combining their studies with a range of extracurricular activities and responsibilities. In later years, residential schools provide support and allow students to make face-to-face contact with their peers and with academics; opportunities that are clearly appreciated by distance education students. Important skills, such as an ability to work in a shared laboratory, are developed during these on-campus sessions. On-campus and distance education students report very similar levels of confidence about their capability in the laboratory on completion of their studies, suggesting equivalent outcomes. Graduate surveys also indicate that this model provides an appropriate preparation for the workplace.

## Acknowledgements

We would like to thank Lauren Burney for her assistance in sourcing student data; and Di Richards and Angela Greenall, who assisted with administration and analysis of surveys of students in their classes and helped to interpret the results.

# REFERENCES

Aziz, S. (2003). *Online technology for enhancing first year experience: A case study at the University of South Australia*. Paper presented at the Uniserve Science Improving Learning Outcomes Symposium, The University of Sydney, Sydney, Australia.

Betz, N.E., & Borgen, F.H. (2000). The future of career assessment: Integrating vocational interests with self-efficacy and personal styles. *Journal of Career Assessment, 8*, 329–338.

Dalgarno, B., Bishop, A.G., & Bedgood Jr., D.R. (2003). *The potential of virtual laboratories for distance education science teaching: Reflections from the development and evaluation of a virtual chemistry laboratory*. Paper presented at the Uniserve Science Improving Learning Outcomes Symposium, The University of Sydney, Sydney, Australia. Retrieved February 26, 2009, from: http://science.uniserve.edu.au/pubs/procs/wshop8/outws004.pdf

Felder, R.M., Felder, G.N., & Dietz, E.J. (1998). A longitudinal study of engineering student performance and retention: Comparisons with traditionally-taught students. *Journal of Engineering Education, 87*, 469–480.

Ford, J.R., Prudente, C., & Newton, T.A. (2008) A model for incorporating research into the first year chemistry curriculum. *Journal of Chemical Education 85*, 929–933.

Fozdar, B.I., Kumar, L.S., & Kannan, S. (2006). A survey of a study on the reasons responsible for student dropout from the Bachelor of Science programme at Indira Ghandi National Open University. *International Review of Research in Open and Distance Learning, 7*(3). Retrieved February 24, 2009 from: http://www.irrodl.org/index.php/irrodl/article/view/291/755

Galusha, J. (1997). Barriers to learning in distance education. *Interpersonal Computing & Technology: An Electronic Journal for the 21st Century, 5*(3/4), 6–14.

Handelsman, J., Ebert-May, D., Beichner, R., Bruns, P., Chang, A., DeHaan, R., Gentile, J., Lauffer, S., Stewart, J., Tilghman, S.M., & Wood, W.B. (2004). Scientific Teaching. *Science, 304*(5670), 521–522.

Hara, N., & Kling, R. (2000). Student distress in a web-based distance education course. *Information, Communication & Society, 3*, 557–579.

Haun, D.E., Zeringue, A., Leach, A., & Foley, A. (2000). Assessing the competence of specimen-processing personnel. *Laboratory Medicine, 31,* 633–637.

Hoit, M., & Ohland, M. (1998). The impact of a discipline-based introduction to engineering course improving retention. *Journal of Engineering Education, 87,* 79–85.

Irizarry, R. (2002). Self-efficacy and motivation effects on online psychology student retention. *USDLA Journal, 16*(12), 55–64.

Kennepohl, D., Baran, J., Connors, M., Quigley, K., & Currie, R. (2005). Remote access to instrumental analysis for distance education in science. *International Review of Research in Open and Distance Learning, 6*(3). Retrieved February 26, 2009, from: http://www.irrodl.org/index.php/irrodl/issue/view/22

Lotkowski, V.A., Robbins, S.B., & Noeth, R.J. (2004). *The role of academic and non academic factors in improving college retention*: American College Testing (ACT) Policy Report, USA. Retrieved February 26, 2009, from: http://inpathways.net/college_retention.pdf

Morgan, P.J., & Cleave-Hogg, D. (2002). Comparison between medical students' experience, confidence and competence. *Medical Education, 36,* 534–539.

Rickinson, B., & Rutherford, D. (1995). Increasing undergraduate student retention rates. *British Journal of Guidance and Counselling, 23,* 161–172.

Trindade, A.R., Carmo, H., & Bidarra, J. (2000). Current developments and best practice in open and distance learning. *International Review of Research in Open and Distance Learning, 1*(1). Retrieved February 26, 2009, from: http://www.irrodl.org/index.php/irrodl/issue/view/6

APPENDIX — QUESTIONS

Students were asked to indicate their level of confidence (from very confident to lacking in confidence) on a scale such as the one shown below. Students' responses were later assigned a value between 1 and 5, depending how the students marked the scale.

**Example question and scale:**
Using the scale provided, place a cross to indicate your ability to perform the following tasks:

Handle biological samples safely

| 5 | 4 | 3 | 2 | 1 |
|---|---|---|---|---|
| very confident | | confident | | lacking in confidence |

**Common questions:**

| Question 1 | Common to all years | "Handle biological samples safely" |
|---|---|---|
| Question 2 | Common to all years | "Draw a reasonable conclusion from experimental data" |
| Question 3 | Common to all years | "Write a scientific report" |
| Question 4 | Common to all years | "Working independently, perform an experiment using written instructions, such as those provided in a lab manual" |
| Question 5 | Common to all years | "Coordinate your work with that of other students working in the laboratory" |
| Question 6 | Common to 2nd and 3rd year | "Manage several experimental tasks concurrently" |
| Question 7 | Common to 1st and 2nd year | "Accurately measure pH" |
| Question 8 | Common to 1st and 2nd year | "Calculate the rate of an enzyme catalysed reaction" |

**Questions asked only of students in 1st year:**

| Question 11 | "Accurately measure 20ml of liquid" |
|---|---|
| Question 12 | "Accurately pipette a 1ml sample of liquid" |
| Question 13 | "Use a microscope to identify features in a tissue section" |
| Question 14 | "Prepare biological samples (e.g., enzymes or chloroplasts) from raw materials" |
| Question 15 | "Monitor a biological process, such as photosynthesis" |

**Questions asked only of students in 2nd year:**

| Question 21 | "Accurately measure 0.35ml of liquid" |
|---|---|
| Question 22 | "Accurately pipette a 220µL sample of liquid" |
| Question 23 | "Accurately measure the absorbance of a solution using a spectrophotometer" |
| Question 24 | "Determine the concentration of a specific metabolite in a solution using a standard curve" |
| Question 25 | "Perform an electrophoretic separation" |

**Questions asked only of students in 3rd year:**

| Question 31 | "Use of an oil immersion lens to distinguish stained micro-organisms" |
|---|---|
| Question 32 | "Successfully isolate a pure culture from a mixed microbial population" |
| Question 33 | "Accurately identify a pure bacterial culture using a rapid test kit" |
| Question 34 | "Working independently, prepare microbiological media" |
| Question 35 | "Perform your experimental work in a totally aseptic manner" |

# Chapter 7
## Low-Cost Physics Home Laboratory

FAROOK AL-SHAMALI AND MARTIN CONNORS

## Introduction

Distance Education (DE) is the presentation of an educational curriculum through self-study materials, often supplemented by regular contact with an instructor. DE is suitable for offering educational opportunities to students in widely dispersed locations. This form of education is gaining momentum and is becoming an increasingly popular form of learning in post-secondary education. Many traditional face-to-face courses have been revised and adjusted to create correspondence (or online) versions. However, due to the pedagogical differences between various subjects and disciplines, it is not always easy to develop correspondence courses that are convincingly equivalent to their face-to-face counterparts. This is particularly evident in science courses with experimental laboratory components. Our focus in this chapter will be on first year undergraduate physics courses and the development of alternative hands-on home lab experiments suitable for DE.

The lab work is an important part of the introductory physics class. It provides the students with a medium to practice their experimental and analytical skills and helps them understand the basis of knowledge and the relation between theoretical and empirical work in physics (American Association of Physics Teachers,

1998). However, a perception exists among students, and also among many instructors, that highly quantitative experiments can only be done in supervised physics laboratories and using specialized and costly equipment. This restrictive view poses an obstacle for the development of correspondence/online physics courses. Therefore, this is currently an open subject for debate, research, and innovation.

Many attempts have been made in the past to develop correspondence physics courses, with a noticeable acceleration in this direction during the past decade. These early efforts can be distinguished and characterized by their delivery of the lab component. One of the pioneering projects was at the UK Open University, which involved a mix of onsite laboratory-based Saturday schools, home experiments with lab kits, and demonstration experiments using purpose-made audiovisual material (Ioannides, 1987). Athabasca University has a rich experience in this regard which will be discussed in detail in Section 4.

## Real versus virtual & to-stay versus to-go labs

"Educational studies indicate that students accept all knowledge as facts, without understanding how it was constructed." (Etkina, 1999). This lack of understanding of how scientific knowledge is constructed and organized creates a fuzzy, and sometimes distorted, picture of the physical world. It is very important for students to understand that theory and experiment are interlocked and cannot be separated. An observation can lead to a theory, which may or may not stand experimental testing. Therefore, properly constructed lab experiments become essential components of an introductory physics course.

With the advancement of personal computers and the wide availability of the Internet, new forms of the physics lab started to emerge, which involve interactive computer simulations (Perkins et al., 2006). Such virtual lab environments are still debatable, with some giving them full support (Finkelstein et al., 2005) while others remain skeptical (Dillon, 2006). We will not enter here into the debate as to whether or not virtual labs have learning outcomes that warrant their use as a replacement of the traditional lab sessions. However, it is important to note that the physical world around us is the reality we try to understand and that physical laws are human attempts to describe this reality. Computer simulations, on the other hand, describe a virtual world as predicted by human-made physical laws. Therefore, we are concerned that the overuse of simulations combined with the underuse of real experiments will add to the existing misconceptions among students about how scientific knowledge is constructed. Nonetheless, this will not be our main concern in this chapter, in which we concentrate on real hands-on home lab experiments.

There are obvious challenges in doing actual hands-on experiments in correspondence courses. In particular, requiring students to come (or even travel) to a central location to do the lab part of a physics course is in conflict with the overall DE concept. One of the attractions of DE is the ability to do courses at home or from a place of the student's choice. Besides, such onsite labs are normally squeezed into a relatively short time period (usually a few days), which might result in a cognitive overdose, thus undermining the benefits of the whole lab experience.

This naturally leads to the next idea: If the student cannot come to the lab, why don't we then send the lab to the student? This is the concept of the home lab, which involves providing students with the necessary equipment, in the form of a lab kit, which allows them to perform real experiments in the convenience of their homes. It should be noted here that such lab kits must have a relatively low cost in order for the whole concept to be financially feasible. Also, due to the nature of DE, the lab kit components must be transportable and allow students to perform the experiments safely with very limited (or even no) supervision. However, this raises a concern about the practicality of this whole idea and also about the level and the quality of such home experiments. It is very important for the devised system not to compromise lab quality.

The idea of science kits is not new. They were previously suggested "as remedies for problems of school science equipment" (Announcements, 1964). However, with the advent of DE, such kits are being looked at as portable mini-laboratories that can substitute for the traditional brick-and-mortar labs located on campuses. We have mentioned the early experience of the UK Open University in this regard. Athabasca University started using lab kits in 1997 (Connors, 2004), as will be elaborated on later. More recently, there is the interesting experience at the North Carolina Community College of developing a very low-cost lab kit to be used in laboratory exercises suitable for a conceptual physics course (McAlexander, 2003). Another example is the apparently successful experience at Murdoch University in Australia (Jennings, 2005). The recent increase in the popularity of lab kits in distance education has even encouraged producing them commercially (Jeschofnig, 2004), which allows some institutions to outsource the handling of the lab material.

In comparing home labs with on-campus labs we should also note that each form of the lab experience has possible advantages and disadvantages. In a regular lab, for example, the student can seek immediate help and advice when it is needed, which can be provided by the instructor, the technician, or even the lab partner. In the home lab, on the other hand, students work almost independently, from the experimental setup to the writing of the lab report. This is normally reflected in the number of trials and the time spent by the student to complete an experiment (Misanchuk & Hunt, 2005). For this particular issue, arguments can be made on both sides. This is because while the lack of immediate guidance in home labs might be perceived as a disadvantage, the increased effort to make the experiment work, and the cognitive process accompanying that, can be argued to be an important part of active learning.

## The lab bill

Traditional laboratories can be equipped with bulky, sophisticated, and costly equipment, whereas home lab kits tend to be far less expensive and very limited in size. The big question, however, is: Can home lab kits substitute for the presumably more specialized equipment found in traditional physics labs?

We do not believe that there is a general consensus regarding an answer to this question. This is because the whole experience of home labs and the use of lab kits is relatively new and limited. Standards have not been laid down yet and the whole idea is still under investigation and requires much more serious research. However, based on our experience at Athabasca University during the past 10 years, we believe that the answer to this question is "yes." Basically, this is because physical phenomena are all around us and are not confined inside a lab room in the physics department on campus. Whether you are adding an ice cube to your drink or going down the slope in a ski resort, you are actually involved in physical phenomena. Besides, many of the important experiments and great discoveries in the early days of physics were conducted at home and using simple tools and equipment. Therefore, we believe that it is time to get away from the stereotyped images of the physics lab and start thinking outside the box.

It is important at this point to differentiate between qualitative demonstrations which are normally used as teaching aids in classrooms and the more genuine highly quantitative experiments that are typically conducted in physics labs. The common belief is that such experiments are costly and require special support and supervision. This also leads to the perception that low-cost home lab experiments are inferior and cannot be considered genuine. This, in our opinion, is a premature judgment. It is not fair at this time to compare a practice that has been developing for more than a century with the alternative that started to develop, in a serious manner, only about a decade ago. Also, we should indicate that most of the cost involved in traditional labs goes toward providing the overhead and support. This is discussed in Chapter 10. When you eat in an expensive restaurant, you mainly pay for the place and the service and only a small fraction of the bill goes toward the food on the plate. This analogy applies, to a great extent, to the traditional physics lab. Therefore, isolating the physical phenomenon from the laboratory apparatus is a first step toward finding cheaper alternatives for observing the same physics. This is especially true in modern homes, which are full of household items (including high-tech devices) that can be used for quantitative physics experiments with sufficient accuracy.

Therefore, we propose that with enough research and imagination, low-cost, high-quality experiments can be designed for the introductory physics courses. We claim to have already developed a wide range of such experiments, which are currently in use. We continue to be active in this direction, and the novelty of home labs noted above suggests that there is plenty of room for improvement. In the next section, we provide examples of home lab experiments that are currently being used in the introductory physics courses at Athabasca University.

## The AU experience

Athabasca University (AU) primarily operates as an asynchronous home-study distance education institution. This means that students can start and progress through courses based on their own schedule (subject to time limits), and do so without the need to travel or commute to a specific location. In the case of physics this includes the ability to do laboratory exercises at a place of the student's choice. AU has an open admission policy so that anyone may enter introductory level courses.

The University started offering its first physics course in 1992. Although the course was based on home study, labs were contracted to be taught on-campus at another institution in Edmonton, and students were required to attend the lab session during the summer.

Enrolment remained low through 1996. In that year, the courses were taught in-house at the Edmonton Learning Centre of Athabasca University, and the lab materials purchased to enable this were used to make the first home lab kits, introduced in early 1997. The courses have subsequently grown dramatically, and now incorporate home lab kits and, increasingly, web technology. Now AU has over 300 physics students, representing over a tenfold increase in a decade.

The three physics courses currently offered at AU are junior, algebra-based courses that cover standard topics in introductory general physics (Connors, 2004). These include classical mechanics, waves, thermodynamics, electricity, magnetism, optics, and the early quantum theory. All three courses are currently based on the widely used textbook (Giancoli, 2005), with a custom-produced study guide detailing learning steps, including readings and solutions to selected problems.

Each of the three courses has an obligatory lab component, done by students using a lab kit. Even though home labs were implemented at some other institutions at least a decade earlier, our kits were independently developed at AU to be an important feature of the physics courses. Since the lab materials are reused, the lab kits are loaned as a library item. The distribution mechanism, through our distance education library, has functioned extremely well. Kits are mailed at no cost to students, and a postal reply coupon pays for return of the kit from within Canada. Our rate of return on the kits is very high, and upon return the kits are checked and refurbished in our Science Lab. Each lab kit is accompanied by a lab manual explaining how the labs work and giving some background information. Vernier Software's Graphical Analysis program (www.vernier.com/soft/ga.html) is also supplied and the students are required to have access to a PC type computer, a requirement which no longer appears restrictive.

The initial PHYS 200 (mechanics) lab kits cost about $800 each, and were largely based on Texas Instruments' Calculator-Based Laboratory (CBL) technology and TI-83 calculators (Taylor,

1995). These were used to obtain data which could be downloaded to a home computer. Later, a second group of kits were developed at a cost of about $410 each and were based on the more restricted Calculator-Based Ranger (CBR) technology, but still with a calculator needed. More information, including photos, are given by Connors (2004). The latest generation of the commercially available motion sensors allowed direct and more convenient connection to the computer (desktop or laptop). This improvement in technology pushed down the lab kit's cost to about $190 each.

Similarly, the laboratory portions of the PHYS 201 (waves, thermodynamics, electricity) and PHYS 202 (magnetism, optics, early quantum theory) courses were initially based on CBL technology. However, due to the relatively high cost, new lab kits were developed with less expensive components. These mainly were constructed based on inexpensive digital multimeters and on sensors developed locally at the AU Science Lab (Connors, 2002). The new PHYS 201 lab kit includes a temperature probe and a circuit board from Vernier Software & Technology (www.vernier.com). This is in addition to a digital multimeter and several other items with a marginal cost. In PHYS 202 the lab kit contains a light sensor and a magnetic field sensor, from the same equipment provider, plus other cheaper items like lenses, diffraction grating, laser pointer, and a LED flash light. Students are also required to supply additional common household lab items in all courses.

The lab manual of the latest generation of PHYS 201 home lab is now available in online mode only. Students in the PHYS 201 course are able to browse the lab website and click on the various sections of each experiment. This format allows coloured pictures and video clips to be easily included and integrated with the rest of the manual. It also allows for including and updating other resources and learning objects related to the content of each experiment. Timely corrections and changes to online material are easily made. Certain parts of the lab manual, such as experimental procedures, are available in Portable Document Format (PDF) to be more printer-friendly.

In addition, the new PHYS 201 manual uses some aspects of the Investigative Science Learning Environment, which is based on physics education research (Etkina, 1999). At the beginning of each experiment, a physics law is introduced. However, for the purpose of the lab the student should not take it as a fact, but rather as a proposed theory (or claim) that may or may not be correct. The student's goal then is to perform a testing experiment and (based on his/her results) to argue and discuss the validity of the theory. A suggested testing procedure is outlined for each experiment, with the major equipment being available in the lab kit. Also, a suggested analysis of the results is given. However, students will have some freedom to follow an alternative procedure and analysis if their proposed new method is correct, rigorous, and addresses the proposed theory. This structure is expected to add more flexibility to the lab and encourages creative ideas which might be useful for future improvement and development of the lab.

Below, we present an outline of three selected experiments from recent versions of our lab manuals.

### Example 1: The simple pendulum

This is a standard experiment on simple harmonic motion. It is also the first experiment in the manual and is designed such that the student can perform it using common household items even before receiving the lab kit. Here are some excerpts from the Student's Manual about this experiment.

**Theory:** In section 11-4 in the textbook (Giancoli, 2005), a theory is introduced to describe the oscillation of a simple pendulum. It is mentioned that "for small displacements, the motion is essentially simple harmonic" and the period of oscillation is given by

$$T = 2\pi \sqrt{\frac{L}{g}}$$

For the purpose of the lab, we will assume that this is just a theory that may or may not be a correct representation of real pendulums. Therefore, like any other physics theory, it has to pass experimental testing before it is validated. This is your goal in this lab.

**Equipment:** To do this experiment, you need to supply a strong, but relatively light, string about 1 m in length. A regular dental floss should work well for this purpose. You also need about 6 coins of the same type, preferably loonies or toonies, to be used as masses. To hold the coins, a medium size binder clip is included in the lab kit. Also, in the lab kit, you will find a protractor and a stopwatch for angle and time measurements. For making length measurements, you need to provide a measuring tape or a meter stick.

**Procedure:** Construct a pendulum by attaching one end of the string to the binder clip and the other end to a fixed support. In the first part of the experiment, you will keep the mass and length of the pendulum fixed and only change the oscillation angle (or amplitude). The purpose is to investigate the relation between the oscillation period and the oscillation amplitude. In the second part of the experiment, you will keep the oscillation angle and pendulum length fixed and only change the mass of the suspended object in order to investigate the relation between the oscillation period and the mass of the pendulum. In the third part, you will keep the oscillation angle and pendulum mass fixed and only change the pendulum length.

**Analysis:** A quick glance at your first data table may give you a feel of how much your data agree with the proposed theory. However, scientifically speaking this cannot be accepted as an appropriate analysis of your results, and more rigorous analysis procedures should be followed. In particular, do the values predicted by the theory agree with the measured values within the estimated uncertainties in your measurements? This is the question that you need to answer in any testing experiment.

## Example 2: Charles's Law

This new experiment was recently developed at AU as a low-cost experiment to be used in the newest, online lab manual. The basic idea behind the experiment is very simple. A disposable plastic dropper is taped (bulb up) to the inside of a clear plastic container, such as a large slurpee cup. The container is then filled with salty water, resulting in the air being trapped inside the dropper. After that the whole container is placed inside the home freezer. As it cools down, the air trapped inside the dropper will shrink. Since the dropper pipet comes with volume marks on it, the volume of the air will be known once the water level reaches one of the marks. This will give the volume of the air inside as a function of temperature.

The only costly device in this experiment is the temperature probe from Vernier. However, there is no reason for the experiment not to work as well using a regular thermometer, which would bring the total cost of the experiment to under $10. Here are some excerpts from the Student's Manual.

**Theory:** In the textbook (section 13-6) it is mentioned that if the pressure "is kept constant, the volume of a gas increases with temperature at a nearly constant rate." It also says that the volume-versus-temperature graph "is essentially a straight line and if projected to lower temperatures E it crosses the ($x$) axis at about -273°C." Assume that this is just a theory and perform an experiment (as suggested in the procedure) to test its validity.

**Equipment:** For this experiment you need three items from the lab kit: plastic dropper, graduated cylinder, and the temperature sensor "Go! Temp". In addition, you need to supply about 200 g of table salt, a clear scotch tape, a juice straw, and a clear plastic container. Note that the plastic container should be at least 3 cm longer than the dropper. A computer with a USB port is also necessary for this experiment.

**Analysis:** In this experiment you measured the volume ($V_w$) of the water that entered the dropper as the temperature decreased. However, since you are investigating the thermal expansion of gasses, you need to determine the volume ($V_a$) of the trapped air inside. E Enter your data into the Graphical Analysis Program and plot $V_a$ versus T. Perform a linear fit to the data and extrapolate to show the temperature at which the volume shrinks to zero. Print the resulting graph. E Based on your experimental results do you support the proposed theory? Provide a detailed discussion (about 400 words) in this regard. In your discussion, make sure that you indicate the limitations of your experiment and the possible sources of error. For example, note that the change in the water column is due to the combined change of the volume of air inside the dropper and the volume of the plastic dropper itself. Also, we know that air contains water vapour which condenses in cold temperatures. Can you estimate the significance of this condensation on your measurements?

### Example 3: Ohm's Law

In this experiment, the student performs two tests of Ohm's law. In the first test he/she measures the voltage drop across a standard resistor versus the current flowing through the resistor. In the second test the student repeats the same measurements using a small light bulb. Since the temperature of the light bulb filament varies significantly, depending on the current flowing in the circuit, the student should notice that Ohm's law does not apply in this case. The experiment described below is the most recent version of an experiment used successfully for many years with parts previously assembled on a push-in breadboard. The current use of a commercial pre-assembled circuit (the Vernier Circuit Board) makes it more convenient for the students and also cuts down the checking and circulation process of returned kits in the Science Lab.

**Theory:** In the textbook (section 18-3) it says: "Exactly how large the current is in a wire depends not only on the voltage, but also on the resistance the wire offers to the flow of electrons E The higher this resistance, the less the current for a given voltage." This is described by Ohm's Law

$V = IR$

"where $R$ is the resistance of a wire or other device, $V$ is the potential difference applied across the wire or device, and $I$ is the current through it."

**Equipment:** All the equipment you need for this experiment are provided in the lab kit. These include the Vernier circuit board, the digital multimeter and their accessories.

Analysis: In the first part of the experiment, you measured the voltage drop across a 68 Ω resistor versus the current flowing through the resistor. Generate a graphical representation of your data. Describe (in about 100 words) your observation and the data collected. E In the second part of the experiment, you measured the voltage drop across a small light bulb. Generate a graphical representation of your data. Describe (in about 100 words) your observation and the trend of your data. E Do your data for the standard resistor support the predictions of Ohm's Law? Do your data for the light bulb support the predictions of Ohm's Law? Provide a detailed discussion (about 400 words) in this regard. In your discussion, make sure that you indicate the limitations of your experiment and the possible sources of error.

## Conclusion

The lab is an essential constituent of an introductory physics course. Students should understand the important relation between theory and experiment in physics. However, the tradition has been to perform physics experiments in especially equipped laboratories and under the direct supervision of a lab instructor. Many of these labs involve standard experiments and use special apparatus purchased from certain lab equipment providers. As a result, there is a general impression that in order to do an experiment you must go to the lab and use the special equipment found there.

We argue that this does not have to be the case. We believe that, with good imagination and adequate research, many high-quality physics experiments can be designed and performed safely by the students at their homes using low-cost materials and devices. As discussed in Section 4, we were able to design home lab experiments for the physics courses at AU using inexpensive equipment, common household items and recycled material. The quality of the results exceeded expectations and is comparable to what is achieved in traditional labs.

While the numbers are hard to come by for other modes of provision of lab experiences, it is likely that home labs are by far the most cost-efficient. This is especially true if the capital cost of construction of on-campus labs is taken into account. We are not advocating here for the closure of traditional labs and the mass conversion to home labs. However, we are observing the rise of an alternative experience that may have at least equivalent (but not exactly the same) learning outcomes as conventional lab sessions in undergraduate physics courses.

REFERENCES

American Association of Physics Teachers (1998). Goals of the introductory physics laboratory. *American Journal of Physics*, 66, 483–485.

Announcements (1964). News and notes: Science kits. *The Physics Teacher*, 2, 39–45.

Connors, M. (2004). A decade of success in physics distance education at Athabasca University. *Physics in Canada*, 60(1), 49–54.

Connors, M. (2002). Measurement and analysis of the field of disk magnets. *The Physics Teacher*, 40, 308–311.

Dillon, S. (2006). No test tubes? Debate on virtual science classes. *N.Y. Times*, October 20. Retrieved February 26, 2009 from: http://www.nytimes.com/2006/10/20/education/20online.html?_r=1&ex=1318996800&e

Etkina, E. (1999). Can we use the processes of physics to guide physics instruction? *unpublished manuscript*, Retrieved February 26, 2009 from: http://paer.rutgers.edu/ScientificAbilities/Downloads/Papers/Pre-ISLE.pdf

Finkelstein, N.D., Adams, W.K., Keller, C.J., Kohl, P.B., Perkins, K.K., Podolefsky, N.S., Reid, S., & LeMaster, R. (2005). When learning about the real world is better done virtually: A study of substituting computer simulations for laboratory equipment. *Physics Review Special Topics — Physics Education Research.*, 1, 010103. Retrieved February 26, 2009 from: http://prst-per.aps.org/abstract/PRSTPER/v1/i1/e010103

Giancoli, D.C. (2005). *Physics: Principles with Applications, 6th ed.* Upper Saddle River, NJ: Prentice-Hall.

Ioannides, A.A. (1987). Open education at a distance: The UK Open University experience in teaching physics. *European Journal of Physics, 8*, 286–296.

Jennings, P. (2005). An external physics degree. In Mendez, A. et al. (Eds.), *Snapshots — Good learning and teaching in physics in Australian universities*, December, 20. Retrieved February 26, 2009 from: http://www.physics.usyd.edu.au/super/AUTC/documents/pdf/Booklet.pdf

Jeschofnig, P. (2004). Effective laboratory experiences for distance learning science courses with self-contained laboratory kits. *Proceedings of the 20th Annual Conference on Distance Teaching & Learning.* Retrieved February 26, 2009 from: http://www.uwex.edu/disted/conference/Resource_library/proceedings/04_1260.pdf

McAlexander, A. (2003). Physics to go. *The Physics Teacher, 41*, 214–218.

Misanchuk M., & Hunt J.L. (2005). Designing problem-solving and laboratory content for a web-based distance education course in introductory general physics. *Proceedings of the Seventh International Conference on Computer Based Learning in Science*, CBLIS, Zilina, Slovakia, (pp. 426–436). Retrieved February 26, 2009, from: http://www.physics.uoguelph.ca/phyjlh/morph/paper2_3MelJim_1.pdf

Perkins, K., Adams, W., Dubson, M., Finkelstein, N., Reid, S., Wieman, C., & LeMaster, R. (2006). PhET: Interactive simulations for teaching and learning physics. *The Physics Teacher, 44*, 18–23.

Taylor R.L. (1995), Using the graphing calculator — in physics labs. *The Physics Teacher, 33*, 312–314.

# Chapter 8
## Laboratories in the Earth Sciences

EDWARD CLOUTIS
University of Winnipeg

**Introduction**

In reviewing and assessing the importance and role of laboratory exercises in earth sciences, we begin with defining the scope of this review. The ensuing discussion is limited to fields of study that have traditionally formed the core of studies of the solid earth, specifically geology, soil science, and geomatics (remote sensing and geographic information systems). Related subjects, such as meteorology and oceanography, have not been reviewed. It also seems reasonable to begin with some general observations which guide the ensuing discussion. Earth science as a discipline is extremely diverse and no consistent definition is available. A robust earth sciences curriculum includes aspects of more traditional disciplines, such as geology, geography, and environmental science. It also generally includes courses that are heavily oriented toward rigorous mathematical treatments (e.g., remote sensing, image processing, geographic information systems), courses with an emphasis on observational inputs (e.g., geomorphology), courses which benefit from hands-on exercises (e.g., mineralogy, petrology), and combinations of theory and observation (e.g., structural geology). In this sense, making the best use of laboratory components in earth science distance education courses can benefit from studies in other disciplines, but earth science possesses some unique characteristics.

In a simplified sense, earth science is a blend of theory and observation. As traditionally practised, earth science attempts to bring scientific rigour to the messy reality of Mother Nature. The development of theories in earth science is normally driven by the desire to understand physical processes, and theories are constantly refined on the basis of observational inputs. The goal is to determine underlying mechanisms of geological processes and to develop predictive explanations. A good example of this is the field of seismology. The long-term goals of seismology are to move from observations (e.g., that earthquakes occur in discrete geographic regions) to understanding why this is so (borrowing observations from other disciplines, such as physics and chemistry), and if successful theoretical mechanisms can be developed, to use these predictive tools for earthquake forecasting, while also feeding back into refining the models of the causes of earthquakes. Earth science is necessarily grounded in a nearly ubiquitous requirement that observation is an essential component of the discipline.

As a result of the diversity in what is termed "earth sciences," it is difficult to develop broadly applicable prescriptions or guidance in terms of optimum delivery methods for associated laboratory course components, or even their appropriateness. Perhaps as a result of the diversity of earth sciences, there is a general paucity of research on the use and effectiveness of earth science laboratories as a component of distance education (e.g., Shea, 1999). Consequently, the ensuing discussion blends reviews of relevant studies, results from affiliated disciplines, and anecdotal observations.

## General observations

The scattered literature on distance delivery as it relates to earth sciences, and in particular on associated laboratory components, either directly or indirectly recognizes the importance of laboratory work in earth science education. Many distance education earth science courses have their laboratory/field components delivered by traditional face-to-face methods; this usually requires that the students be present at a central location for a specified period of time. Other earth science courses supplement multimedia/hypermedia course materials with physical objects, such as rock and mineral samples in geology courses (e.g., Andris, 1996; Mose & Maney, 1993), or periodic face-to-face visits or instruction (Butler & Gore, 1997; Mose & Maney, 1993). This seems to be driven by a number of imperatives: (1) that laboratory/field work is considered to be an essential component of earth science education; (2) that proper training in field-based earth science subdisciplines is driven by coupling "book-learning" to laboratory/field work; (3) that a "local perspective" is a useful teaching approach (i.e., enabling students to see how concepts learned in class are relevant to their local environment or immediate surroundings); and (4) that much earth science knowledge is observation-driven or -enabled. In addition, it appears that inclusion of distance-based visual components after exposure of students to hands-on laboratory exercises further facilitates learning and retention.

Previous researchers have found that earth science students have diverse learning styles (Andris, 1996; Healey et al., 2005), and that this affects student satisfaction, performance, and method of utilization of hypermedia-based course materials (Andris, 1996). This may actually be of benefit to earth science distance education, as many earth science subdisciplines are an amalgam of theories/concepts and observations, and hence lend themselves quite readily to delivery via different pedagogical approaches; the same learning outcomes can be accessed via different mechanisms and pathways (Bishop, Schroder & Moore, 1995; Andris, 1996; Healey et al., 2005; Reuter, 2007). This potential diversity in delivery styles comes with a price: learning outcomes and skills development must be clearly enunciated and considered in light of the proposed teaching strategies (Blowers, Sarre & Smith, 1992; Williams, 1992; de Caprariis,

2000; Reed & Mitchell, 2001; Harvey, 2002), and an estimate of expected time requirements on various aspects of a course should be provided to students (Blowers, Sarre & Smith, 1992). In addition, navigation through hypermedia-based materials should be straightforward (Bishop, Schroder & Moore, 1995; Lemke & Ritter, 2000). Course delivery mechanisms should be cognizant of the characteristics of the target audience (Buckley & Donert, 2004), which may differ from those of traditional undergraduate students (Dibiase, 2000; Solem et al., 2006). It also appears that a variety of learning and contact methodologies need to be employed to ensure effective learning (Tremblay, 2006). Related to this is a perception that multimedia and internet resources can serve as effective supplemental teaching tools (Warf, Vincent & Purcell, 1999; Schroder et al., 2002; Veal, Brantley & Zulli, 2004).

Distance delivery of earth science programs often involves some component of group work. While admirable in concept, for example by promoting a sense of community among geographically dispersed students, its record in terms of providing a satisfactory learning experience appears to be negative on balance. Common shortcomings include comminication problems, scheduling conflicts, uneven levels of contribution from team members, and difficulties in assigning proper levels of credit to individual team members (e.g., Shea, 1995; Reed & Mitchell, 2001; Buckley & Donert, 2004; Vassala, 2006).

### Essential need for field/laboratory/hands-on work
Here we subdivide earth science courses into "technique" and "physical geography" categories. Technique courses are those that emphasize development of analytical skills for diverse earth science applications. Courses under this category include remote sensing/image processing, and geographic information systems (GIS). These tools are applicable to a wide range of earth science issues, such as environmental monitoring and geological exploration. For these courses, the emphasis is on the technique as opposed to the ultimate

end use. Image processing and geographic information systems are now almost exclusively computer-based techniques, and this migration from analogue to digital environments has transformed their utility to the point where they are considered core capabilities in an earth scientist's "tool kit" of skills.

To become proficient in utilizing image processing and geographic information systems, hands-on laboratory exercises provide two significant benefits: (1) understanding the essential capabilities and limitations of these techniques in a digital environment; and (2) providing an understanding of how image processing and GIS concepts are applied operationally (Bishop & Schroder, 1995). A third benefit is that students become proficient in digital data analysis utilizing a particular software package. Working with a different software package is likely facilitated by having had some exposure to some form of image processing/GIS software.

As mentioned earlier, one of the overarching objectives of the earth sciences is inherent in its title: applying scientific techniques to understanding the earth. In the physical geography subdisciplines, being able to relate scientific principles to direct observation is widely considered to be an essential element of earth sciences (e.g., Gober, 1998). Field work provides a "sense of place" (Gober, 1998) and is frequently cited as one of the most enjoyable aspects of earth science courses or programs of study (e.g., Kern & Carpenter, 1984, 1986; Moles, 1988; Camman, 1992; Gober, 1998; Vassala, 2006). There is also evidence that incorporating a field component into earth science courses results in higher overall program satisfaction (Kern & Carpenter, 1984).

Observation is an important component of physical geography. For this reason, laboratory work and field schools remain essential components of earth science education (e.g., Camman, 1992; Mose & Maney, 1993). Depending on resources and other factors, observation-based laboratory or field work can be undertaken in a traditional setting or via multimedia delivery (Schroder et al., 2002; Buckley & Donert, 2004). The proliferation of multimedia educational resources for earth sciences allows for a much richer visual experience for students, reducing the traditional gap between merely seeing and experiencing (Lemke & Ritter, 2000; Schroder et al., 2002). Newer publicly available resources, such as Google Earth, whose utility in earth science distance education has not yet been assessed, and third party utilities built upon this resource, can also be used to greatly enrich the visual aspects of earth science education.

Some aspects of earth science education are more sensory in nature than mere observation. The best example would be the laboratory component normally associated with mineralogy and petrology. Training in these areas normally includes working with rock and mineral hand specimens, and other more visual techniques, such as examining thin sections with petrographic microscopes. The latter could be delivered reasonably effectively via appropriate multimedia; for example, virtual thin sections and how individual minerals display different interference figures under plane polarized light as the sample stage is rotated could be presented in a video or still picture mode with, likely, little negative impact on comprehension.

In the case of hand specimen examination, rock and mineral identification is often based on a number of identifying characteristics. Concepts such as colour, cleavage, and crystal habit could be presented using visuals in distance delivery mode, but other key mineral identification properties such as specific gravity, hardness, taste, and lustre are more amenable to direct sensation. It is difficult to convey the lustrous feel and softness of talc, the greasy feel of graphite, the bitter taste of sylvite, the surprising heaviness of barite, or the iridescent nature of labradorite through means other than providing actual mineral specimens to students. This also allows students to see how multiple properties are often necessary for proper mineral identification. Multiple properties often "go together" to enable mineral identification. This is one of the main reasons that introductory level geology courses at Athabasca

University include a rock and mineral specimen kit as part of the course materials.

A similar rationale can be applied to historical geology courses. An important aspect of these courses is fossil identification, which serves a number of purposes: to illustrate principles of extinction (clearly unfamiliar species once existed on the earth) and evolution/succession (how body plans and species have changed over time), and to show how the process of fossilization can radically alter (or preserve) once-living organisms. While images can convey much of what is important concerning fossils, an opportunity to physically handle remains of long-dead organisms is both satisfying and compatible with almost any form of distance delivery.

Some courses within an earth science curriculum require mastering certain mathematical/geometric concepts. The most apparent of these are structural geology and some aspects of cartography. Becoming proficient in structural geological analysis requires mastering, or at least understanding, the basic principles of a stereonet or Wulff net. Essential concepts such as small and great circles are difficult to understand initially. However, the use of analogies has proven to be useful for student understanding of stereonets and basic types of map projections. The basic analogy which is used to aid in student comprehension of stereonets and map projections is to imagine (or actually construct) a hemisphere or sphere with a light bulb in the centre (a bowl can be used for this purpose with line of latitude and longitude drawn on its surface). A piece of paper placed outside but in close proximity to the sphere/hemisphere/bowl then allows students to visualize how lines of latitude and longitude appear in projection. This follows from the principle that projection is required to represent a three-dimensional curved surface (e.g., the earth's surface) on a two-dimensional (flat) surface. Students can also use the sphere/hemisphere-piece of paper analogy to understand how essential properties of features on, or properties of, the earth's surface (direction, distance, shape, area) may be distorted depending on the particular type of projection that is used. Cylindrical projection and its inherent distortions can be visualized by observing how lines of latitude and longitude may be distorted when the piece of paper used for the projection is formed into a cylinder and placed around the sphere/hemisphere. Similarly, the piece of paper can be formed into a cone (for conical projection) or laid flat (for planar projection) and the resulting distortions observed.

## Review of previous studies

In this section we review the available literature on distance delivery of earth science laboratories. Once again, because of the diversity of what constitutes earth sciences, the relevance of most of these studies is likely limited to only some aspects of earth science. Appendix provides a more detailed review of previous studies on an individual basis.

The review of previous studies has found that there are few studies that critically assess the outcomes of distance education in the earth sciences: the bulk of the studies discuss anecdotal data. A further shortcoming of many of the previous studies is that they often deal with selected components of earth sciences courses; many of the studies involve assessment of courses in which only selected components are delivered via distance education, most commonly the laboratory or field-study component.

Nevertheless, as this review shows, there is much anecdotal evidence that earth science courses can be effectively delivered via distance education, provided that such offerings are well designed and take into account the needs of the students. Hands-on components, either in the form of laboratory exercises or field work, are also generally well received. Group assignments generally fare less well with students, although there are significant variations in student satisfaction, and this seems to be a function of the students' backgrounds and expectations.

## Lessons learned

Some common themes emerge from the studies available on distance delivery of earth science courses, and many of these themes transcend political boundaries and specific courses. One of the most consistent observations is that some level of face-to-face contact with course instructors or tutors is beneficial (Camman, 1992; Butler & Gore, 1997; Warf, Vincent & Purcell, 1999; Buckley & Donert, 2004). Related to this is the consistent positive feedback from students concerning field trips and related group activities (Kern & Carpenter, 1984, 1986; Camman, 1992; Finstick, 1997; Gober, 1998; Vassala, 2006).

An additional common theme is that careful consideration needs to be given to the interrelationships between learning objectives, skills development, mode of delivery, and support services (Blowers, Sarre & Smith, 1992; Gerber & Lundin, 1992; Williams, 1992; Reed & Mitchell, 2001; Harvey, 2002; Lieblein et al., 2005; Reuter, 2007). Continuous or periodic assessment of learning progress, through self-testing or other mechanisms, is also a useful aspect of distance delivery (Camman, 1992).

An additional theme that commonly arose was the need to keep course materials "fresh" and engaging, and this can commonly be achieved by including course materials that are of local or direct relevance to students or are current (Camman, 1992; Lieblein et al., 2005). In earth sciences, this is probably easier than other disciplines, as many natural phenomena have an earth science origin (e.g., volcanic eruptions, earthquakes, tsunamis) and such stories appear frequently in the media.

Much of the past research on distance delivery of earth sciences is anecdotal. Many potentially valuable earth science distance education programs seem to suffer from a lack of systematic evaluation and follow-up (e.g., Camman, 1992; McDowell & Yockney, 1992; Neal, 2007). Due, probably in part, to the lack of systematic evaluations of distance-delivered earth science courses, their effectiveness is still somewhat uncertain (e.g., Warf, Vincent & Purcell, 1999; Reed & Mitchell, 2001).

At a more anecdotal level, certain approaches have been found to be very effective at enhancing student comprehension of certain concepts or course materials. In the case of structural geology, having students physically construct a globe and experiment with it to understand concepts of projections and stereonets appears to be particularly effective. It has also been found that some sort of field geology component can be undertaken by students regardless of their location. This could involve analysis of stratigraphy in areas with appropriate geological environments, or something as simple as examining rock types used to make headstones in a cemetery or a visit to a local museum, for students located in areas of "bland" geology. Appropriate exercises can be constructed that allow for some level of field observation in nearly any environment. An ability to conduct field observations in a locally relevant context is found to be advantageous to students and builds on the more rigorous studies cited above that demonstrate the benefits of local relevance in earth science courses.

The type of laboratory exercises that are incorporated into an earth science curriculum or course must of course be driven by the learning objectives. Some courses lend themselves well to the use of physical "props," in particular mineralogy and petrology. There appears to be no effective substitute for students being given the opportunity to physically handle geological samples. In the larger context, and as discussed above, laboratory/field-based activities are felt to be particularly important in the earth sciences because of the essential coupling between theory, observation, and understanding that underpins much of the earth sciences.

Some earth science programs, such as that at Athabasca University, permit students to begin a particular course at the start of any month of the year. As a result, group projects are not feasible in this setting. However, effective group work has been found to be difficult to implement in a number of cases (Shea, 1995; Reed & Mitchell, 2001; Vassala, 2006), and thus a lack of group interaction is not considered to be an impediment to effective earth science education.

Returning momentarily to the issue of distance versus face-to-face instruction, the success or satisfaction level of a particular student will depend on their particular circumstances, and a number of studies have shown that some types of students perform better in a distance education environment than they would in a traditional setting (Camman, 1992; Mose & Maney, 1993; Warf, Vincent & Purcell, 1999; Dibiase, 2000).

## Conclusions

With such a wide-ranging topic as earth sciences, it is difficult to draw universally applicable conclusions. This difficulty is coupled to the general lack of rigorous evaluations of the effectiveness of distance-delivered earth science courses. However, some general observations can be made from the preceding overview:

- field-based study of some sort appears to be beneficial for earth science students
- geology courses should include "hands-on" exercises for students involving the use of rock/mineral/fossil samples
- techniques-based courses, such as structural geology, remote sensing/image processing, and geographic information systems, should include a laboratory component, as this provides a number of simultaneous benefits
- courses should be subdivided into discrete modules which, while allowing for a logical flow, facilitate updating and revision
- all aspects of an earth science laboratory (e.g., learning outcomes, time requirements, student expectations, course materials) need to be well integrated to ensure student satisfaction and skills development

There appear to be no major impediments to distance delivery of effective earth science laboratories. It is, however, imperative that earth science laboratory courses be well designed prior to delivery, and constantly evaluated in terms of effectiveness and student satisfaction.

REFERENCES

Andris, J.F. (1996). The relationship of indices of student navigational patterns in a hypermedia geology lab simulation to two measures of learning style. *Journal of Educational Multimedia and Hypermedia, 5,* 303–315.

Bishop, M.P., Schroder Jr., J.F., & Moore, T.K. (1995). Integration of computer technology and interactive learning in geographic education. *Journal of Geography in Higher Education, 19,* 97–110.

Blowers, A., Sarre, P., & Smith, D. (1992) Exploring interdisciplinary issues at a distance: Teaching environment at the Open University. In R. Gerber & M. Williams (Eds.), *Distance education and geography teaching,* (pp. 26–33). Swansea, Wales, United Kingdom: Department of Education, University College of Swansea.

Buckley, C., & Donert, K. (2004). Evaluating e-learning courses for continuing professional development using the Conversational Model: A review of UNIGIS. *European Journal of Open, Distance and E-Learning, 2004.* Retrieved February 24, 2009 from: http://www.eurodl.org/materials/contrib/2004/Buckley_Donert.html

Butler, J.C., & Gore, P. (1997). Another node on the internet. *Computers & Geosciences, 23,* 607–608.

Camman, M. (1992) Telelearning project. In R. Gerber & M. Williams (Eds.), *Distance education and geography teaching,* (pp. 71–93). Swansea, Wales, United Kingdom: Department of Education, University College of Swansea.

de Caprariis, P.P. (2000). Creating or adapting courses for on-line presentation. *Journal of Geoscience Education, 48,* 673–678. Retrieved February 24, 2009 from: http://www.nagt.org/files/nagt/jge/abstracts/v48n5p673.pdf

Dibiase, D. (2000). Is distance education a Faustian bargain? *Journal of Geography in Higher Education, 24,* 130–135.

Finstick, S.A. (2002). Field trips — their importance in an undergraduate general education distance learning geology course. Presented at: 54th Annual Meeting of the Geological

Society of America; Cedar City, IO, USA, May 7–9, 2002. Abstract 34015.

Foote, K.E. (1999). Building disciplinary collaborations on the World Wide Web: Strategies and barriers. *Journal of Geography, 98,* 108–117.

Gerber, R., & Lundin, R. (1992). Strategies for distance education in geography. In R. Gerber & M. Williams (Eds.), *Distance education and geography teaching,* (pp. 108–127). Swansea, Wales, United Kingdom: Department of Education, University College of Swansea.

Gerber, R., & Williams, M. (Eds.) (1992). *Distance education and geography teaching.* Swansea, Wales, United Kingdom: Department of Education, University College of Swansea.

Gober, P. (1998). Distance learning and geography's soul. *AAG Newsletter, 33*(5), 1–2.

Harvey, L. (2002). The end of quality?. *Quality in Higher Education, 8,* 5–22.

Healey, M., Kneale, P., Bradbeer, J., with other members of the INTL Learning Styles and Concepts Group (2005). Learning styles among geography undergraduates: An international comparison. *Area, 37,* 30–42.

Kern, E.L., & Carpenter, J.R. (1984). Enhancement of student values, interests and attitudes in earth science through a field-oriented approach. *Journal of Geological Education, 32,* 299–305.

Kern, E.L., & Carpenter, J.R. (1986). Effect of field activities on student learning. *Journal of Geological Education, 34,* 180–183.

Lemke, K.A., & Ritter, M.E. (2000) Virtual geographies and the use of the internet for learning and teaching geography in higher education. *Journal of Geography in Higher Education, 24,* 87–91.

Lieblein, G., Moulton, M., Sriskandarajah, N., Christensen, D., Waalen, W., Breland, T.A., Francis, S., Salomonsson, L., & Langer, V. (2005). A Nordic Net-based course in agroecology — integrating student learning and teacher collaboration. *European Journal of Open, Distance and E-Learning.* Retrieved February 24, 2009 from: http://www.eurodl.org/materials/contrib/2005/Lieblein.htm

McDowell, W., & Yockney, J. (1992). Distance learning: Great Britain's Royal Navy and the study of geography. In R. Gerber & M. Williams (Eds.), *Distance education and geography teaching,* (pp. 57–70). Swansea, Wales, United Kingdom: Department of Education, University College of Swansea.

Moles, J.A. (1988). The classroom and the field: A necessary unity. *Journal of Experiential Education, 11*(2), 14–20.

Mose, D., & Maney, T. (1993). An experiment in distance learning of geology. *Journal of Computers in Mathematics and Science Teaching, 12*, 5–18.

Neal, E. (2007). A critical response to Jerald G. Schutte's virtual teaching in higher education: The new intellectual superhighway of just another traffic jam? Retrieved February 24, 2009 from: http://www.informatikdidaktik.de/HyFISCH/Teleteaching/VirtualTeachingCritics.html

Reed, M., & Mitchell, B. (2001). Using information technologies for collaborative learning in geography: a case study from Canada. *Journal of Geography in Higher Education, 25*, 321–339.

Reuter, R. (2007) Introductory soils online: An effective way to get online students in the field. *Journal of Natural Resources and Life Sciences Education, 36*, 139–146.

Schroder Jr., J.F., Bishop, M.P., Olsenholler, J., & Craiger, J.P. (2002). Geomorphology and the World Wide Web. *Geomorphology, 47*, 343–363.

Shea, J.H. (1995). Problems with collaborative learning. *Journal of Geological Education, 43*, 306–308.

Shea, J. (1999). Education "research" at the annual meeting. *Journal of Geoscience Education, 47*, 110.

Solem, M., Chalmers, L., Dibiase, D., Donert, K., & Hardwick, S. (2006). Internationalizing professional development in geography through distance education. *Journal of Geography in Higher Education, 30*, 147–160.

Tremblay, R. (2006). Technical evaluation report. 55. Best practices and collaborative software in online teaching. *International Review of Research in Open and Distance Learning, 7*(1). Retrieved February 24, 2009 from: http://www.irrodl.org/index.php/irrodl/article/view/309/513

Vassala, P. (2006). The field study as an educational technique in open and distance learning. *Turkish Online Journal of Distance Education, 7*(4), 10–17. Retrieved February 24, 2009 from: http://tojde.anadolu.edu.tr/tojde24/articles/article_1.htm

Veal, W., Brantley, J., & Zulli, R. (2004). Developing an online geology course for preservice and inservice teachers: Enhancements for online learning. *Contemporary Issues in Technology and Science Teacher Education, 3*, 382–411. Retrieved February 24, 2009 from: http://www.citejournal.org/vol3/iss4/science/article1.cfm

Warf, B., Vincent, P., & Purcell, D. (1999). International collaborative learning on the World Wide Web. *Journal of Geography, 98*, 141–148.

Williams, M. (1992) Distance learning and geographical education: Introduction. In R. Gerber & M. Williams (Eds.), *Distance education and geography teaching*, (pp. 1–8). Swansea, Wales, United Kingdom: Department of Education, University College of Swansea.

## APPENDIX — REVIEW OF PREVIOUS STUDIES

Andris (1996) conducted a hypermedia geology lab simulation which utilized actual rock and mineral samples as part of the laboratory. He found that students' learning style affected how students utilized the accompanying hypermedia resources.

Bishop, Schroder & Moore (1995) provide a discussion of integrating internet-based resources into earth science teaching. They concluded that such materials are proliferating rapidly and provide new opportunities for distance education beyond those available through more traditional media, as well as being applicable to a wide range of pedagogical tasks.

Blowers, Sarre & Smith (1992) reviewed the development of interdisciplinary courses in environment science at the Open University in the United Kingdom. They found that well-developed objectives and time requirements are essential elements for such courses.

Buckley & Donert (2004) conducted a review of the UNIGIS program from the perspective of continuing professional development and student interaction. They found that the program delivers many benefits but that some shortcomings remain.

Butler & Gore (1997) briefly reviews his delivery of introductory-level geology courses via distance delivery. He found that periodic face-to-face visits were beneficial from a number of perspectives. These courses were also supplemented by traditional face-to-face laboratories.

Camman (1992) provides an overview of a telelearning project in geography at the secondary school level. She found that well-planned and delivered course materials were essential to student satisfaction and that group projects and field excursions were well received by the students.

De Caprariis (2000) discusses the general lack of research on distance education in earth sciences. He has determined that various modes of feedback should be included in course design. Course design should also include careful consideration of objectives, skills, and teaching strategies.

Dibiase (2000) discusses some of the larger issues surrounding geography distance education. He contends that educators have an obligation to serve as wide a constituency as possible. He also finds that distance learners are qualitatively different from traditional undergraduate students and that they can be properly served by distance delivery.

Finstick (2002) discusses the use of field trips in the context of an undergraduate distance learning course. The field work component of the course was consistently rated as one of the most enjoyable parts of the course.

Foote (1999) presents a discussion of how the Internet can be used to develop collaborative distance offerings in geography. He has found that the multiplicity of resources allows for the development of high-quality courses and laboratory modules that can be widely adopted.

Gerber & Lundin (1992) reviewed the findings of a committee on distance education. It was found that important elements in distance delivery of geography programs include carefully developed materials, small modules of study, the availability of counselling, and credit transferability. In addition, the particular needs and learning styles of students need to be considered during course development.

Gerber & Williams (1992) provided a compendium of studies and presentations conducted by the IGU Commission on Geographical Education. Many of the contributions discuss specific examples of distance delivery of geographic courses. While some of the findings, particularly as they relate to the impact and use of computer resources for distance delivery, are now somewhat dated, it is an excellent overview of some of the early efforts in this area.

Gober (1998) presents an impassioned case for including field work as a component of earth science education. Such work provides a number of perceived benefits, including developing a "sense of place" among geography students.

Harvey (2002) provides a summary of discussions and presentations of papers presented at a seminar entitled "The End of Quality," held in 2001. One of the themes that emerged from this meeting is the need to pay close attention to course organization and clarity in the design of distance education courses.

Healey, Kneale & Bradbeer (2005) conducted a study of learning styles among geography undergraduate students. They found that students in this group possess different learning styles, as expected, and that the proportion of different learning styles varies among different countries.

Kern & Carpenter (1984) describe results of an experimental introductory level earth science course delivery study where students took an essentially identical course, with or without a fieldwork component. Students who participated in the fieldwork-enhanced course reported greater levels of enjoyment and interest.

Kern & Carpenter (1986) report results from a study similar to that reported in their 1984 paper. In their 1986 study both groups of students had identical levels of lower-order learning, while the group enrolled in the section with a fieldwork component demonstrated significantly higher levels of comprehension, application, analysis, and synthesis of knowledge.

Lemke & Ritter (2000) discuss the use of the Internet for distance education in geography. They found that this is a potentially valuable educational resource, but that instructors must pay careful attention to ensure that it is used as an effective teaching tool.

Lieblein et al. (2005) conducted an evaluation of a Net-based ecology course offered through Nordic Net. This study involved students from a number of countries and diverse backgrounds. Among their findings was that providing a local perspective to the course (in this case farming practices), even if the local perspective was used for comparison with the case study used in the course, was beneficial to the learning experience of the students. They also emphasized the importance of designing the course starting from clearly defined learning objectives.

McDowell & Yockney (1992) reported on distance delivery of geography courses for the British Royal Navy. They concluded that effective geography teaching can be provided for students in a wide variety of geographic and operational settings.

Moles (1988) offers personal perspectives on the values to be derived from experiential teaching (i.e., field work). He found that the inclusion of a field-based component to his agricultural courses added immeasurably to the students' educational experiences.

Mose & Maney (1993) provide a discussion of an introductory level geology course offered via distance learning. They found that students who utilized computers for communications showed improvements in their grades over the first (non-computer) semester.

Neal (2007) provides a brief critique of an earlier unpublished study by J.G. Schutte concerning serious errors in evaluating distance versus direct learning courses. He found that the distance and direct learning courses were very different and hence meaningful comparisons could not be made.

Reed & Mitchell (2001) report on their experiences in designing and delivering a distance collaborative learning course in geography. They found that a number of challenges arose in this exercise, with a major issue being the need to clearly define objectives and expectations.

Reuter (2007) discusses the success in offering hands-on/distance delivered lab components of an introductory level soil science course. They found no significant differences between the distance delivered and face-to-face versions of this course. The distance education laboratory component was designed to ensure that students could perform the necessary experiments through simplified experiments.

Schroder et al. (2002) discuss resources available on the World Wide Web that are relevant to teaching geomorphology, either by direct or distance delivery. They find that the use of such resources can enhance a student's learning experience, but that they must be used judiciously.

Shea (1995) described anecdotal evidence gathered over many years of teaching, documenting a number of shortcomings associated with collaborative learning in the earth sciences. These shortcomings include scheduling constraints and unequal levels of participation by team members.

Shea (1999) bemoans the general lack of rigorous education research in the earth sciences. While the volume of such work has increased its usefulness has not.

Solem et al. (2006) discuss the issues behind international professional development in geography through distance education. They examine the potential of distance learning and conclude that it can be used to reach non-traditional learners and other underserved constituencies. They also identify a number of challenges, including quality assurance and inter-institutional certification.

Tremblay (2006) provides an overview of collaborative software available for distance delivery. He believes that a number of tools should be available or used to ensure that a rewarding learning experience is provided to all students.

Vassala (2006) provides some lessons learned from the use of field work in open and distance learning in geology. She finds that field study was enthusiastically embraced by her students, but that special care must be taken to effectively undertake field studies given the external demands on students' time.

Veal, Brantley & Zulli (2004) provide a discussion of techniques for developing and delivering an online geology course. They found that interpersonal interactions were perceived by the students as being influential to their learning. As with other distance delivery courses, a number of procedural hurdles needed to be overcome.

Warf, Vincent & Purcell (1999) discuss the use of the Internet for international collaborative learning in geography. Among their conclusions, they believe that Web-based interactive learning is an "imperfect substitute" for traditional face-to-face interaction.

Williams (1992), in his introduction to the volume by Gerber & Williams (1992), discusses some of the essential elements that need to be considered during course development for distance education in geography. He concludes that geography distance education can be adapted for in-service teacher education, provided that learning objectives are identified initially, followed by needs analysis and determination of appropriate delivery methods and support services.

# Chapter 9
## Remote Control Teaching Laboratories and Practicals

DIETMAR KENNEPOHL
Athabasca University

## Introduction

A strong laboratory or practical component is at the heart of many university-level science courses. Yet, it is still also one of the more challenging elements of a course to deliver effectively at a distance (Kennepohl & Last, 1997). Experimentation is regarded as a fundamental part of the education and training of most scientists and so university science programs require practical components to be considered *bona fide* or recognized within the scientific community. The rationale for having practical work in the sciences, the role of the teaching laboratory, and its changing nature have been discussed and will continue to be discussed at great length (Bennett & O'Neale, 1998; George, 2003; National Research Council, 2003; Lagowski, 2005). A variety of methods have been employed to address delivery of practical components at distance, including (1) supervised face-to-face sessions offered in a concentrated format on campus or at regional sites or in the field; (2) home study laboratory kits; (3) video demonstrations of experiments; and (4) interactive computer simulations. There is no one correct solution in delivering laboratories for distance students and often an assortment of methods are used in concert to overcome challenges (Kennepohl & Last, 2000). However, some educators have now directed their efforts toward allowing students remote access to real experiments via the Internet. These remote experiments have benefits for both distance and residential environments alike. They are increasingly appearing in a variety of disciplines and quickly becoming a viable part of a science educator's teaching arsenal. This work will provide a brief review of how remote controlled experiments are being used, some observations on creating remote experiments, the advantages and challenges associated with remote access, and expected trends for the future.

## Remote control over the Internet

Remote control devices are well incorporated into our growing technological world. We have automatic car starters on our key chains, unmanned reconnaissance drones are used by the military, police bomb squads regularly make use of robots, and most of us use a remote control to change television channels. The idea of remote controlled experiments is not a new one for scientists either. Remote control is often used when an experiment or instrument is physically inaccessible by virtue of location or danger. For example, safety demands that all nuclear fission reactors are operated remotely, unmanned spacecraft and deep sea craft are used for exploration, and the location of the orbiting Hubble space telescope makes remote control a necessity. Scientists also find that remote access is an excellent method for sharing expensive equipment and facilities with other researchers.

Although remote control has been with us for some time, remote control over the Internet for teaching experiments was only first established in the early 1990s (Cox & Baruch, 1994; Penfield & Larson, 1996). Over the years it has primarily been used in the areas of robotics, computing, and engineering and, not surprisingly, the bulk of the literature contributions have come from these fields. In addition to the use of these laboratories for teaching students, the disciplinary interest has focused on such topics that include: physical control and manipulations (Yeung & Huang, 2003; Sebastian, Garcia & Sanchez, 2003; Doulgeri & Matiakis, 2006), electronics and electrical engineering (Arpia et al., 1998; Ko et al., 2000; Jimenez-Leube et al., 2001; Ferrero et al., 2003; Nedic, Machotka & Nafalski, 2003), physical measurements (Chang et al., 2005), and the system architecture (Arpia et al., 1998; Das, Sharma & Gogoi, 2006; Yan et al., 2006) . The examples cited give only an indication of the work being done and are not by any means an exhaustive listing. A summary of remote laboratory sites found online (Teichmann & Faltin, 2002) and an online bibliography of recent literature (DiscoverLab, 2007) give a good initial overview of what is available.

In contrast, the use of remote access for teaching laboratories in the natural and physical sciences has not been as common. A recent worldwide inventory done in 2006 indicates that about 60–70% is in engineering, 30% is in physics (this includes electronics labs), and less than 10% occur in other disciplines (Gröber et al., 2007). In the past, the complexity and technology involved have often dissuaded universal adoption of remote controlled experimentation as a part of regularly run university-level science courses. However, with the increasing availability and robustness of new technologies, the use of remote laboratories and remote access is being explored by many educators in the sciences as a viable method of offering a first-class practicum experience for the student. Despite the increasing interest, the formal literature on remote access for teaching in the sciences is meagre and sporadic. Much of the work being done in this area is presented at conferences or is quite often only reported on the website of the remote lab itself, rather than in refereed publications. In addition, the use of remote laboratories is often experimental and fleeting, resulting in many websites that are outdated or inaccessible. Jodl and co-workers carried out a worldwide remote controlled laboratory inventory in 2004 and again in 2006. Although the total number of remote labs increased in that time from 70 to 120, free access to those labs dropped from 70% to 30%. More striking is that of those with free access only 20% worked without problems (Gröber et al., 2007).

## Not a virtual laboratory

With the advent of the World Wide Web there has been a great deal of effort placed on bringing the student laboratory experience online. In many instances, the online laboratory components are simulated and offer the virtual laboratory experience (Kennepohl, 2001; Jara et al., 2009). In discussing the role of remote laboratories it is vital to realize the difference between a virtual laboratory environment and remote teaching laboratories. A virtual environment is created through interactive computer simulations of instrumentation and experiments. The role of virtual laboratories can prepare students for a real laboratory environment or, conversely, reinforce concepts from theory or experiment. In contrast, remote access achieves many of the same things as a virtual laboratory, but also allows learners to physically carry out real experiments over the Web. Students obtain real results using real substances and make real conclusions, just as they would if they were in the laboratory with the equipment.

Remote laboratories are a step beyond the virtual realm and their computer generated laboratory simulations. They represent the best alternative to working in a real laboratory. Although there is a variation in use, remote teaching laboratories are being employed in four basic ways:

> 1. to allow observations of natural phenomenon or experiments;
> 2. to carry out measurements;
> 3. to manipulate instruments or physical objects in experiments;
> 4. to facilitate collaborative work at a distance.

*Observation*
Facilitating observations remotely is by far the simplest and most robust version of a remote experiment. Usually the observer interaction is minimal and is often limited to controlling the camera. For example, the astronomical camera called "Stardial" delivers images of the night sky in real time (McCullough & Thakkar, 1997), and our own university houses a geomagnetic observatory to study the northern lights that includes spectacular 360° images of the night sky which can be accessed remotely (Donovan et al., 2006). There are also Internet controlled electron microscope sites such as "Bugscope" (Potter et al., 2001) and "POIT-EM" (Furuya et al., 2005), which accept and prepare mailed-in specimens for observation. Students then log on at scheduled times to carry out their observations. The importance of observation in supporting measurements and manipulations is also often cited (Lang et al., 2007).

*Measurement*
Other remote experiments go beyond observation, and the core activity is to carry out some measurements. A few examples include measuring the elasticity of a metal beam as a function of temperature (Alhalabi et al., 2001), reaction kinetics in chemistry (Senese, Bender & Kile, 2000), measuring and analyzing remote sound waves (Forinash & Wisman, 2005), thermal conductivity experiments in food engineering (Palou et al., 2005), chemical analysis using gas chromatography (Baran, Currie & Kennepohl, 2004), and carrying out single crystal X-ray diffraction measurements (Szalay, Zeller & Hunter, 2005). There is also an excellent series of online physics experiments on the RCL—Remotely Controlled Laboratories site, with such experiments as a wind tunnel, Millikan's oil drop experiment, diffraction, and interference (Gröber et al., 2007).

*Manipulation*
In addition to observing and measuring, some remote experiments will require actual physical control of objects. This could be

the control of an electric motor (Yeung & Huang, 2003) or a scale model greenhouse for climate and irrigation control (Guzmán et al., 2005) or more interactive robotic operations, such as manipulating a mechanical arm or moving a toy vehicle through a maze (Gröber et al., 2007). It is important to note that although observation, measurement, and manipulation are separately identified and illustrated in our discussion above, it is common to incorporate combinations of these into one experiment. For example, a remotely controlled simple ball-drop apparatus used by physics students to determine g (gravitational constant) is described in the literature (Connors, 2004). A steel ball is physically moved to a specific height determined by the student and released (manipulation), the student reads the output from a timer which automatically starts upon the ball's release and stops when the ball passes by an optical sensor (measurement), and the entire process is captured on a Web camera (observation).

### *Collaboration*

Certainly one advantage of Internet access is that it can facilitate sharing not only of experiments and instruments, but also of data. A recent remote laboratory example is in animal behaviour, involving following a mouse in an arena. This employed observation and measurement, along with collaboratively pooling individual student findings to gain better statistical results (Fiore & Ratti, 2007). Others are also taking advantage of the remote control environment to incorporate a collaborative component to their teaching practicals, such as collecting kinetic data from an entire class (Senese, Bender & Kile, 2000). Indeed, the idea of using remote laboratories to facilitate collaboration has already been employed to a limited degree by science researchers during these last two decades and is described as a "collaboratory" (Sonnenwald, 2003). Applying the concept of the collaboratory in a teaching environment is being explored by some groups (Johnston et al., 2001).

## Pedagogy and learning

Among science educators, there is a collective wealth of practical experience in using the laboratory to teach undergraduate students. There is also an increasing awareness of teaching and learning models that underpins many existing best practices and can potentially lead to new approaches for improvement. Earlier parts of this book discuss some of these fundamentals of how science students learn that also extend discussion to the practical and laboratory components. Bailey and Garratt provide an excellent review of teaching and learning theories as they apply to chemical education and to science education in general (Bailey & Garratt, 2002). In addition, more generalized reference sources are available for those interested in how students learn (Driscoll, 2005).

Despite a general interest in the scholarship of learning, the literature around remote practicals and laboratories has mainly focused on the technology and feasibility of the access rather than on its educational value. Yet in developing a remote laboratory component for science students, educators should have many of the same aims and intuitively employ many of the same strategies, such as the incorporation of appropriate feedback, creating an active learning environment, and providing sufficient logical structure and guidance to form a cognitive foundation for the student to build on. They should also be aware of challenges surrounding the matching of teaching and learning styles (Krause 2003; Yeung, Read & Schmid, 2005) and feel compelled to provide a level of meaningful engagement that will motivate students (Newstead & Hoskins, 2003). However, the real question on everyone's mind is whether there is equivalent learning using remote access as opposed to the traditional supervised laboratories.

There are two criticisms often levelled against remote laboratories. First, they are seen as not offering the identical laboratory environment with all its atmosphere, noises, smells, and haptic experience of experimenting. Secondly, the student-student and student-instructor interactions are usually altered and reduced.

The underlying epistemological assumptions of these criticisms are that both laboratory environment and human interaction are needed to give the student an effective laboratory experience. Indeed, laboratory environment and human interaction can and do lead to both formal and informal learning. However, we know that other forms of interaction in other environments can also lead to learning. Our own experience has been that there are no substantial overall differences in student performance between proximal and remote modes. Other researchers have also reported similar findings (Ogot, Elliot & Glumac, 2003; Scanlon et al., 2004; Doulgeri & Matiakis, 2006; Fiore & Ratti, 2007). One well-controlled systematic study goes even further in its evaluation by identifying differences between learning outcomes of students carrying out the same experiment onsite, remotely, or as a simulation (Lindsay & Good, 2005). Overall learning is equivalent, but particular components of that learning are better suited to different modes of delivery. For example, students in the non-proximal modes of this experiment were more likely to identify and understand consequences of non-idealities in their results. Lindsay and Good also caution against using student surveys in evaluating learning by showing that their students' perceptions of learning objectives and actual learning outcomes are mismatched.

The challenge for the educator now becomes more than just building the technological means to carry out remote experiments or teaching the disciplinary principles through a remote laboratory. The student also needs to learn how to be comfortable with and effectively operate in that remote laboratory environment. Successful remote laboratories are self-contained, intuitive, and designed with a seamless pedagogical front end to facilitate the high level of student learning and skills development necessary to carry out an experiment at a distance. Some components employed to do just that have included FAQs and help sections, video or audio clips, tutorials, simulations, access to the instructor and other students, qualifier exercises, self-tests, library or database access, supplementary materials or related links, note-taking functionality, and live images of the equipment and laboratory. It is vital that student interaction with the experiment be free of excessive time delays and have sufficiently clear feedback for the student to know their commands are being executed. The instructional design, reliability, and functionality of the online remote laboratory environment need to be at a level where the student is not distracted from learning or discouraged from exploring. As with any experiment in science or engineering, it does not necessarily need to be sophisticated or complex — just effective.

## Creating a remote experiment

Developing the laboratory or a practical component of a course requires consideration of many factors. Each laboratory type (whether real, virtual, or remote) offers both advantages and limitations. Those associated with remote laboratories will be discussed in more detail later in this chapter. There are very basic logistical considerations that often seem very obvious in hindsight, but should be addressed up front. The experiment itself should be kept as simple and robust as possible, proper physical space needs to be secured to house the experiment, ongoing maintenance needs to be arranged, and certainly ongoing financing should be in place. As with any laboratory component, there should be a clear vision of what learning objectives and outcomes are intended for the remote experiment being developed. As we have discussed in the last section, a solid didactic foundation is desirable before moving to the technology solutions needed to achieve those intended goals.

There is a certain degree of novelty in the technology being used that has, in effect, become a double-edged sword. At the onset of introducing a new mode of experiment there is a Hawthorne effect. The laboratory designer, the teacher, and the student have a keen interest and usually respond positively for an initial period. That effect, coupled with the realization of the benefits a remote laboratory can bring, has been identified by Lindsay & Good as an amplification effect. The downside, of course, is the attenuation effect, which results from technology getting in the way. That negative effect is often a result of focusing on the technology itself rather than what the technology is supporting (Lindsay & Good, 2005).

Still, technology needs to be properly addressed. There are several commercial software packages available (e.g., PC Duo, PC Anywhere, Labview) that allow clients to access and take control of a remote experiment with just a web browser. The strength of keeping the specialized software on the delivery side is that it allows more universal access for students, while removing other logistical problems associated with distributing sofware. Issues of security, multiple users, and compatibility with other software and hardware are certainly very specific to each situation. It is therefore imperative that professional information technology (IT) support be locally available to address issues like this and ensure success.

In contemplating the design for a remote laobratory environment used by the student, the educator who has the local and disciplinary knowledge is often best suited to lead its development. However, having an experienced instructional designer participate in the creation of the site is advantageous to the process. As much as possible, the technology should not get in the way of learning and everything needed to carry out the experiment should be readily available for the student. That usually means a self-contained site that is seamless and intuitive from the students' perspective. The following are a few online features that might be considered in building such a remote environment.

1. Public information describing the project, the researchers, and funding sources.
2. Password protection (if needed) to limit access to areas that may be damaged.

3. Scheduler function to help students and instructors assign unique and secure instrument time to qualified operators.
4. Searchable FAQ and Help sections to address common problems encountered by students.
5. Tutorials to introduce students to the software, the equipment, and the particular experiment being undertaken.
6. Experiment simulations (in some cases) to allow practice.
7. Qualifier exercises to establish a minimum skill level for students before moving onto actual instrument access.
8. Actual remote access to carry out real experiments.
9. Web camera to allow real-time viewing of the instrument during the experiment. The purpose is to make the instrument real for the remote student (i.e., "seeing is believing").
10. Connection to the instructor and other students to further address problems and provide moral support.
11. eLogbooks to allow students to make comments and house data collected from the experiment. This is especially useful for the facile handling of large data sets collected, so students are not immersed in the details.
12. Supplementary resource materials provided for each experiment such as a database reference library or remedial resources (e.g., statistics review) or other useful links for further study.
13. An area to submit individual data and retrieve pooled results.

## Advantages and disadvantages

Each laboratory type (whether real, virtual, or remote) comes with its own advantages and disadvantges (Nedic, Machotka &

Nafalski, 2003). Computer simulations in virtual laboratories have advantages over real laboratory work such as allowing students to do more complicated and hazardous experiments, obtain reproducible results more quickly, and aquire a deeper understanding of the experiments, just to name a few. Disadvantages such as the lack of human contact, boredom, and lack of experimental errors are also associated with laboratory simulations. Employing remote laboratories is way to add flexibility while still working on real experiments.

The importance of the opportunity to do real experiments as opposed to simulations cannot be understated and has often been stressed by researchers in the area (Nedic, Machotka & Nafalski, 2003; Kennepohl et al., 2005; Cooper, 2005). Since these remote laboratories exist in the physical world with real experiments on real samples, there is also the possibility of operational problems, errors, and non-ideal results. In moderation, this is beneficial for the student. Ironically, creators of some simulated experiments spend a lot of effort incorporating errors into their programs to make them more real and place the learner into a problem-solving environment. Real-life experiments, whether accessed in-lab or remotely, seem to do this automatically and we should see this as an opportunity to encourage learning.

The role of the laboratory experience is to promote learning and reinforce theoretical concepts covered in the course. It is also used to develop practical skills and encourage problem solving. Educators are reporting that remote laboratories are not only providing viable alternatives to a real laboratory experience, but also providing their own distinctive advantages. As with a real laboratory, a remote laboratory provides:

- an experience with real equipment and experiments;
- presence and control of experiments in the laboratory;
- an opportunity to explore through trial and error;
- generation of real data.

The remote laboratory also has other potential benefits when compared to a real laboratory and can also provide:
- the ability to do more complicated and hazardous experiments;
- a network for learners and teacher to facilitate collaboration;
- increased access to experiments irrespective of geography;
- increased flexibility and the opportunity for more experimentation and exploration;
- better use of institutional resources;
- opportunities for students with disabilities.

Limitations and disadvantages in using remote laboratories include:
- a dependence on a reliable technological platform for delivery;
- the continued perception that there is a decreased educational value;
- financial commitment necessary to build and maintain the experiment;
- extra effort needed to design a high-quality learning environment.

## Trends

Currently the use of remote laboratories over the Internet for teaching is just developing. There are examples of several initial efforts on various websites that reflect that interest. Unfortunately, the fact that many of those remote laboratory websites are currently not functional indicates the very exploratory nature of this mode of delivery and perhaps also a serious underestimation of what is needed to maintain working experiments. There has been little formal study on the effectiveness of remote laboratories, especially from a pedagogical perspective. One recent review of engineering laboratories suggests we have been lingering at a technological crossroads awaiting the next generation of remote experiments that will hopefully address such issues as reusability, interoperability, collaborativeness, and convergence with Learning Management Systems (Gravier et al., 2008).

With newer technologies becoming more reliable and available, teachers will continue to explore remote laboratory use and develop more experiments. For example, one upcoming trend is the increased availability of mobile devices and interest in m-learning (Wu, Kuo & Lin, 2005; López-de-Ipiña, García-Zubia & Orduña, 2006; Wattinger et al., 2006). Development in this area offers the possibility of increasing access to remote laboratories to an even larger degree. With a handheld wireless device one could literally be almost anywhere and carry out an experiment remotely. As current and new technologies become more commonplace, the emphasis should also shift from the novelty around the mechanics of setting up a remote access connection for a specific experiment to designing and evaluating the learning experience for the student in a remote environment. A more systematic evaluation of the learning experience will be absolutely necessary to inform the larger discussion on how remote laboratories can and should be used in science and engineering curricula.

Much of the continued exploration with new technology will no doubt be driven by interest, but there will also be increasing fiscal pressure to bring laboratory costs down. To do that, administrators will be constantly seeking cost-effective alternatives to the traditional teaching laboratory. Although the upfront investment in setting up a quality remote laboratory environment is significant, the ability to remotely share experiments and equipment would reduce costs for students and individual institutions. This aspect of remote laboratories is attractive not only to distance educators, but also to traditional residential institutions seeking to extend the use of current facilities.

Sharing experiments and equipment is not limited to single institutions. The accessible nature of remote laboratories also has the potential to foster collaborations at many levels. In fact, various inter-institutional collaborations and consortia have already been created to share the cost and the benefits of remote laboratories. Although not operational since 2003, the PEARL project (Practical Experimentation by Accessible Remote Learning) was a consortium of European Union (EU) institutions developing remote experiments in spectrometry, cell biology, manufacturing engineering, and electronic engineering (Scanlon et al., 2004). *ProLearn* is a network of research groups financed by the Information Society Technology program of the European commission dealing with technology-enhanced professional learning (ProLearn, 2007). The German *LearNet* initiative is a consortium of eight German universities sharing remote engineering laboratories (LearNet, 2007). Another EU consortium called *Network for Education — Chemistry* uses mostly interactive simulations, but it is also exploring online remote process control using a residence time distribution experiment (Zürn et al., 2003). There are many more collaborations as well as some commercial interests in offering remote laboratory services. For example, the *World Wide Student Laboratory* has partial funding from the National Science Foundation in the United States and offers delivery of science and engineering education over the Internet. As remote experiments become more common one can envisage networks of laboratories sharing experiments. Rather than everyone duplicating experiments, there would be a coordinated system of hosting specific laboratories. One institution might host an electron microscope, another an analytical chemistry instrument, while another might have an interactive optics laboratory.

## Conclusion

The use of remote teaching laboratories offers residential as well as distance educators another tool to integrate a strong laboratory component within a science course. The experience is not necessarily identical to supervised on-campus laboratories, but it is equivalent. Students obtain real results using real substances to arrive at real conclusions, just as they would if they were in a physical laboratory with the equipment; this approach allows students to access to science experiments, thus providing them with an advantageous route to upgrade their laboratory skills.

## REFERENCES

Alhalabi, B., Hamza, M.K., & Marcovitz, D.M. (2001). Innovative distance education technologies: remote labs in science & engineering education. *ISTE Journal of Online Learning*, June. Retrieved February 25, 2009 from: http://www.iste.org/Content/NavigationMenu/Membership/SIGs/SIGTel_Telelearning_/SIGTelBulletin/Archive/20012/2001_June_-_Alhalabi.htm

Arpia, P., Baccigalupi, A., Cennamo, F., & Daponte, P. (1998). A measurement laboratory on geographic network for remote test experiments, IEEE Instrumentation and Measurement Technology Conference, St. Paul, 18–21 May.

Bailey P.D., & Garratt J. (2002). Chemical education: theory and practice. *University Chemistry Education*, 6, 39–57.

Baran, J., Currie, R., & Kennepohl, D. (2004). Remote instrumentation for the teaching laboratory. *Journal of Chemical Education*, 81, 1814–1816.

Bennett, S.W., & O'Neale, K. (1998). Skills development and practical work in chemistry. *University Chemistry Education*, 2, 58–62.

Chang, G.-W., Yeh, Z.-M., Chang, H.-M., & Pan, S.-Y. (2005). Teaching photonics laboratory using remote-control web technologies. IEEE Transactions on Education, 48, 642–651.

Connors, M. (2004). A decade of success in physics distance education at Athabasca University. *Physics in Canada*, 60, 49–54.

Cooper, M. (2005). Remote laboratories in teaching and learning — issues impinging on widespread adoption in science and engineering education. *International Journal of Online Engineering*, 1, 1–7.

Cox, M.J., & Baruch, J.E.F. (1994). Robotic telescopes: An interactive exhibit on the World-Wide Web. *Proceedings of the 2nd*

*International Conference of the World-Wide Web*, Chicago, 17–20 October.

Das, S., Sharma, L.N., & Gogoi, A.K. (2006). Remote communication engineering experiments through Internet. iJOE International Journal on Online Engineering, 2. Retrieved February 25, 2009 from: http://www.ijoe.org/ojs/include/getdoc.php?id=139&article=37&mode=pdf

DiscoverLab (2007). Publications and reference materials about the WWSL and related Projects. Retrieved February 25, 2009 from: http://www.discoverlab.com/publications.html

Donovan, E., Mende, S., Jackel, B., Frey, H., Syrjäsuo, M., Voronkov, I., Trondsen, T., Peticolas, L., Angelopoulos, V., Harris, S., Greffen, M., & Connors, M. (2006). The THEMIS all-sky imaging array — system design and initial results from the prototype imager. Journal of Atmospheric and Solar-Terrestrial Physics, 68, 1472–1487.

Doulgeri, Z., & Matiakis, T. (2006). A web telerobotic system to teach industrial robot path planning and control. IEEE Transactions on Education, 49, 263–270.

Driscoll, M. (2005). Psychology of learning for instruction (3rd ed.). Boston: Pearson Education.

Ferrero, A., Salicone, S., Bonora, C., & Parmigiani, M. (2003). ReMLab: A Java-based remote, didactic measurement laboratory. IEEE Transactions on Instrumentation and Measurement, 52, 710–715.

Fiore, L., & Ratti, G. (2007). Remote laboratory and animal behaviour: An interactive open field system. Computers & Education, 49, 1299–1307.

Furuya, K., Tanaka, M., Mitsuishi, K., Ishikawa, N., Tameike, A., Date, M., Yamada, A., & Okura, Y. (2005). Public-opened Internet electron microscopy 2005 in Japan — Remote-control SEM and TEM for high-school users. *Microscopy and Microanalysis*, 11(S02), 68–69.

Forinash, K., & Wisman, R. (2005). Building real laboratories on the internet. *International Journal of Continuing Engineering Education and Lifelong Learning*, 15(1/2), 56–66.

George, S. (2003). Robert A. Millikan Award Lecture (August 2002): Global study of the role of the laboratory in physics education. *American Journal of Physics*, 71(8), 745–749.

Gravier, C., Fayolle, J., Bayard, B., Ates, M., & Lardon, J. (2008). State of the art about remote laboratories paradigms — Foundations of ongoing mutations. *International Journal of Online Engineering*, 4(1), 19–25.

Gröber, S., Vetter, M., Eckert, B., & Jodl, H.-J. (2007). Experimenting from a distance—remotely controlled laboratory (RCL). *European Journal of Physics, 28*, S127–S141.

Guzmán, J.L., Berenguel, M., Rodríguez, F., & Dormido, S. (2005). Web-based remote control laboratory using a greenhouse scale model. *Computer Applications in Engineering Education, 13*, 111–124.

Jara, C.A., Candelasa, F.A., Torresa, F., Dormido, S., Esquembrec, F., & Reinoso, O. (2009). Real-time collaboration of virtual laboratories through the Internet. *Computers & Education, 52*, 126–140.

Jimenez-Leube, F.J., Almendra, A., Gonzalez, C. & Sanz-Maudes, J. (2001). Networked implementation of an electrical measurement laboratory for first year engineering studies. IEEE Transactions on Education, 44, 377–383.

Johnston, M.V., Cox, F.J., Forte, G.J., Nairn, D.C., Sacher, R.S., Schwartz, A.Z., & Vertes, A. (2001). Remote experimentation over the net: Our first year with MALDI. *Analytical Chemistry, 73*, 440A-445A.

Kennepohl, D., & Last, A. (1997). Science at a distance. Journal of College Science Teaching, 27(1), 35–38.

Kennepohl, D., & Last, A. (2000). Teaching chemistry at Canada's Open University. *Distance Education, 21*, 183–197.

Kennepohl, D. (2001). Using computer simulations to supplement teaching laboratories in chemistry for distance delivery. *Journal of Distance Education, 16*(2), 58–65.

Kennepohl, D., Baran, J., Connors, M., Quigley, K., & Currie, R. (2005). Remote access to instrumental analysis for distance education in science. *International Review of Research in Distance Education, 6*(3). Retrieved February 25, 2009 from: http://www.irrodl.org/index.php/irrodl/article/view/260/831

Ko, C.C., Chen, B.M., Chen, S.H., Ramakrishnan, V., Chen, R., Hu, S.Y., & Zhuang, Y. (2000). A large-scale web-based virtual oscilloscope laboratory experiment. *Engineering Science and Education Journal, 9*, 69–76.

Krause, L.B. (2003). How we learn and why we don't: Student survival guide (4th ed.). Ohio: Thompson Learning.

Lagowski, J.J. (2005). A chemical laboratory in a digital world. *Chemical Education International, 6*, 1–7.

Lang, D. Mengelkamp, C., Jäger, R.S., Geoffroy, D., Billaud, M., & Zimmer, T. (2007). Pedagogical evaluation of remote laboratories in eMerge project. *European Journal of Engineering Education, 32*, 57–72.

LearNet (2007). Lernen und Experimentieren an realen technischen Anlagen im Netz. Retrieved February 25, 2009 from: http://www.learnet.de

Lindsay, E.D., & Good, C. (2005). Effects of laboratory access modes upon learning outcomes. *IEEE Transactions on Education, 48*, 619–631.

López-de-Ipiña, D., García-Zubia, J., & Orduña, P. (2006). Remote control of Web 2.0-enabled laboratories from mobile devices. *Second IEEE International Conference on e-Science and Grid Computing (e-Science'06)*, 123.

McCullough, P.R., & Thakkar, U. (1997). Stardial: An Autonomous Astronomical Camera on the World Wide Web, *Publications of the Astronomical Society of the Pacific, 109*, 1264–1268.

National Research Council (2003). BIO 2010: Transforming undergraduate education for future research biologists. Washington (D.C.): The National Academies Press.

Nedic, Z., Machotka, J., & Nafalski, A. (2003). Remote laboratories versus virtual and real laboratories. *33rd Annual Frontiers in Education Conference, 1*, T3E1-T3E6.

Newstead S.E., & Hoskins S.L. (2003). *Encouraging student motivation.* In Fry S., Ketteridge F. & Marshall S. (Eds.), *A handbook for teaching and learning in higher education* (2nd ed.). Kogan Page, London/New York, 62–74.

Ogot, M., Elliot, G., & Glumac, N. (2003). An assessment of in-person and remotely operated laboratories. *Journal of Engineering Education, 92*, 57–64.

Palou, E., Welti-Chanes, J., Singh, R. P, López-Malo, A., Guerro, L.G., Carrillo, J., Ramírez, J.M., & Athmaram, K. (2005). Remote experiments for food engineering. *Journal of Food Engineering, 67*, 129–133.

Penfield Jr., P., & Larson, R.C. (1996). Education via advanced technologies. *IEEE Transactions on Education, 39*, 436–443.

Potter, C.S., Carragher, B., Carroll, L., Conway, C., Grosser, B., Hanlon, J., Kisseberth, N., Robinson, S., Thakkar, U., & Weber, D.

(2001). Bugscope: A practical approach to providing remote microscopy for science education outreach. *Microscopy and Microanalysis, 7,* 249–252.

ProLearn (2007). Main website. Retrieved February 25, 2009 from: http://www.prolearn-project.org/index.html

Scanlon, E., Colwell, C., Cooper, M., & Di Paolo, T. (2004). Remote experiments, re-visioning and re-thinking science learning. *Computers & Education, 43,* 153–163.

Sebastian, J.M., Garcia, D., & Sanchez, F.M. (2003). Remote-access education based on image acquisition and processing through the Internet. *IEEE Transactions on Education, 46,* 142–148.

Senese, F.A., Bender, C., & Kile, J. (2000). The Internet chemistry set: Web-based remote laboratories for distance education in chemistry. *Interactive Multimedia Electronic Journal of Computer-Enhanced Learning, 2*(2), 1696–1698.

Sonnenwald, D.H. (2003). Expectations for a scientific collaboratory: A case study. *Proceedings of the 2003 international ACM SIGGROUP conference on supporting group work,* 68–74, New York: ACM Press.

Szalay, P.S., Zeller, M., & Hunter, A.D. (2005). The incorporation of single crystal x-ray diffraction into the undergraduate chemistry curriculum using Internet-facilitated remote diffractometer control. *Journal of Chemical Education, 82,* 1555–1557.

Teichmann, T., & Faltin, N. (2002). Übersicht über Fernlabore. Retrieved February 25, 2009 from: http://www.l3s.de/i_labs/docs/Uebers_Fernlabore/uebersicht_fernlabore.html

Wattinger, C., Nguyen, D.P., Fornaro, P., Guggisberg, M., Gyalog, T., & Burkhart, H. (2006). Problem-based learning using mobile devices. *Proceedings of the Sixth International Conference on Advanced Learning Technologies (ICALT'06),* 835–839.

Wu, P.-H., Kuo, C.-H. & Lin, C.-C. (2005). Design and implementation of the remote control lab using PDA. *Proceedings of the 2005 IEEE International Workshop on Wireless and Mobile Technologies in Education (WMTE'05),* 70–72.

Yan, Y., Liang, Y., Du, X., Saliah-Hassane, H., & Ghorbani, A. (2006). Putting labs online with Web services. *IEEE IT Professional, 8*(2), 27–34.

Yeung, A., Read, J., & Schmid, S. (2005). Students' learning styles and academic performance in first year chemistry. *UniServe Science*

*Blended Learning Symposium Proceedings*, 137–142. Retrieved February 25, 2009 from: http://science.uniserve.edu.au/pubs/procs/wshop10/2005Yeung.pdf

Yeung, K., & Huang, J. (2003). Development of a remote-access laboratory: A dc motor control experiment. *Computers in Industry, 52*, 305–311.

Zürn, A., Paasch, S., Thiele, S., & Salzer, R. (2003). Linked curriculum chemistry: Different from a virtual university. CHIMIA, *57*, 105–115.

# Logistics

# Chapter 10
## Needs, Costs, and Accessibility of DE Science Lab Programs

LAWTON SHAW AND ROBERT CARMICHAEL
Athabasca University

## Introduction

The issue of how to deliver science labs at a distance goes back to distance education (DE) pioneers at the Open University (UK). In his book "The Open University," Walter Perry, first Vice-Chancellor of the Open University, described how he was often asked, "How are you possibly going to be able to teach science and technology, where laboratory work is a significant part of the total course?" His response was:

> I used to argue that we could teach the laboratory element of scientific disciplines in three ways. The first was by television where demonstrations of experiments can usually be carried out more efficiently than in the classroom... The second way in which we could approach laboratory teaching was by developing what we called a "home experiment kit" for each course where needed. This used to be laughed at, since for most people it conjured up the vision of sort of child's chemistry set. But what we actually designed over the years was very much more sophisticated than that. The third way

> in which we could provide laboratory experience was at summer school, where the whole week could be devoted to laboratory work... (Perry, 1976)

Perry's answer covers the essential possibilities for DE science laboratory programs. As he noted, one way to deal with the challenge is to make use of multimedia, for example videos of experiments. This can be extended to the host of interactive computer simulations that are available today. But when it comes to hands-on experimentation, the only options are home lab kits and concentrated residential laboratories, where students physically attend a lab session that lasts several days. Indeed, at Athabasca University, these are the two primary ways that students complete science laboratory work. Athabasca University's science program has been described previously (Kennepohl & Last, 1997).

However, there is no guidebook on how to implement a DE science laboratory program. There is virtually no common, shared knowledge among science academics and educators that enables us to implement such a program, which is very different from semestered, residential lab programs that almost all of us were trained in. One of the aims of this chapter is to share, at least in part, what it takes to run science labs at a distance. There are a number of requirements, in particular institutional supports, which can easily be overlooked.

The choice between home labs and on-site, supervised labs can be controversial. The whole purpose of home labs is to increase student accessibility, and we present data showing that home labs do this. At the same time, there are the persistent ideas that home labs are expensive to run (Ross & Scanlon, 1995) or that they impose a high development cost on instructors (Forinash & Wisman, 2001). We attempt to answer the question of cost through an actual costing of different laboratory delivery modes in general chemistry.

## A. What is needed to run a DE science lab?

*Core science lab staff*

Athabasca University Science Lab's main purpose is to deliver an accessible, individualized, distance-delivered university level science lab education to all our science lab students. The Science Lab at Athabasca University has three full-time staff members who are responsible for laboratory coordination and logistical support, and provide information to students and academic staff for all science lab courses (biology, chemistry, physics, geology, and geography).

The Science Lab Coordinator's main role is to ensure the smooth and efficient delivery of home and residential supervised lab courses. This is accomplished by coordinating and developing teamwork between the course professor, lab instructors, the science lab staff, and other departments; to make the lab learning experience safe, enjoyable, and as educational as possible for the student. The Lab Coordinator is the primary contact for all science students who have questions about lab courses and experiments.

The Science Lab Technician is involved in lab kit design, construction, and maintenance, all of which involve finding technical solutions. For supervised labs, the Lab Technician prepares all the lab supplies. In addition, at AU, the Lab Technician is also the Lab Purchasing Officer, and therefore is responsible for ensuring that all the lab materials, reagents, and supplies are on site when the Science Lab Kit Manager needs them for kit restocking and maintenance, or for a residential DE supervised lab session.

The Lab Kit Technician has a very broad range of responsibilities. From the construction and restocking of kits, to the receiving and processing of lab kit requests, to maintaining a lab kit shipment database, the Lab Kit Manager is expected to ensure that lab kit standards are implemented and followed in all aspects. Technical ability is also required, as electronic equipment and other delicate kit components need to be frequently tested and repaired. The Lab Kit Manager must work closely with the Lab Technician, and the

Lab Coordinator, to make sure each science course professor is satisfied with the home lab component delivery for their course.

*Home lab programs*

Home lab kits can take from two to four years of design and planning, with kit prototypes often being sent to select students before mass kit construction begins. Logistics such as availability of critical supplies and best student outcomes must be considered during the development stage.

One of the key requirements in operating a home lab program is a dedicated laboratory space for the construction, packaging, refurbishing, and storage of the lab kits. The amount of space required is a function of the size of the kits, the nature of kit contents, and kit turnover — how many kits are in circulation, how long it takes to replenish and refurbish a kit, how fast kits are returned, etc.

There are significant coordination and communication functions required to operate a home lab program. Once a student has registered in a course with a home, the student will want to know more about the lab component, how to get their kit, and what to do with it. From the moment the student requests the home lab kit online until they receive, use, and return the kit, the laboratory staff try to communicate with the student as much as possible to make sure the student understands and knows what to do with the kit. The kit request, shipping, and return are tracked using an online kit records system.

*Residential DE lab programs*

DE residential lab sessions are frequently planned over one year in advance. This is partly due to student demand, so that students can do long-range planning of their science program. However, on the more practical side, it is necessary and prudent to book lab facilities well in advance, and prepare and post lab schedules online. In addition, logistical considerations play a role as to when supplies must be ordered and then eventually transported to the appropriate lab site. Lab instructors must also be contacted and contracted for their services.

The online student lab registration database serves as a hub of information and data for lab staff, professors, lab instructors, and students to conveniently find out when, where, and who will be attending a lab session. Lab contingency planning must be considered should a lab session have to be cancelled or moved. Finally, lab session debriefing among instructors and including student feedback help us plan and offer improved lab sessions on an ongoing basis.

*Laboratory instructors*

The laboratory instructors who supervise residential labs are critical to the student's laboratory experience. As such, they must be highly qualified in their discipline and have demonstrated teaching ability. Due to the intermittent nature of AU labs, lab instructors work under short-term contracts. Lab instructors often work as AU tutors on a part-time basis. Some lab instructors are graduate students studying at other universities. AU lab instruction contracts are particularly attractive to graduate students because of the good compensation and because labs are often run on weekends and are not disruptive to their graduate work. Further, AU lab instructors are not responsible for marking lab reports; marking is the responsibility of course tutors who are in contact with students throughout their course.

Residential lab sessions are usually scheduled to run for an 8–9 hour day, depending on the course. Because of the intensity, length, and nature of lab instruction, we use a minimum of two lab instructors for each session. Residential labs that run for 2–4 days require a high degree of organization and timing throughout the days in order to complete all of the experimental work. When one instructor is interacting with students, the other instructor is often preparing for the next experiment. Further, having two instructors provides the opportunity for breaks and gives flexibility when lab activities need to be altered unexpectedly.

### Relations with external institutions

In several AU science courses, labs are offered using laboratory space at external institutions. This is always done at times when the laboratories are not being used, such as weekends, reading weeks, and spring/summer intersession periods. For the external institution, AU teaching labs provide a way to get something from underutilized space. In all cases, the usage agreements involve some sort of cash or in-kind payment for the use of laboratory facilities. Costs vary depending on the institution and the lab space being used. Typical costs are provided in the next section.

External publicly funded institutions that host AU laboratories also gain a degree of political advantage with government funding agencies because they are able to show their ability to cooperate with 'sister' institutions within the province.

At the present time, AU residential labs are only offered within the province of Alberta. This is partly because post-secondary education is within provincial, not federal, jurisdiction. If AU were to offer on-site educational programs, such as labs, in other provinces, it would potentially create an intergovernmental turf war arising from the competition of AU with public institutions that are funded by their home province. At the same time, however, other provinces have no way of preventing students from enrolling in the distance education courses and programs from outside their province.

One of the ways to get around this interprovincial barrier to running science laboratories in other provinces is informal partnerships with universities located there. For example, Athabasca University has an arrangement with McMaster University, in southern Ontario, whereby McMaster University offers residential organic chemistry labs over four days in the summer months when their facilities are not being used. These labs are operated entirely by McMaster and instructed by full-time McMaster staff. AU students pay a fee directly to McMaster to attend these labs. McMaster provides AU with pass/fail grades of students, and the students who pass are considered to have met the AU lab requirement. For many students located in southern Ontario, the cost to attend McMaster labs is significantly lower than the cost to travel to Alberta for AU residential labs. Just as in the residential lab arrangements with Alberta institutions, the out-of-province partner benefits from a revenue stream associated with little investment.

*Institutional support*

Distance delivered education requires a number of institutional services that go beyond the typical teaching-related activities that are part of the function of an academic department. For example, IT support is necessary for running an online laboratory booking service. Other institutional supports include facilities management, legal advice, financial services, library services, and shipping & receiving — a function that is crucial to home lab programs. The exact organization of these supporting activities is institution-dependent, but it is important that these supports are present when new distance delivered courses are introduced.

## B. Full costs of DE lab programs

It has been suggested that laboratory programs based on home lab kits are significantly more expensive to develop and to operate than residential labs (Ross & Scanlon, 1995). We are unaware of any published work that quantifies the difference in cost, despite the obvious importance of the question to DE institutions. Decisions about laboratory programming must take into account the sustainability of any particular delivery mode for the laboratory component of a course. For this purpose, we present a full costing of different laboratory delivery modes, based on a first-year general chemistry in the North American system of three-credit, one-semester courses. Table 1 shows the estimated total costs of running the same general chemistry labs in different delivery formats.

**Table 1.** Per Student Costs of General Chemistry Labs in Different Delivery Modes*

| | DELIVERY MODE | | |
|---|---|---|---|
| Item | On Campus, Semestered Labs | Residential DE Labs | Home Lab Kits |
| **Location Costs ($)** | 56 | 50 | 21 |
| **Labour** | | | |
| Instructors ($) | 49 | 43 | n/a |
| Lab preparation ($) | 3 | 4 | 47 |
| **Materials** | | | |
| Equipment ($) | 8† | 3 | 24 |
| Consumables ($) | 9 | 9 | 7 |
| **Shipping ($)** | n/a | n/a | 33 |
| **Total Cost per Student ($)** | 125 | 109 | 132 |

*All figures are in Canadian Dollars.
† See Appendix for details.

Location costs represent the amortized, per student construction cost (or capital cost) of laboratory facilities. These were calculated using the current laboratory construction costs of a wet chemistry lab, as estimated by Athabasca University's department of Facilities & Services, of $700 CDN per square foot. This estimate compares reasonably with current published chemistry research laboratory construction estimates of $490–530 US per square foot, which does not include architectural and design fees which are typically worth 30% of the overall construction costs (Stark, Hammer & Mermelstein, 2007). It is assumed that a new laboratory space is designed for 25 years of use, at which time renovations and refurbishing would be expected.

In semestered, on-campus laboratory programs in North America, lab sessions are often three hours in duration, and three lab sections can be scheduled back-to-back, every working day. Thus, over a single week, it is easy to schedule 15 lab sections in a single laboratory room. For this arrangement, the calculation of location cost per student is done by assuming a 1200-square-foot laboratory, used by 15 lab sections per week, each with 20 students. Thus, in two 13-week semesters in a given academic year, it is possible for 600 students to use a single laboratory per course. Then, using the above laboratory construction cost estimate and depreciation, a location cost of $56 per student, per course, is found.

For AU's residential DE lab sessions that use laboratory space at other institutions, we have estimated the location cost based on our rental costs in the form of cash or in-kind payments. The location cost is competitive with semestered, on-campus programs. There are significant benefits for the laboratory host instititutions. The use of their laboratory space by a DE institution increases the usage of expensive buildings during underutilized periods, such as weekends or reading weeks when the space is not being used for their own programs. In this sense, it provides a revenue stream that is associated with virtually no additional cost. Further, at least in the Canadian system, institutional co-operation is viewed favourably by the governments that fund public institutions.

The location costs for a home lab program are much lower than for the residential DE or on-campus semestered programs. In our Chemistry 217 program, the home lab kits are prepared, restocked, and shipped from a 150-square-foot space. At any given time, most of the lab kits are in the hands of students and are not taking up any storage space in university facilities. The same assumptions of construction cost and depreciation were used to calculate location costs. We have recently been turning over home lab kits on the order of 200 kits per year. Thus, we calculate a location cost of $21 per student (i.e., per kit).

Laboratory programs have two types of ongoing labour costs. One is the cost of instructors. Lab instructors are often hired on a contingent, contract basis at a particular hourly rate of pay. Lab instructor costs for residential DE labs and on-campus, semestered labs were calculated using an hourly pay rate of $25/hour. For the on-campus, semestered labs, we assume 13 weeks of 3-hour lab sessions for every 20 students. This gives an instructor cost of $49/student. In the case of residential DE labs, we have calculated the instructor cost based on having two instructors present over 17 hours of instructional time, for 20 students. In this case, instructor costs are somewhat lower than for on-campus, semestered labs. This is mainly because of the reduction in instructional time required to complete a similar number of experiments. This can be done with no change to the experiments performed by significantly reducing the time spent by students on set-up and clean-up between experiments, and having two instructors present to increase student performance through a greater degree of one-on-one instruction. In the home lab program, instructor costs are not applicable because the student works through the entire set of experiments using comprehensive learning materials (i.e., a highly detailed lab manual).

The second ongoing labour cost is for lab preparation. On-campus lab programs often have a full-time staff member who is responsible for setting up equipment and reagents for undergraduate laboratories. For on-campus labs, we assume that approximately 3 hours is spent on preparing labs for a given week of experiments, for the 15 sections of 20 students per week who are enrolled in a given laboratory space. At $25/hour, the preparation cost is around $3 per student. For residential DE labs, the lab preparation cost is similar, with the lab coordinator spending approximately 3 hours preparing for a weekend lab session of 20 students. Using $25/hour, the lab preparation cost is $4 per student. The preparation cost for home lab kits is significantly higher because the work involves unpacking, restocking, and packing individual kits that will be sent to students. For our Chemistry 217 kits, we have tracked the length of time this requires. Our labour cost is $47 per kit.

Materials for a laboratory program include all lab equipment such as glassware and balances, and consumables such as reagents, disposable pipets, and paper towels. For a typical first-year chemistry laboratory with 20 seats, the initial cost of equipment is estimated at around $75,000 (see Appendix). Much of this equipment has a shorter life span than the laboratory itself. In this costing, we have estimated lab equipment lifetime to be 15 years. For a single laboratory used for an on-campus, semestered lab program, the equipment cost per student is $8. For residential DE labs in which some of the host laboratory equipment is used, this cost is reduced. However, when AU labs are offered in this fashion, AU equipment is often brought in. Our estimate of equipment cost per student is $3.

Consumable materials in on-campus, semestered, and residential DE labs is estimated at $9 per student. At least $2 of this goes to cleaning supplies like soap and paper towels. For a home lab program, consumable materials have been calculated at $7 per kit.

Shipping costs represent a significant portion of the total costs of running a home lab kit program. As will be discussed below, a home lab kit program can result in a larger number of students studying in geographically distant locations. This naturally means a higher average shipping cost per student.

We have not attempted to make estimates of the different costs of developing lab programs. It could be argued that development costs of a home-based lab program are higher than for a residential lab program. However, all laboratory programs have development costs, usually in the form of time spent by academic staff who research and test experiments and write laboratory manuals. In short, lab program development activities are similar between home-based and residential lab programs and we see little benefit in parsing out specific development costs.

From Table 1, it can be seen that a general chemistry home lab program has approximately the same per student cost as a similar on-campus, semestered lab program, using this set of assumptions. For DE, the most cost-efficient lab format is concentrated, residential labs. However, this is highly dependent on the number of students attending the residential DE labs. The calculation in Table 1 used 20 students. At AU, general chemistry labs are frequently attended by much fewer students. When only 10 students attend a 2-day residential lab, the cost per student can exceed $200 because of fixed labour and location costs.

The cost of home labs shown in Table 1 is based on the assumption that each kit has a lifetime of 20 uses. At this time, many of the AU Chemistry 217 kits are approaching this number of uses. There has been very little breakage of lab kit contents and it is quite possible that the kits will survive much longer than 20 uses. This would obviously decrease the unit cost of equipment to the point where the home-lab program is the most cost-efficient for institutions.

This discussion has focused on the departmental and institutional costs of running different lab programs, and has not addressed the costs to students. For DE students, the home lab program is by far the most affordable because it eliminates the need for expensive travel to attend a residential laboratory session. Even if students were required to pay the round trip shipping costs for the lab kit, it would still be more affordable than travel and accommodation costs. Our conclusion is that, in terms of costs, a home lab program is of the greatest benefit to DE providers and the students of general chemistry.

### *Costs of labs in the other natural sciences*

The preceding costing was for introductory chemistry. The picture is somewhat different for the other natural sciences that employ practical laboratory programs — physics, biological sciences, and earth sciences such as geology. Without embarking on full cost comparisons of laboratory delivery modes in these areas, we can make general observations based on the AU experience.

In physics and geology, introductory laboratory experiments are very suitable for the home lab delivery mode, for a number of reasons. First, home kits tend to be affordable to build. For example, electronic circuit boards for electricity and magnetism experiments and diode lasers for optics experiments are all very affordable. An introductory physics kit can be prepared for under $200 (see Chapter 7).

In geology, hardness testing kits and sets of small fossil samples are also affordable. Second, kits in these areas do not generally require consumable materials, reducing the cost of home labs. Third, shipping costs of physics and geology kits are much lower than for chemistry home lab kits because of the weight of materials and because packaging is not required to be spill-proof.

In the realm of biological sciences, there is a great deal of variability. In some courses, it is not feasible to operate a home lab program. For example, microbiology experiments require large, expensive lab equipment like autoclaves and incubators that obviously cannot be shipped to the student. And in ecology, field-based teaching laboratories are appropriate. In such courses, students must attend residential supervised labs.

In other areas of biology, it is possible to operate a home lab kit. For example, one introductory biology course at AU has a home lab kit that is surprisingly affordable ($30), partly because it relies on students obtaining many consumable materials on their own. This lab kit has been described elsewhere (Holmberg & Liston, 1998). On the other hand, physiology home kits are an order of magnitude more expensive due to the costs of an electronic balance and a spirometer.

## C. Home labs: accessibility and enrolment growth

Accessibility is perhaps the most important reason that students register in distance education courses and programs. For the purposes of this chapter, accessibility is a function of the student's opportunity cost to complete a course. The opportunity cost is the sum total of the costs of time, travel, and other inconveniences that students must incur during the course. As has been described repeatedly in the Laboratory section of this volume, in science courses, the laboratory component is often the most expensive in terms of opportunity cost for students.

In the Chemistry 217 course at AU, the laboratory program has undergone two significant changes in delivery format. Prior to 1996, all of the labs were delivered as two-day residential labs. From 1996 to 2002, approximately half of the experiments were delivered as home-based experiments — a "partial lab kit." These experiments have been described by Kennepohl (Kennepohl, 1996). The partial home lab kits were picked up by students when they attended residential labs to complete the other experiments. From 2003 to the present time, Chemistry 217 labs have been delivered entirely as home lab kits.

The switch in Chemistry 217 from a residential lab program to one that is based on home labs provides the opportunity to look for changes in enrolment patterns that result from the switch. Enrolment patterns in Chemistry 217 can be compared to those in the second half-course of general chemistry, Chemistry 218, which has always had a residential lab component. We assume that enrolments in a given course are a function of overall demand for the course and the student's opportunity cost to complete the course. Converting a laboratory program to home-based experiments is an obvious way to lower the opportunity cost for students by removing the requirement to travel to residential labs. Such a change should lead to an increase in enrolments in the course with home experiments, as compared to other, similar courses with residential labs.

Figure 1 shows the enrolment growth in Chemistry 217 and 218, from the fiscal years 1990/91 to 2006/07. Yearly enrolments, N, are normalized to the number of enrolments in 1990/91, N. This provides a way to compare cumulative enrolment growth as a simple factor increase in the two courses, rather than comparing raw numbers of registrations. Over the 17 years shown, the overall trend is an increase in enrolments in both courses. Until 2002/03, enrolment changes in the two courses are very similar, with Chemistry 218 showing slightly higher growth than Chemistry 217. This is likely due to an increase in the number of students returning from Chemistry 217 to complete Chemistry 218. From the introduction of the complete home lab program in 2003, growth in Chemistry 217 clearly outpaced growth in Chemistry 218.

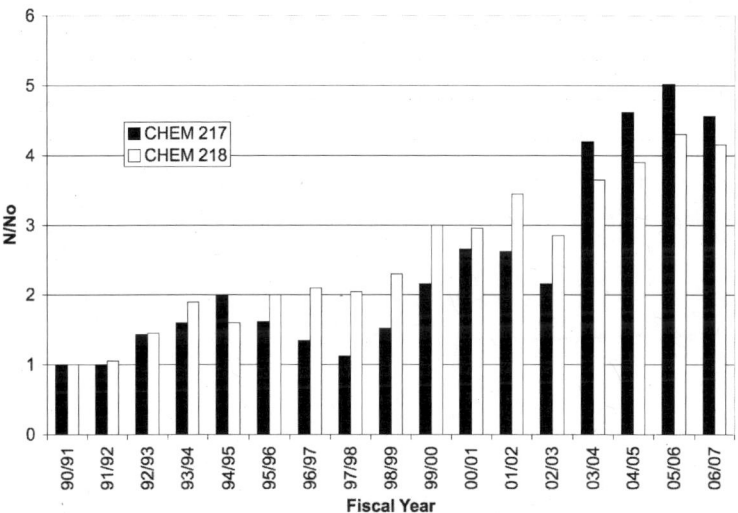

**Figure 1.** Normalized Enrolments in General Chemisty from 1990 to 2007. This shows cumulative growth in enrolments over this period. Enrolments excluded all early withdrawls.

The introduction of partial home lab kits does not appear to have had a significant positive effect on enrolments in Chemistry 217, from 1996 to 2002, as compared to enrolment changes in Chemistry 218. During this period, the laboratory program still used residential labs. Thus, there would have been only a minimal decrease in the students' opportunity cost to complete the labs; student travel to lab sessions was still required.

The introduction of a full home lab program in 2003 resulted in an increase in cumulative growth in Chemistry 217, relative to Chemistry 218. On examination of Figure 1, it is clear that much of this additional cumulative growth occurred between the 2002/03 and 2003/04 fiscal years, corresponding perfectly to the introduction of the full home lab program. The actual year-to-year growth in Chemistry 217 enrolment between 2002/03 and 2003/04 was a stunning 94%.

The opportunity cost of attending residential chemistry labs is expected to be highest for those students who reside outside of the province of Alberta. Thus, it is expected that the introduction of a full home lab program in Chemistry 217 would lead to an increase in the fraction of out-of-province students. Figure 2 shows the percentage of out-of-province students in Chemistry 217 and 218 from 1990 to the present. During this time, the fraction of out-of-province students has increased significantly. The out-of-province fractions in the two courses have been similar through most of this period, and have increased in step with each other until 2003/04, when the full home lab program was introduced. In that year, the percentage of out-of-province students in Chemistry 217 increased by over 20%. Since that year, the percentage of out-of-province students in Chemistry 217 has been consistently higher than in Chemistry 218. This result is consistent with the notion that home lab programs significantly decrease the opportunity cost of completing a DE chemistry course, especially for students who reside in other provinces.

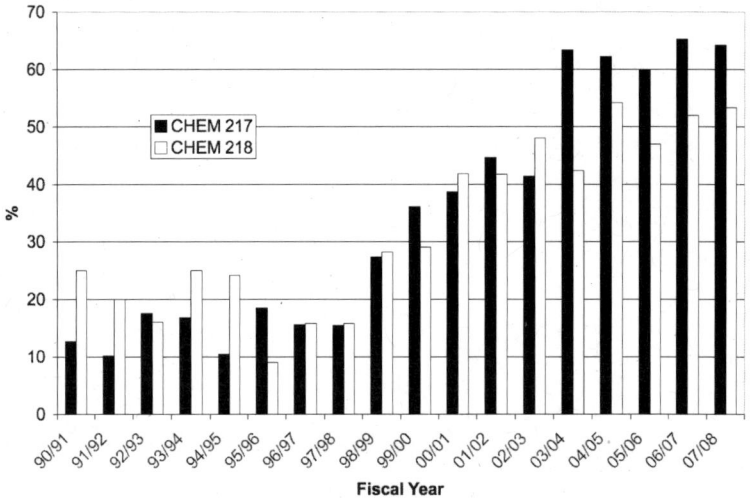

**Figure 2.** Percentage of Out-of-Province Students in General Chemistry from 1990 to 2007.

## Conclusion

DE laboratory programs are delivered through two primary modes: the home-based lab and the residential DE lab. The organizational structure required to operate these delivery modes is different from that of traditional on-campus, semestered lab programs. Perhaps surprisingly, the full institutional costs of operating different laboratory programs in chemistry are not significantly different. Home-based laboratory programs are not associated with student travel costs, so we conclude that this delivery mode is the best choice for making DE labs accessible. This is borne out in enrolment data that shows an increase in student enrolments and an increase in geographically remote students when a full home lab program is introduced.

## Acknowledgments

We acknowledge Mr. Sami Houry of Athabasca University's Institutional Studies unit for providing information on chemistry enrolments. Mr. Neil Sexton provided information on lab kit costs. Ms. Elaine Goth-Birkigt assisted with checking the accuracy of the manuscript. Mr. Greg Wiens of Athabasca University's Facilities & Services provided an estimate of laboratory construction costs. We thank Athabasca University for supporting this work.

REFERENCES

Gravois, J. (2006). Tracking the invisible faculty. *The Chronicle of Higher Education, 53*(17), A8.

Forinash, K., & Wisman, R. (2001). The viability of distance education science laboratories. *T.H.E. Journal, 29*(2), 38–45. Retrieved February 26, 2009 from: http://www.thejournal.com/articles/15590

Holmberg, R.G., & Liston, M.L. (1998). Home lab activities for introductory biology delivered at-a-glance. In S.J. Karcher (Ed.), *Tested studies for laboratory teaching, Volume 19, Proceedings of the 19th Workshop/Conference of the Association for Biology*

Laboratory Education (ABLE) (pp. 362–365).
Kennepohl, D. (1996). Home-Study Microlabs. *Journal of Chemical Education, 73*, 938–939.
Kennepohl, D., & Last, A.M. (1997). Science at a distance. *Journal of College Science Teaching, 27*(1), 35–38.
Perry, W. (1976). *Open University.* Milton Keynes: The Open University Press.
Ross, S., & Scanlon, E. (1995). *Open science: Distance teaching and open learning of science subjects.* London: Paul Chapman Publishing.
Stark, S., Hammer, T., & Mermelstein, E. (2007). Construction boom boosts new lab costs. *R&D Magazine*, July, 27–30, Retrieved February 26, 2009, from: http://www.rdmag.com/pdf/RD0707_Lab.pdf

## APPENDIX — GENERAL CHEMISTRY LABORATORY MATERIALS AND EQUIPMENT

| No. | Item | Quantity | Cost / item $* | Total $ |
|---|---|---|---|---|
| 1 | Battery, 9 volt | 20 | 1.09 | 21.80 |
| 2 | Beaker, 50mL | 100 | 4.04 | 404.00 |
| 3 | Beaker, 100mL | 100 | 2.90 | 290.33 |
| 4 | Beaker, 150mL | 100 | 4.04 | 404.00 |
| 5 | Beaker, 250mL | 100 | 2.81 | 280.75 |
| 6 | Beaker, 400mL | 100 | 2.81 | 280.75 |
| 7 | Beaker, 600mL | 100 | 4.23 | 423.17 |
| 8 | Beaker, 1000mL | 20 | 7.80 | 155.90 |
| 9 | Beaker, 1000 mL plastic | 20 | 0.55 | 11.00 |
| 10 | Bottle, 30 mL | 140 | 1.95 | 273.00 |
| 11 | Bottle, 60 mL | 60 | 2.00 | 120.00 |
| 12 | Burette, 50mL | 20 | 72.11 | 1442.20 |
| 13 | Burner, Bunsen | 20 | 26.40 | 528.00 |
| 14 | Clamps, burette | 20 | 20.51 | 410.20 |
| 15 | Clamps, iron ring | 20 | 10.21 | 204.20 |
| 16 | Clamps, utility | 40 | 53.28 | 2131.20 |

| | | | | |
|---|---|---|---|---|
| 17 | Cylinder, 10 mL grad. | 30 | 12.14 | 364.20 |
| 18 | Cylinder, 25 mL grad. | 30 | 15.57 | 467.10 |
| 19 | Cylinder, 50 mL grad. | 30 | 2.44 | 73.20 |
| 20 | Cylinder, 100 mL grad. | 30 | 2.44 | 73.20 |
| 21 | Dessicator | 1 | 130.75 | 130.75 |
| 22 | Flask, 50 mL Erlenmeyer | 20 | 5.04 | 100.80 |
| 23 | Flask, 125 mL Erlenmeyer | 20 | 4.81 | 96.20 |
| 24 | Flask, 250 mL Erlenmeyer | 100 | 4.15 | 414.58 |
| 25 | Flask, 500 mL Erlenmeyer | 20 | 17.40 | 347.96 |
| 26 | Flask, 250 mL Filter | 20 | 13.86 | 277.13 |
| 27 | Flask, 500 mL Filter | 20 | 17.79 | 355.73 |
| 28 | Flask, 10 mL Vol. | 20 | 17.46 | 349.20 |
| 29 | Flask, 25 mL Vol. | 20 | 19.05 | 381.00 |
| 30 | Flask, 50 mL Vol. | 20 | 19.33 | 386.60 |
| 31 | Flask, 100 mL Vol. | 20 | 22.16 | 443.20 |
| 32 | Flask, 200 mL Vol. | 20 | 42.83 | 856.67 |
| 33 | Flask, 250 mL Vol. | 20 | 45.35 | 907.03 |
| 34 | Flask, 500 mL Vol. | 20 | 56.98 | 1139.60 |
| 35 | Flask, 1000 mL Vol. | 20 | 70.70 | 1414.00 |
| 36 | Funnel, Buchner, 4.25 cm | 20 | 43.27 | 865.40 |
| 37 | Funnel, Buchner, 5.5 cm | 20 | 51.42 | 1028.40 |
| 38 | Funnel, Buchner, 7.0 cm | 20 | 67.61 | 1352.20 |
| 39 | Funnel, burette | 20 | 8.18 | 163.60 |
| 40 | Funnel, glass long stem 55 mm | 20 | 12.68 | 253.65 |
| 41 | Funnel, glass short stem 60 mm | 20 | 10.94 | 218.70 |
| 42 | Funnel, glass short stem 80 mm | 20 | 12.20 | 244.03 |
| 43 | Funnel, plastic | 20 | 2.80 | 56.00 |
| 44 | Pipette, 1 mL Vol. | 20 | 7.33 | 146.60 |
| 45 | Pipette, 5 mL Vol. | 20 | 7.33 | 146.60 |
| 46 | Pipette, 10 mL Vol. | 20 | 7.24 | 144.80 |

| | | | | |
|---|---|---|---|---|
| 47 | Pipette, 25 mL Vol. | 20 | 27.55 | 551.00 |
| 48 | Pipette, 50 mL Vol. | 20 | 31.73 | 634.60 |
| 49 | Pipette, 10 mL serological | 20 | 0.79 | 15.80 |
| 50 | Pipette bulb(1) | 20 | 8.01 | 160.20 |
| 51 | Safety glasses | 20 | 5.61 | 112.20 |
| 52 | Spatula | 20 | 5.62 | 112.40 |
| 53 | Stand, retort 14×23cm | 20 | 28.22 | 564.40 |
| 54 | Stir bars, magnetic, teflon set | 10 | 50.98 | 509.80 |
| 55 | Stir rod, glass | 20 | 0.65 | 13.00 |
| 56 | Stopper, rubber #7 | 20 | 1.49 | 29.75 |
| 57 | Stopper, rubber #5 | 20 | 1.49 | 29.75 |
| 58 | Stopper, rubber 0 | 20 | 1.20 | 24.04 |
| 59 | Stopwatch | 20 | 23.61 | 472.20 |
| 60 | Test tube, small | 80 | 0.04 | 3.20 |
| 61 | Test tube, large | 40 | 0.05 | 2.00 |
| 62 | Test tube rack | 30 | 19.99 | 599.70 |
| 63 | Thermometer, 0–110°C | 20 | 3.75 | 75.00 |
| 64 | Tubing, latex | 60 | 1.10 | 66.00 |
| 65 | Tubing, vacuum 50ft roll | 60 | 1.92 | 115.20 |
| 66 | Tweezer | 20 | 1.78 | 35.60 |
| 67 | Vial, glass — 1 dram(9) | 180 | 0.31 | 55.80 |
| 68 | Vial, plastic — 3 dram (3) | 60 | 0.33 | 19.80 |
| 69 | Vial, glass — 3 dram(10) | 200 | 0.38 | 76.00 |
| 70 | Vial, calorimetric | 30 | 0.33 | 9.90 |
| 71 | Watch glass, 65mm | 30 | 1.37 | 40.98 |
| 72 | Watch glass, 100mm | 30 | 2.15 | 64.59 |
| 73 | Wire, Nichrome (1-30 cm) | 30 | 0.14 | 4.20 |
| 74 | Wire, Copper stir (1-30 cm) | 30 | 0.50 | 15.00 |

|  |  |  |  |  |
|---|---|---|---|---|
| 1 | Centrifuge | 1 | 4010.29 | 4010.29 |
| 2 | Conductivity Tester | 1 | 706.15 | 706.15 |
| 3 | Hot plate/stirrers | 20 | 512.92 | 10258.40 |
| 4 | Lab Jack, 15×15 cm | 20 | 73.02 | 1460.40 |
| 5 | Power supply, 12 V | 10 | 303.18 | 3031.80 |
| 6 | Multimeter | 20 | 20.00 | 400.00 |
| 7 | Oven | 1 | 1363.00 | 1363.00 |
| 8 | pH meter (Denver Ultrabasic) | 20 | 404.26 | 8085.2 |
| 9 | Refridgerator | 1 | 500 | 500 |
| 10 | Spectrophotometer (educ 400 to 1000nm) | 10 | 862.79 | 8627.90 |
| 11 | Water Bath | 4 | 968.73 | 3874.92 |
| 12 | Analytical Balance | 1 | 2900.00 | 2900.00 |
| 13 | General Pan Balance 610G/0.01G | 5 | 612.48 | 3062.40 |
|  |  |  | **Total** | **73271.21** |

\* Prices taken from Fisher Scientific 2007 Catalogue, retrieved September 12, 2007 from http://www.fishersci.ca/

# Chapter 11
## Challenges and Opportunities for Teaching Laboratory Sciences at a Distance in a Developing Country

MD. TOFAZZAL ISLAM
Bangladesh Open University

## Introduction

Education *per se* is widely seen as a necessary precondition for economic growth within the knowledge-based economies of early twenty-first century. Educating and training a vast population of people for both preparatory and in-service purposes is a huge and expensive venture, which is very difficult to manage in the developing countries due to budgetary constraints. This is further compounded when the education and training have to be delivered in scientific and technical subjects. Conventional systems of delivering science-based education and training have often failed to meet the current and anticipated demand for the skills in the said areas. Innovations in delivery systems must be part and parcel of the solution to the above-mentioned constraints, requiring further exploration. The use of distance and open learning methodologies is one such innovation. This is why the last century has witnessed the establishment of hundreds of distance learning institutions in both developed and developing countries like Bangladesh. The challenges and prospects for distance education in the developing countries have been studied by a number of researchers (Arger, 1990, 1993; Ramanujam, 2001; Fozdar, Kumar & Kannan, 2006; Jung & Latchem, 2007).

Bangladesh is a developing country (GDP growth rate 6%) with the highest population density (1,020 persons per sq km) in the world, excepting city-states like Singapore. About half of her population is struggling to survive as they are living under the poverty line. Illiteracy and a high dropout rate at all levels of education are major challenges in attaining sustainable economic development and thereby improving quality of life. Vocational and technical education provides employment-oriented knowledge and skills to the unemployed youth force. However, the current strength of conventional institutions satisfies only a small portion of the huge demand for such education and training. Moreover, the conventional system cannot provide training for people of all ages and from diverse locations, or satisfy demands for easily accessible alternatives such as open and distance learning.

To create an opportunity for the huge numbers of unskilled and less educated people, the Bangladesh Open University (BOU) was established in 1992 as the only public university to introduce different levels of education, ranging from junior secondary to higher education, through distance mode. Over the years, it has launched 21 formal and 19 non-formal academic programs under seven schools, namely the School of Agriculture and Rural Development, the School of Business, the School of Education, the School of Law, the Open School, and the School of Social Science, Humanities and Languages. For pedagogic delivery, BOU uses both the conventional face-to-face tutorial system based on the print module and electronic technologies such as CD, audiovisual cassettes, and radio and TV broadcasts. The response to BOU programs has been so phenomenal that current enrolment of students in each year (BOU Diary 2008, 271,630) is several times higher than that of any of the public and private universities in the country. Thus BOU has emerged as a new exemplar of the mega-university (Daniel, 1996). In several studies, it has been found that BOU education is flexible, cost-effective and of a standard comparable to that of the conventional universities (Anonymous, 2002; Islam, Rahman & Rahman, 2006; Islam & Selim, 2006a). However, scepticism has persisted as to whether current delivery methods are effective enough in imparting knowledge and practical skills to students attending science and technical courses that have substantial practical/laboratory works (Islam, 2007). Generally, infrastructure and facilities for laboratory experiments are not practically up to date and adequate even in conventional institutions in the developing countries. Obviously, hands-on experience is essential for effective transfer to students of technical skills which are often limited in distance education (Fozdar, Kumar & Kannan, 2006; Jung & Latchem, 2007). Several innovative approaches have therefore been proposed to overcome this barrier and do laboratory science in an environment that is flexible for learners (Rudd, 1994; Ross & Scanlon, 1995; Kennepohl, 2001; Boschmann, 2003; Casanova et al., 2006; Kennepohl, 2007; Nigam & Joshi, 2007).

It has been a concern of educators how to effectively deliver laboratory-based science and technology courses through distance mode. The aim of this chapter is to discuss the challenges and opportunities for effective delivery of lab-based and field-oriented practical science subjects through distance mode in the developing countries, with special reference to Bangladesh.

## Distance education in Bangladesh

Distance education and correspondence courses are a hundred-year-old concept, initiated in the western world. The history of open and distance learning in Bangladesh (then East Pakistan) dates back to 1956 when the then Education Directorate distributed 200 radio receivers to educational institutions, which in turn led to the establishment of an audio-visual cell and later the Audio-visual Education

Center (AVEC) in 1962. Upon the creation of an independent Bangladesh in 1972, a pilot project School Broadcasting Program was undertaken during 1978–1980, which was later merged with AVEC to establish the National Institute of Educational Media and Technology (NIEMT). The NIEMT was later transformed into the Bangladesh Institute of Distance Education in 1985. Bangladesh Open University (BOU) was established in 1992 by an Act passed in the national parliament. The BOU Act 1992 stated the purpose of the establishment of the university as follows:

> …to spread multimedially instruction of every standard and knowledge, both general and scientific, by means of any kind of communications technology, to raise the standard of education and to give the people educational opportunities by democratizing education and to create a class of competent people by raising the standard of education of the people generally.

To bring education to the doorsteps of the people, BOU has set up 12 regional centres (RCs), 80 coordinating offices (COs) (Fig. 1) and nearly 1,000 tutorial centres (TCs) geographically distributed throughout the country. Although RCs and COs are BOU's own infrastructures, the TCs are situated at selected government and non-government institutions which have sufficient facilities and experts to conduct tutorial services for the students of respective BOU programs during weekends and holidays.

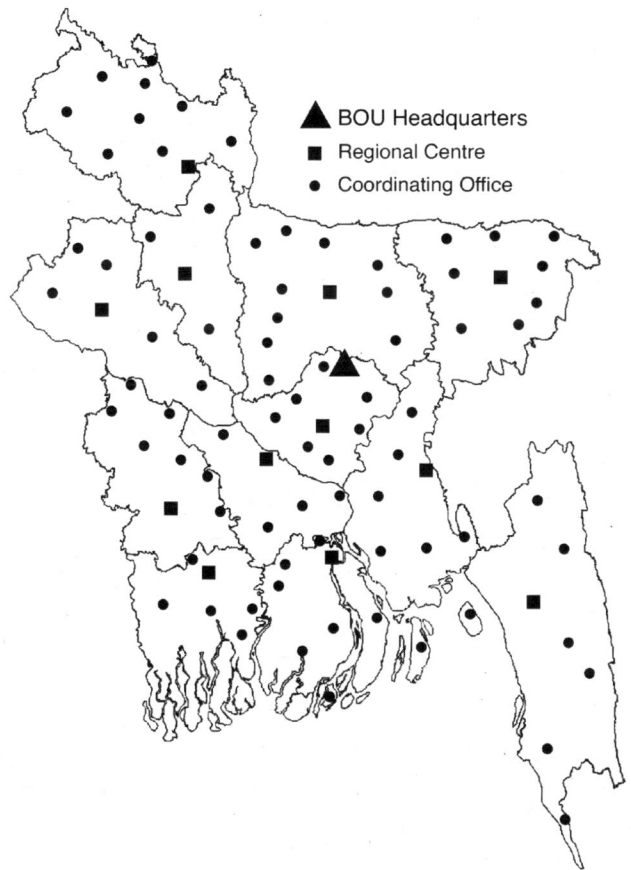

**Figure 1.** Locations of BOU's main campus, regional centres (RCs) and coordinating offices (COs) in Bangladesh map.

## Materials development and delivery

*Science programs in BOU*

Out of twenty-one academic programs, seven programs, namely Bachelor of Agricultural Education (B.Ag.Ed.), Bachelor of Science in Nursing (B.Sc.Nurs.), Diploma in Computer Science and Application (DCSA), Certificate in Poultry and Livestock (CLP), Certificate in Pisciculture and Fish Processing (CPFP), Higher Secondary Certificate (HSC), and Secondary School Certificate (SSC), have substantial or minor science courses. The detail descriptions and trends of student enrolment in these programs are given in Table 1 and Fig. 2. Among these programs, three in agricultural sciences (B.Ag.Ed., CLP and CPFP) and one in health science (B.Sc.Nurs.) and another one in engineering (DCSA) have substantial practical or laboratory work along with theoretical lessons in almost in every course. So far several thousand students have successfully completed these science-based programs. The modes of delivery and student support systems in all science courses are more or less similar, and hence, these are discussed together. To give a detailed view of the whole process of the choice of media, preparation, and delivery of materials for teaching science courses, each component is discussed separately in the following sections.

Table 1. List of BOU programs having major or minor science courses with practical/lab work.

| Programs | Year of launch | Level | Admission requirement | Min./ max. duration (years) | Freq. of enrolment in a year | Semester[a] (total credit hours) | Practical or lab. activity needed |
|---|---|---|---|---|---|---|---|
| B.Ag.Ed. | 1997 | Bachelor | HSC/Dip.Ag. | 3/6 | Twice | 6(95) | Major |
| B.Sc.Nurs. | 2003 | Bachelor | Dip. Nurs. | 3/5 | Once | 6(100) | Major |
| DCSA | 1998 | Diploma | HSC or equiv. | 1.5/5 | Once | 3(35) | Major |
| CLP | 1999 | Certificate | SSC or equiv. | 0.5/2.5 | Twice | 1(16) | Major |
| CPFP | 1999 | Certificate | SSC or equiv. | 0.5/2.5 | Twice | 1(15) | Major |
| SSC | 1995 | Certificate | Grad.8 or equiv. | 2/5 | Once | 02(60) | Minor |
| HSC | 1998 | Certificate | SSC or equiv. | 2/5 | Once | 02(72) | Minor |

Data retrieved from BOU website (http://www.bou.edu.bd/SARD.html) on February 13, 2008. B.Ag.Ed., Bachelor of Agricultural Education; B.Sc. Nurs., Bachelor of Science in Nursing; DCSA, Diploma in Computer Science and Application; CLP, Certificate in Livestock and Poultry; CPFP, Certificate in Pisciculture and Fish Processing; SSC, Secondary School Certificate; HSC, Higher Secondary Certificate; Dip.Ag., Diploma in Agriculture; Dip.Nurs., Diploma in Nursing. [a]Each semester duration in all programs is 6 months except in SSC and HSC (1 year in each semester).

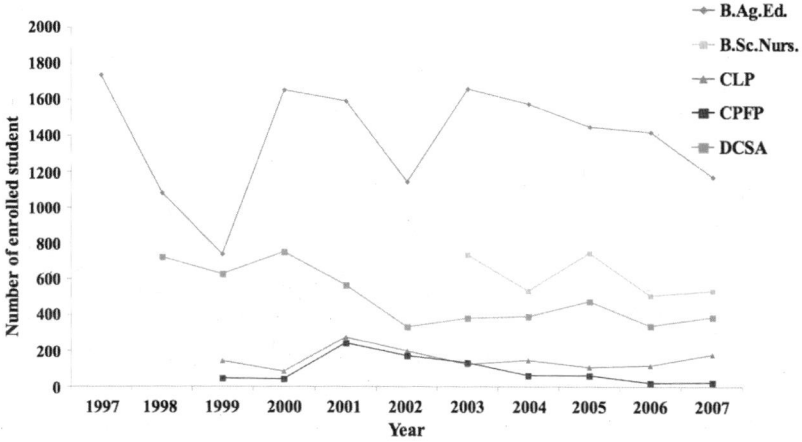

**Figure 2.** Annual student enrolment in BOU science programs. (Source: Student Support Services Division, BOU).

## *Media of delivery*

Global Distance Education (DE) has progressed very rapidly during the last few decades.

Now DE is defined as the education system where learners are able to communicate and interact with voice, video, and data, in real time with their teachers and other learners through modern information and communication technologies (Islam, 2007; Daniel, 1996). Learning through electronic technologies and mobile electronic devices is popularly known as electronic learning (e-learning) and mobile learning (m-learning), respectively, and has been expanding most rapidly in the developed countries (Islam & Selim, 2006b; Islam, 2007). Although different universities have some common features in terms of distant delivery and its objectives, the actual actions vary greatly to meet specific local challenges. Faced with economic and infrastructural limitations, most of the universities in developing countries like BOU are still far behind in adopting all modern technologies to teach their distant students. However, BOU has adopted such technologies where they are affordable and easily accessible to its distant students. BOU is using (1) print; (2) radio and television; (3) audiocassettes; and (4) occasional face-to-face tuition to teach its learners (Islam & Selim, 2006b; Islam, Rahman & Rahman, 2006). It has not yet adopted the computing media and technologies (5th medium) for teaching due to costliness and poor access, but it has adopted a spectrum of four out of the five media and makes use of four technologies (Islam, 2007). Almost similar delivery methods are being used in Indira Gandhi National Open University in India to teach distant students (Fozdar, Kumar & Kannan, 2006).

In each science course, a printed course book written in modular format is provided to the students. Each book is divided into several units and each unit is further divided into 3-5 lessons. The lesson containing the practical or laboratory work is designed in step-by-step fashion with enough illustrations, drawings, and examples so that students can do exercises in their home environment and/or nearby farm/field. The practical/labwork—related lessons are added consistently together with theoretical lessons within the printed course books of the respective courses. To supplement print, radio and television programs (every day 25-45 minutes, which is expected to extend up to 4 hours in the near future) are broadcast through state-owned radio and TV channels. Students are invited to perform laboratory or practical work at their nearby tutorial centres (TCs) under the supervision of specialist tutors.

*Print materials*

Print is still a powerful medium in many open universities in the developing as well as the developed countries (Gaba & Dash, 2004). BOU has introduced a course team approach for developing effective printed course materials for distant students. Each course team comprises specialist course writer(s), editor, trained style editor, graphic designer, illustrator, audio-visual producer and anonymous referees (see detailed process in Fig. 3). An editorial board is responsible for the final approval of publishing materials for students. This approach has proven to be effective, but has also appeared to be complicated and time-consuming (Islam, Rahman & Rahman,

2006). Once the course is in operation, the university monitors the performance of the course books and begins to collect data on errors identified by the learners and the tutors. The university strongly encourages students and tutors to report errors and difficulties they encounter while going through the course materials during or immediately after the course delivery. The information or feedback is collected and analyzed by the concerned course teams of the relevant school. If significant criticism is found along with the positive reactions, the course is then revised and reprinted; otherwise, errata pages for the mistakes suffice. The BOU policy of developing a course book incrementally, refereeing its materials meticulously, inviting criticisms, collecting feedback, observing course presentation and assessment, correcting errors, and revising the whole work is designed to ensure that quality assurance is maintained (Islam, Rahman & Rahman, 2006). This traditional approach is nothing but a synthesis of the BS 5750 (i.e., quality loop) Approach and the Iterative Approach (Freeman, 1991), and the whole process has proven effective (Islam & Rahman, 1997; Islam, 1998).

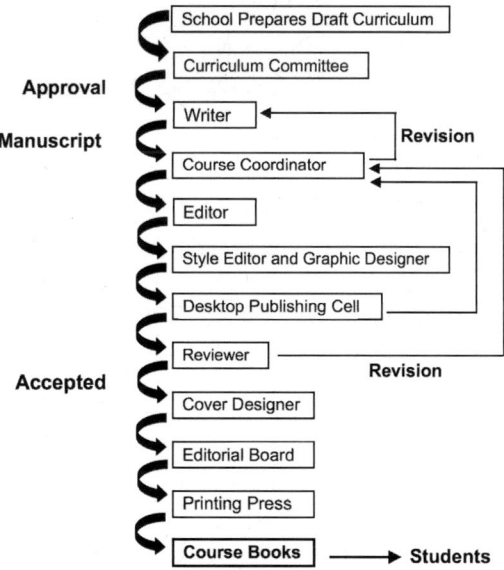

**Figure 3.** Schematic diagram of the processes of course book production in BOU (Islam, Rahman & Rahman, 2006).

A survey of student opinion revealed that the overall quality of BOU curricula and course books is rated good to very good as self-study learning materials (Anonymous, 2002; Rahman et al., 2005, Shah et al., 2005, Islam, Rahman & Rahman, 2006). Although BOU generally revises course books every five years, this interval was not found to be appropriate/effective in the science and engineering courses due to the continual and substantial influx of new knowledge in the areas of science and technology. The appropriate solution in the cases of science and engineering courses is to revise course books every two years. It has also been suggested that practical lessons should be revised more elaborately and written in a step-by-step manner with appropriate photographs, artwork, and suitable examples and print as a separate manual (Islam, Rahman & Rahman, 2006; Fozdar, Kumar & Kannan, 2006).

## Audio and audio-visual media

As with course book production, strict principles are followed in audio and audio-visual productions (Islam, Rahman & Rahman, 2006; Islam, 2007). Evaluating the difficulty level and relative effectiveness of media, the school selects topics from different courses for audio and audio-visual production. The presenter is selected from in-house faculty and/or reputable academics from outside. The selected presenter prepares a script on the basis of a particular topic of the concerned course. The school checks the quality of the script and then sends it to the respective producer of Media Division. The producer arranges recording and editing of the materials with a media editor and then presents the edited program before a preview committee prior to its radio or TV broadcast. The preview committee consists of the following members: Director (media), Dean or his/her representative, subject specialist, video specialist, producer, program specialist, and one external member. If the committee approves, the program will go on air. Although audio cassettes are provided to supplement printed course material in some language teaching programs (English or Arabic — CELP, CALP), there are no audio cassettes for the science courses.

The quality of BOU radio and TV programs is rated good to very good by the students (Islam & Rahman, 1997; Islam & Islam, 2008). However, as one-way delivery is followed without any real-time discussion and interaction, these programs are practically contributing less in transferring knowledge and skills, especially in the science courses (Rahman et al., 2005). The thirst for instant response/solutions/suggestion/clarifications by asking questions and participation cannot be quenched by these two media. In addition, there are several other reasons behind the lower effectiveness of radio and TV programs in BOU. Access to TV and radio programs is to some extent restricted due the short daily interval of broadcasting by the government-owned TV and radio channels. A survey result further indicated other problems such as unstable supply of electricity, poor connectivity of TV and radio broadcasts in some remote areas, lack of prior information regarding the topic of the program to the students, unexpected variation from the scheduled broadcast time and insufficient number of programs per course. One of the suggested solutions is to make available those audio and audio-visual programs in RCs, COs and even TCs for the students' as well as for the tutors' use (Islam & Selim, 2006c; Islam, Rahman & Rahman, 2006). Some of those programs could be added in the course package on CD-ROMs. These attempts would surely improve the effectiveness of these programs in a cost-effective manner.

## Face-to-face tutorial services for laboratory and practical work

Effective transfer of skills in any technical or science work to the students requires hands-on experience and human interaction. BOU has introduced face-to-face tutorial services in the designated TCs to support students in theoretical lessons and to perform practical experiments under the direct supervision of subject specialist tutors. Each tutorial session for practical/laboratory work is 55–110 minutes long, depending on the program. The tutors are appointed on a part-time basis, and are usually engaged in government or nongovernment organizations. They render academic services following a routine provided by the concerned school of BOU. Nominal logistic support is provided to the TCs to conduct practical and laboratory work; however, it varies from program to program. It has been found from students' examination records that their performances in the laboratory courses are very good, as they receive facilities, direct guidance, and feedback for practical work at the TCs. Students' participation in the tutorial session is not mandatory, and therefore, a high rate of absenteeism in the laboratory or field work is common (Rahman et al., 2005; Shah et al., 2005; Islam, 2008). It has also been found that students who did not attend the tutorial sessions failed in great numbers in the practical part of the examinations (Rahman et al., 2005; Islam, Rahman & Rahman, 2006). A high rate of absenteeism in tutorial sessions has also been found in distance education other developing countries (Fozdar, Kumar & Kannan, 2006).

The concept of freedom and individual choice for distant learners is an important driver for success. Although students get current hands-on experience in doing laboratory work under guidance of specialist tutors in the TCs, this approach is obviously quite inflexible and offers students little independence and freedom in their learning. Low attendance of BOU students in the tutorial sessions is a strong indicator that distant students need an approach that is flexible as to time, pace, geographical location, and environment. Therefore, innovative and flexible methods are needed for effective transfer of cognitive and practical skills in science courses at a distance (Fozdar, Kumar & Kannan, 2006). There have been numerous approaches to addressing this challenge, including using regional laboratory sites, concentrating laboratory sessions, and offering flexible hours (weekends and evenings), as well as employing computer simulations and remote laboratories (Kennepohl, 2001). Laboratory work performed by distance students in their home environment using appropriate kits or computer simulations was found to be more or less equivalent to on-campus experiments (Rudd, 1994; Ross & Scanlon, 1995; Boschmann, 2003; Casanova et al., 2006; Kennepohl, 2001, 2007). The high cost of kits and/or lack of student access to electronic devices are two major concerns in introducing these innovative approaches in developing countries.

Most of the practical lessons in agricultural sciences, such as seed germination testing, analysis of soil texture (sand/silt/clay) by the filed method, identification of nutrition deficiency in plants by leaf color chart, and identifications of weeds, insects, etc., can easily be done at home and nearby farms by following protocols written in the course books. However, nearly 30% students do not perform these works alone (Rahman et al., 2005; Islam, 2008). This is probably due to isolation and lack of motivation and scope for collaborative learning practices. To overcome this situation, it has been suggested that students' participation in the practical session should be encouraged by allocating 10–20% marks for attendance (Islam 2008). But this would certainly limit the flexibility and freedom of students. Several other reasons have also been identified for lower attendance in tutorial sessions such as transportation difficulties, engagement in personal matters, and costs. As BOU students do not receive any kits for practical work, a both tutors and students often appeal for increased facilities (materials, equipments, transportation) and duration of tutorial sessions. Insufficient support from the study centre as the cause of student withdrawal in a BSc program in IGNOU has been reported (Fozdar, Kumar & Kannan, 2006). However, face-to-face counselling in the study centre has been found effective in meeting the demands of distance learners in many developing countries (Fung & Carr, 2000; Fozdar, Kumar & Kannan, 2006).

*Evaluation methods*

To assess acquired knowledge and skills, an appropriate evaluation method is needed. BOU has introduced two types of evaluation for assessing students' performance. One is the tutor-marked assignment (TMA), a tool for continuous assessment, and the other is the semester-end examination. In science courses, questions for TMAs are usually practice-oriented. Each course is evaluated in terms of a total of 100 marks. The marks distributions for TMAs, theory, and laboratory or practical components are 10, 70, and 20, respectively. Marks allocated for laboratory works are further divided into three parts; 5, 10, and 5 for laboratory notebook, an experiment/job, and *viva voce*, respectively. All questions are prepared centrally by anonymous subject specialists and moderated by the examination committee under direct coordination by the respective school of BOU and printed and distributed by the controller of the examinations. However, evaluation of the practical/lab examination is done by two examiners (internal and external) during or immediately after the examination and sent to the controller of the examination through TC. As with the theory portion, a student must get a minimum of 50% of the marks in the practical portion in order to complete the course. Results are expressed in cumulative grade point average on a scale of 5 (Islam & Selim, 2006c). To maintain quality, all question papers are prepared by anonymous experts under the supervision of an examination committee in the respective school and then printed and distributed to TCs by the controller of the examination. Analysis of examination results of different science courses revealed that students who passed the laboratory or practical component generally passed in other components of the course. In BOU, transfer of practical skills in the laboratory courses is highly emphasized. The current evaluation method seems less flexible, and it takes a long time to conduct examinations in the TCs and publish results thereafter.

# Challenges and opportunities in specific science programs

## Science at secondary and higher secondary

In the SSC program, there is a compulsory integrated science course, while in HSC, there are three courses such as Biology, Chemistry, and Physics for science group students. Enrolment in these two programs is very high in Bangladesh (Table 1). As BOU selects the best government and non-government high schools or colleges as tutorial centres, facilities for laboratory work and the expertise of tutors are supposed to meet the national standard. However, so far no study has been conducted on how effectively BOU students are learning practical skills in science courses at the secondary and higher secondary levels.

## Agricultural sciences

Agriculture is the mainstay of the national economy of Bangladesh. Nearly two thirds of the population of this country is engaged in agriculture. Therefore, it is agreed that agricultural and associated education should create effective human capital which is capable of increasing profitability in agriculture enterprise and that it should be able to create social capital (Rahman et al., 2005). Considering the socio-economic conditions and high dropout rates in both SSC and HSC levels, the School of Agriculture and Rural Development of BOU introduced three challenging programs in agricultural sciences. These three programs have been designed to provide essential know-how, skills, and professional knowledge for various categories of people interested in generating self-employment through crop, fisheries, livestock, and poultry farming and in participating in technology transferring activity through working in government and non-government organizations. The B.Ag.Ed. program was designed to gradually produce nearly 300,000 teachers who teach agricultural science in secondary schools or madrashas, while the CLP and CPFP programs are intended for skilled youths who will engage themselves in small farming by self-employment. A survey report revealed that most of the students are coming from rural areas with an expectation to create their own farms or engage in teaching and extension works in agricultural technology transfer after completion.

Current media and delivery methods in these programs were found to be effective in transferring knowledge but a little less effective than expected by students in transferring practical skills (Rahman et al., 2005; Shah et al., 2005; Islam, 2008). There are several reasons behind this phenomenon. The most notable one, mentioned earlier, is that all TCs are not well equipped and the materials and transportation facilities provided by BOU for laboratory work and visiting farms are not adequate. Obviously, student freedom and individual choice are very limited by pre-scheduled tutorial sessions in the TCs. However, overall performance of students in these programs is rated satisfactory as a significant number of the students have started farming or have engaged themselves in teaching after completion of the CLP and CPFP and B.Ag.Ed. programs, respectively (Rahman et al., 2005; Shah et al., 2005; Islam, 2008).

*Health science*
The B.Sc. in Nursing has been designed for diploma nurses who have completed three years post-diploma training in the hospital. There are about 16,000 diploma nurses (mainly female) and only about 1,500 graduate nurses for more then 150 million people in the country. In Bangladesh there is only one graduate College of Nursing at Dhaka with a capacity of about 150 students every year. But due to a number of reasons only 50–60 nurses can graduate from the college each year for about 1,200 diploma nurses coming out of 38 nursing institutes (Numan, 2001a, 2001b). Much emphasis has been placed on applied subject areas such as English, Applied Sciences, Nutrition, Behavioural Science, Maternal and Child Health Nursing, Community Health Nursing, Nursing Research, Administration and Management, Teaching Methodology and Project in Senior Focus Elective. This program has been developed with 52%

practical components in comparison to 48% theory components, with 25 courses.

In health science courses, each theory and practical course is evaluated in terms of a total of 100 marks. Each course has two TMAs of 15 marks each that are usually practice-oriented. The marks distributions for theory courses are TMAs 30, theory 50, and objectives 20. Marks allocated for practical courses are further divided into three parts: 60, 20 and 20 for continuous assessment, which comprises periodical laboratory work, ward activities, two to four prescribed assessments related to the course, an experiment/job at the final exam and *viva voce*, respectively. However, evaluation of the practical/lab examination is done by two examiners (internal and external) during the examination. A student must get at least 50% in each component of the theory and practical courses to pass/ or complete a course.

*Computer science and application*
This program is designed to produce skilled manpower in the ICT sector, which is expanding very rapidly in Bangladesh. Hands-on practical training is offered to students in the well-equipped TCs in government and non-government computer training centres and universities. As it is a practice-oriented technical program, attendance in tutorial sessions was found to be high.

## Problems and suggestions for improvement

Bangladesh Open University has taken up the challenge of introducing several undergraduate, diploma, and certificate programs in agriculture, health science and engineering through distance mode in this resource-poor developing country. The responses to these programs have been phenomenal, as they are very cost-effective and flexible for adult learners (Fig. 2). There are several reasons behind the success and cost-effectiveness in BOU programs. These are (i) as a public university BOU has access to any government and non-government infrastructure and facilities without cost or with nominal costs and can engage specialists from any institution for tutoring with a small honorarium; (ii) it broadcasts programs free of cost through government-owned radio and TV channels which have coverage throughout the country; (iii) the demand for higher and technical education in Bangladesh is very high, as due to seat limitations only 4% of students get the chance to enrol in universities after their HSC; (iv) the degree/diploma/certificate of BOU is accepted by all as equivalent to that of any other public university; and (v) the faculties of BOU are highly qualified and obviously equivalent to those of conventional public universities. In spite of all these opportunities, scepticism has remained as to the flexibility and effectiveness of current media for laboratory science and practical work. Most of the current media offer only one-way delivery with limited freedom and individual choice for learning. Therefore, innovative approaches are needed to improve the current situation.

Although Bangladesh is a developing country with 50% of the population living below the poverty line, it is surprising to note here that access to cellular phones has increased tremendously in this land within the past decade. Subscribers to mobile phone companies now total nearly 30 million citizens of the country, irrespective of their income levels. Survey results have indicated that 50–70% of BOU students have access to a mobile phone (Islam, 2008). Obviously, an acceleration in the speed of access to modern ICTs in Bangladesh will happen due to mass acceptance of the government's visionary plan to develop a digital Bangladesh by the year 2021. However, BOU does not yet offer any mobile learning facility which is considered as a credible, cost-effective component of blended open and distance learning provisions, adaptable to an institution's needs and situation. Recently, all government-run secondary and higher secondary education boards offered students the opportunity to obtain their results through an automated short message service (SMS) immediately after the results are published. This approach was found very successful in Bangladesh. Obviously, learning through mobile phone (mobile learning or m-learning) is a personal, spontaneous, "anytime, anywhere" way to learn and enlarges access to education for all. It reinforces learners' sense of ownership of the learning experience, offering them flexibility as to how, when, and where they learn. Therefore, as a leading body in distance education, BOU should conduct necessary studies to include the mobile phone as a tool for teaching students at a distance. Similarly, the Internet is also expanding rapidly in the country, which offers an opportunity for electronic learning (e-learning). It is therefore reasonable to inititate Web-based information dissemination for admissions and examination schedule and result publication, as has already been done in conventional universities. Studies are needed to develop innovative approaches for teaching science subjects through electronic media such as the Internet (e.g., e-mail, Web-based delivery) and computer that would be flexible and offer more scope for student-teacher and student-student interactions.

## Conclusion

Teaching science at a distance is undoubtedly a challenging task in the developing countries. This report discusses how a mega-university in a resource-poor developing country like Bangladesh teaches science courses in different disciplines at a distance using some older generation media such as print, radio, and TV broadcasts and face-to-face tutorials. Although these media are less flexible, they were found effective in transferring both theoretical and practical skills in a cost-effective manner in the context of Bangladesh. Review of several studies identified the problems in the current system and proposed alternatives to mitigate them by applying innovative approaches, which may have practical implications in research and effective teaching of laboratory science through open and distance learning in the developing countries.

## Acknowledgments

I am grateful to the Alexander von Humboldt Foundation, Germany, for a Georg Forster Research Fellowship during this study. My sincere thanks are due to my colleagues Sharker Md. Numan, Prof. AQMB Rashid, and Mostafa Azad Kamal for their critical reading and comments for improvement of this manuscript. Prof. Dietmar Kennepohl of Athabasca University, Canada, deserves special thanks for encouragement and valuable comments during preparation of this chapter.

### REFERENCES

Ali, M.S., Haque, A.K.E., & Rumble, G. (1997). The Bangladesh Open University: Mission and promise. *Open Learning*, 12(2), 12–28.

Anonymus (1997). Basic trade programme for students of secondary schools and Madrashas: The resource and time saver programme. Directorate of Technical Education, Dhaka.

Anonymous (2002). Project performance audit report on Bangladesh Open University project in Bangladesh (Loan 1173-BAN [SF]).

Anonymous (2007). Only 4pc go for higher education after college. *The Daily Star*, Dhaka, Bangladesh, December 2 (Sunday).

Arger, G. (1990). Distance education in the third world: critical analysis on the promise and reality. *Open Learning*, 5(2), 9–18.

Arger, G. (1993). Australia. In *Distance Education in Asia and the Pacific: Country Papers*, Vol. 1, UNESCO.

Boschmann, E. (2003). Teaching chemistry via distance education. *Journal of Chemical Education*, 80, 704–708.

Casanova, R.S., Civelli, J.L., Kimbrough, D.R., Heath, B.P., & Reeves, J.H. (2006).Distance Learning: A viable alternative to the conventiona lecture-lab format in general chemistry. *Journal of Chemical Education*, 83, 501–507.

Daniel, J.S. (1996). *Mega-universities and knowledge media: Technology strategies for higher education*. London, Kogan Page.

Freeman, R. (1991). Quality assurance in learning materials production. *Open Learning*, 6(3), 24–31.

Fozdar, B.I., Kumar, L.S., & Kannan, S. (2006). Study of the factors responsible for the dropouts from the BSc programme of Indira Gandhi National Open University. *The International Review of Research in Open and Distance Learning*, 7(3). Retrieved

February 25, 2009 from: http://www.irrodl.org/index.php/irrodl/article/view/291/755

Fung, Y., & Carr, R. (2000). Face-to-face tutorials in a distance learning system: Meeting students need. *Open Learning, 15,* 35–46.

Gaba, A.K., & Dash, N.K. (2004). Course evaluation in open and distance learning: A case study from Indira Gandhi National Open University. *Open Learning, 19,* 213–221.

Islam, M.T. (1998). Developing course materials: An experience of Bangladesh Open University. *Proceedings of the 12th Annual Conference of Asian Association of Open Universities,* Hong Kong, Part II, pp. 189–198.

Islam, M.T. (2007). *Information and communication technologies in education.* Paragon Enterprises Ltd., Mohakhali, Dhaka (ISBN 984-32-3872-9) *(in Bangla).*

Islam, M.T. (2008). Appropriateness of curricula, technology choice and methods of assessment: A study of vocational education programmes in agriculture through distance mode. Presented in the *5th Meeting of the Pan Commonwealth Forum,* 13–27 July, 2008, University of London, UK (http://www.wikieducator.org/PCF5:_Children_and_Youth).

Islam, M.A., & Islam, M.N. (2008). Effectiveness of the different medium of education to imparting knowledge at Bangladesh Open University. *Turkish Online Journal of Distance Education,* 9(1), 44–53.

Islam, M.T., & Rahman, A.N.M. (1997). Quality assurance in distance and open learning: Bangladesh Open University experience. *Proceedings of the 11th AAOU Annual Conference* (pp. 187–194), Kuala Lumpur, Malaysia.

Islam, M.T., & Selim, A.S.M. (2006a). Information and communication technologies for the promotion of open and distance learning in Bangladesh. *Journal of Agriculture & Rural Development,* 4(1/2), 35–42.

Islam, M.T., & Selim, A.S.M. (2006b). Current status and prospects for e-learning in the promotion of distance education in Bangladesh. *Turkish Online Journal of Distance Education,* 7(1), 114–119.

Islam, M.T., & Selim, A.S.M. (2006c). Quality assurance in distance education on 'agriculture and rural development': A workshop at Bangladesh Open University. *Indian Journal of Open Learning, 15,* 196–198.

Islam, M.T., Rahman, M.M., & Rahman, K.M. (2006). Quality and processes of Bangladesh Open University course materials development. *Turkish Online Journal of Distance Education*, 7(2), 130–138.

Jung, I., & Latchem, C. (2007). Assuring quality in Asian open and distance learning. *Open Learning*, 22, 235–250.

Kennepohl, D. (2001). Using computer simulations to supplement teaching laboratories in chemistry for distance delivery. *Journal of Distance Education*, 16(2), 58–65.

Kennepohl, D. (2007). Using home-laboratory kits to teach general chemistry. *Chemistry Education Research and Practice*, 8, 337–348.

Nigam, A., & Joshi, V. (2007). Science education through open and distance learning at higher education level. *Turkish Online Journal of Distance Education*, 8(4), 20–33.

Numan, S.M. (2001a). Health education through distance mode to enhance the health status of Bangladesh. *Journal of Bangladesh Open University*, 2, 58–65.

Numan, S.M. (2001b). Networking as a means to deliver distance-mode health education in Bangladesh. *Higher Education in Europe*, 26, 125–130.

Rahman, A.N.M.A., Shah, A.K.M.A., Alam, M.S., Alam, M.S. (2005). Skills for development: a study of vocational programme in livestock and poultry through distance mode. *Indian Journal of Open Learning*, 14(2), 139–149.

Ramanujam, P.R. (2001). Distance open learning in the developing asian countries: Problems and possible solutions. ZIFF Papiere 117, FernUniversität, Germany.

Ross, S., & Scanlon, E. (1995). *Open science: Distance teaching and open learning of science subjects*. Paul Chapman Publishing Ltd., Great Britain, pp. 137–145.

Rudd, V. (1994). Happy birthday to yOU. *Education in Chemistry*, 31, 87.

Shah, A.K.M.A., Rahman, A.N.M.A., Alam, M.S., Alam, M.S. (2005). Vocational education in fisheries through open and distance mode: A case study of Bangladesh Open University. *Journal of Agriculture & Rural Development*, 3(1/2), 17–24.

# Chapter 12
# Distance and Flexible Learning at University of the South Pacific

ANJEELA JOKHAN AND BIBHYA N. SHARMA
University of the South Pacific

## Introduction

The University of the South Pacific (USP) was set up in the South Pacific region in 1968 by its 12 member countries — Cook Islands, Fiji Islands, Kiribati, Marshall Islands, Nauru, Niue, Samoa, Solomon Islands, Tokelau, Tonga, Tuvalu, and Vanuatu. A total of 14 campuses and 8 smaller centres are spread over an area of 30 million square kilometres of the Pacific Ocean (See Figure 1). The smaller centres are parts of the larger campuses spread in remote locations or on the smaller islands in some countries.

The size of the campuses in member countries varies significantly, with a range of student numbers, courses offered, and facilities available. At one end of the spectrum is the main Laucala Campus (based in the Fiji Islands), which is the largest of all the campuses, enrolling about 14,000 students (full-time and part-time) at any one time. At the other end is the smallest campus in Tokelau, which has only about 20 students enrolled each semester. The regional campuses and centres are predominantly utilized to cater for the students enrolled in the Distance and Flexible Learning (DFL) mode of study. Most campuses have been appropriately equipped and provided with other resources which may be utilized by the students enrolled in the DFL mode to help them complete their courses. Nonetheless, most of the "essentials" are located at the Laucala Campus, which has the central administration, including the registry, library, student academic services, vice-chancellors' office, and the faculties and divisions. The main campus also acts as a central repository of exams, student and staff records, and other important documentation. These materials are shared with other campuses and centres if and when the need arises.

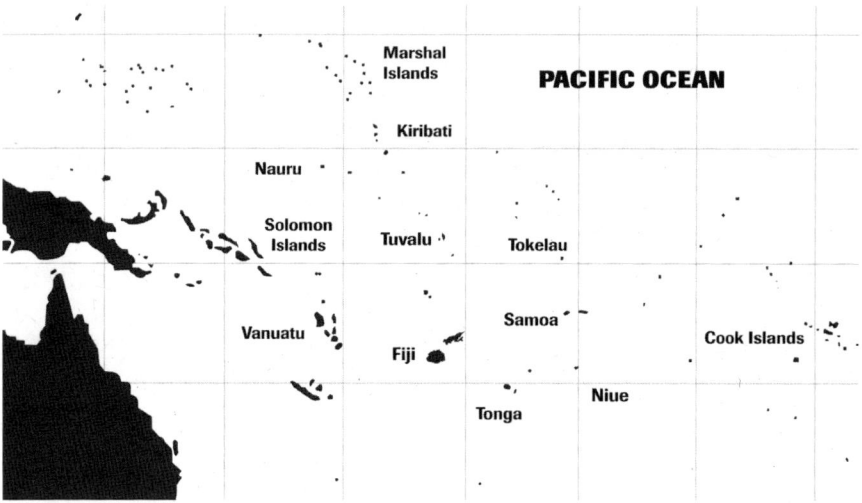

**Figure 1.** Map showing the 12 member countries of the University of the South Pacific. Map courtesy of the University of the South Pacific. Used with permission.

The University of the South Pacific is mandated to play a leadership role in overall capacity building and developing skills for knowledge-based societies within the South Pacific region. The university treats DFL as a matter of top priority due to the geographical isolation of the member countries and heavy work commitments that make it difficult for many students to attend classes during normal hours. There is a great demand for the DFL courses, as can be seen from the growing DFL enrolments and the increased number of courses offered via this mode. Currently, 70% of USP students are studying (at least partially) by the DFL mode in the region.

In 1971, the university first began offering courses through the DFL mode of delivery, making them available to its off-campus students (Mataki and Koshy, 2004). Since then, the university has actively engaged in the development of high-quality DFL services and products for the region. The university has funded/co-funded a number of studies to help pilot its DFL deliveries across the region. Findings and recommendations from these studies have continuously improved DFL delivery.

A historic need that the university addresses with DFL delivery is the shortage of Year 13 (pre-university) education in most of the member countries. These member countries are unable to support education at the senior secondary level and to prepare the students for higher studies. Since they do not have Year 13, the students either have to go abroad to attain this university entrance qualification or enrol in the Foundation program offered by the university via the DFL mode. The initial focus of the Foundation year program in the member countries was for preparation for university studies. This demand still exists in parallel with the demand for undergraduate and postgraduate courses and programs even after four decades of continued service from the university.

There are a number of programs that are offered partially by the DFL mode. The students enrolled in these programs are able to complete most, if not all, 100-level and a few higher level courses through DFL mode and later complete their programs at the main campus. This would include most of the social science, mathematics, computing science, and information system disciplines. However, the process of conversion to DFL delivery in the area of science (core science disciplines) has been relatively slow, due in part to the challenges of delivering science education discussed below. Nonetheless, absence of full DFL delivery of programs is treated as a barrier to literacy and equity throughout the region (Lockwood, Smith & Yates, 2000) and as such the university is committed to expand and diversify programs already offered in the DFL mode.

The University of the South Pacific offers a wide spectrum of distance and flexible learning options, including online delivery and print-based distance delivery. A full description of DFL at USP is available (University of the South Pacific, 2007). The DFL options for science courses are presented in Table 1.

**Table 1.** Distance and Flexible Learning (DFL) Delivery Modes for Science Courses at University of the South Pacific.

| Distance and Flexible Learning Delivery Mode | Description |
| --- | --- |
| Print-based | Students receive all the materials for a course in the beginning of an academic semester and are required to follow the course schedule. First year chemistry and biology and Foundation courses are offered in this mode. |
| Flexi-schools | Four to six weeks of intensive teaching, mostly carried out by staff travelling from the Laucala Campus to the flexi-school venues; offered during semester breaks. Some Foundation courses are offered as flexi-schools. |
| Video Broadcast | Lectures from the face-to-face delivered courses at the main campus are broadcast to the local campuses and centres for the benefit of the DFL students. First year physics courses are offered by video broadcast. |

USP provides academic support for its DFL students in a number of ways. Satellite tutorials are commonly utilized by the teaching staff for sharing knowledge with students from all the member countries simultaneously. Video conferencing is also used, and incorporates the benefits of conventional face-to-face teaching. Tutorial visits are normally held during the mid-semester breaks at various campuses in the region. Tutors and lecturers travel to the member countries and hold tutorial and/or lecture sessions for the courses offered by their divisions for a short duration (normally a week). Other visits can also be accommodated based upon the requests from the various campuses. Finally, email/phone/fax facilities are in place for one-to-one transactions between the course coordinator or tutor and the student. Course materials and other important documents can also be exchanged via the fax and e-mail facilities.

## Challenges and opportunities for DFL delivery in science

*Practical work*

Although science courses are in high demand in the USP region, their practical component imposes constraints on DFL delivery.

Laboratories in the regional campuses are adequately equipped to carry out the practical component of Foundation science courses. These Foundation science courses are offered in the print-based mode and/or as flexi-school courses. If offered as a flexi-school course, the course will usually run with the same assessment portfolio as the face-to-face offering, while the practical component of the assessment is left to be carried out at a centre or campus that has the appropriate laboratory facilities. On the other hand, if offered through print mode, the assessment portfolio will usually consist of a tutorial component, assignments, and mid-semester test as well as weekly practicals. Laboratory demonstrators and other helpers are employed either locally or from the region to help prepare and mount these practicals. Local tutors are also appointed, either full-time or part-time, to assist in the delivery.

One of the biggest challenges is the lack of proper laboratory equipment in the senior schools of the member countries. While some countries that teach Year 12 initially had partially equipped laboratories, schools in other countries had to be funded by the university to upgrade their laboratories for the practical work in Foundation science courses. In the larger campuses, for example in Tonga, Samoa, and the Solomon Islands, the university has fully funded the construction of the science laboratories.

Another challenge in delivering practicals in regional locations is that most of these member countries do not have the technical support necessary to maintain and run the laboratories. For example, regional countries are not equipped for the storage and use of chemicals. Also, there is a lack of sufficient expertise to maintain equipment such as microscopes. In some instances it is necessary to transport the equipment to and from the regional campuses to complete the practical component of the courses. The equipment and consumables are ordered through the main campus in Laucala and transported to the regional campuses, since there is no system or staff in the regional campuses to do this.

First year (or 100-level) practical science courses are not offered at all the regional campuses, mainly because of the lack of adequate laboratory facilities. Also, some of the smaller campuses have very few students (normally less than five), and to run laboratory classes in these campuses is a very expensive exercise. As a consequence, the first year science courses are only offered in campuses where adequate laboratory facilities exist together with a sizable enrolment.

All of the first year biology and chemistry courses are in print mode, while the physics courses are run in the video broadcast format from the Laucala Campus. The courses offered through print mode are run as 30-week courses (as opposed to the 15-week on-campus courses), and in most cases, the laboratory classes are run as a block toward the end of the year at the regional campuses. Students registered in the science courses in the other two campuses in Fiji travel to the main campus to do block laboratories during the second half of the year, as there are no laboratories set up at the other two campuses in Fiji for this purpose. In the other countries, the practical work is organized and run by staff travelling from the Laucala Campus. Staff are also required to take the consumables from the main campus with them to run these sessions. This is not only an expensive exercise but is also very labour-intensive.

In the case of first year courses in plant and animal biology, transportation of specimens and consumables for the laboratory work is critical because many of the atoll islands have distinctly fewer plant and animal species and so the availability of teaching materials is rather limited. The introduction to students of the plant and animal kingdoms requires many unique biological specimens that are frequently not found in countries with limited flora and fauna.

There have been numerous discussions on the possibility of using virtual laboratories in the regional campuses. In 1996, the Biology Division experimented by sending out videotapes of laboratories designed and demonstrated at the main campus. At that time, the laboratory facilities for Foundation science courses were still inadequate. The response from the regional campuses was that because of poor understanding of the English language the students did not benefit much from these videos. Since then the campuses have become better equipped to hold Foundation laboratories and there are now local tutors who run tutorials and laboratory sessions in the regional campuses for Foundation science courses.

For baccalaureate level courses, regional practical laboratories have not been used because of the lack of teaching support in the regional campuses. The university is trying to increase the face-to-face component of the courses offered in the regional campuses because experience and post-implementation reviews have clearly shown that this is more effective for the students than totally independent learning. The laboratory component has been seen as one way of doing this, but the fact remains that this is an expensive method of delivery. The university is considering other options for the laboratory component, such as laboratory kits.

The spatial vastness of the USP region is an added challenge for the university. In the member countries where adequate infrastructure is not available to support the practical component, the offering of the practical science courses presents an even bigger challenge. Firstly, travel within the region is limited by the infrequency of flights to most of the member countries. Normally flights are available only once a week, and because of economic considerations these are relatively more expensive flights. Travel to Tokelau, which is a very small country, takes three days and even requires travel by boat for a considerable part of the journey, an example of the other extreme of remoteness. In some instances quicker travel is possible transiting through Australia or New Zealand; however, costs for these travels escalate. As a consequence, members of the academic staff are unable to travel from Laucala Campus as often as would be desirable to the region to provide much-needed support to students and ensure quality of delivery of the courses. As a result, the academic sections in Laucala Campus rely on staff in the regional campuses as much as possible to ensure that the delivery on the ground is of high quality and that the support staff situated at the local campuses provide the necessarysupport for students. The cost of employing academic support staff on each campus for every discipline is very high, hence only some disciplines are able to employ the required numbers of staff. These would normally be those disciplines that are able to attract an economically viable number of students. The other disciplines need to either rely on remote support from the Laucala Campus or provide support in the form of staff travelling from the Laucala Campus.

Some of the member countries are very small, and so hiring academic support staff locally provides the university with a real challenge. This is not because there is a lack of qualified locals but rather due to the fact that these qualified locals would already hold good jobs (mostly within the government) and therefore not be available to be employed either as full-time or part-time staff of the university. This means that hiring expatriate staff (from Fiji or elsewhere) becomes a necessity and the expenses escalate even more.

### Challenges for students

Students in the region face the challenge of studying in the English language. In some countries English may be the third language and English may not necessarily be used in schools, either formally or informally. For example in Vanuatu some schools are teaching in the French or Bislama languages so it can become increasingly difficult for students to study in English at tertiary level. The main obstacle is the understanding of text in the English language. Experience has shown that most students read text in English, translate it as best they can into their own language in order to understand it and then either learn or respond to it. They learn or respond in their own language initially, and then attempt to translate it back to English before writing or speaking. In all this translation, information can be lost or misrepresented. This is perhaps more serious where scientific vocabulary is used (Jokhan, 2003).

Language barriers are a major challenge to delivering university education. The university is expected by its member countries to provide distance education to students from rural areas as well as the regional campuses, but there is a question of sustainability when so many students need extra support to study in the English language. The university is always challenged to arrive at a reasonable compromise between maintaining sustainable programs and providing as much support as possible for the DFL students.

The secondary education system in the region is still quite traditional and has limited resources. For example, a high percentage of the students in the region would have completed their secondary schooling without ever having had any experience using a computer. So, in some academic programs more than others, the university must address fundamental computer skills in addition to the disciplinary content.

Many students are not prepared for the independent nature of DFL courses. This may derive from the traditional secondary system, where there is a strong culture of respect in terms of always accepting what the teacher says. The transition to learning in the DFL mode is a bigger shift in study culture than going from school to face-to-face university studies.

The need for making student orientation at the regional campuses more focused toward preparing students for study in the DFL mode and improving time management has been identified. A number of campuses are implementing a project developed by the Centre for Educational Development and Technology (CEDT) to build these study skills as a pilot study. It is anticipated that this important initiative will become essential in improving the success of students studying in the distance and flexible modes.

*Traditional academic culture*

A hard-to-change constraint on healthy growth of high-quality DFL products and services in USP is the difficulty in changing the organizational culture. Teaching staff around the world are not very comfortable changing from the traditional forms of delivery. Many lecturers are apprehensive and resistant to change and innovation. Nonetheless, support (in terms of training and personnel) and a reward system can change the organizational culture and persuade lecturers to contribute more to the DFL mode of study. The university has taken a number of steps in this direction. Firstly, it has restructured the existing University Extension unit to the Distance and Flexible Learning Support Centre (DFLSC) situated in the main campus. The support centre now champions the DFL delivery, provides staff and student training, makes media decisions and administers the DFL activities across its campuses and centres. Secondly, the university has proposed that its Graduate Certificate in Tertiary Teaching (GCTT) program be made compulsory to all academic staff without formal teaching qualifications, to help them to facilitate and service the DFL mode of study properly. In the past few years, many USP faculty members have benefited tremendously from this program, and it has led to increased favourable responses from student course evaluation reports and formal/informal correspondences with respect to their classroom teaching and DFL deliveries. Finally, the university has made sure that commitment to DFL work is now an additional performance indicator for the academic staff. A reward system is put into place where staff involved in DFL work are incremented or given cash bonuses during their performance review or renewal of contract.

## Conclusion

The University of the South Pacific plays a large role in developing skills for knowledge-based societies within the South Pacific region. USP's commitment to the DFL mode of study has achieved international recognition. This is demonstrated by the substantial funding that USP attracts from donors such as Australia, New Zealand, and Japan specifically dedicated to DFL activities. In addition, the university continues to be recognized in the form of international awards that it receives in the DFL area. USP delivers a range of science courses in the DFL mode, but challenges related to geography, language, and culture need to be overcome in order to successfully offer science courses through DFL. USP has achieved some success in this area and is committed to expanding and diversifying programs offered in the DFL mode.

## Acknowledgments

We wish to acknowledge the Pro-Vice Chancellor Regional at USP for agreeing to allow us to use USP information for this work.

### REFERENCES

Jokhan, A.D. (2003). Teaching science in the region. In A. Kirkness & N. Fanene (Eds.), *Teaching and learning with Pasifika students: A Colloquium for Tertiary Teachers* (pp. 73–77). Auckland, New Zealand: Centre for Educational and Professional Development, Auckland University of Technology. Retrieved February 25, 2009 from: http://www.aut.ac.nz/resources/staff/cepd/proceedingsofpasifikacolloquiumfeb03.pdf

Lockwood, F., Smith, A., & Yates, C. (2000). *Review of distance and flexible learning at the University of the South Pacific*. University of the South Pacific: Suva, Fiji. Retrieved February 25, 2009 from: http://www.usp.ac.fj/fileadmin/files/academic/pdo/digitised/ReviewOfDistance%26FlexibleLearningAtUSP-2000.pdf

Mataki, M., & Koshy, K. (2004). *Learning methods and networking to bridging the knowledge and learning gaps in small island developing states.* (USP Assessment Report for IDRC-UNDP Project). University of the South Pacific: Suva, Fiji. Retrieved Febraury 2009 from: http://www.usp.ac.fj/fileadmin/files/Institutes/pacesd/Research/USP_DFL_Assessment_Report.pdf

University of the South Pacific (2007). *2007 Distance and flexible learning handbook.* Suva, Fiji. Retrieved February 25, 2009 from: http://www.usp.ac.fj/fileadmin/files/public_relations/2007_dfl_handbook.pdf

# Chapter 13
## Institutional Considerations: A Vision for Distance Education

**ERWIN BOSCHMANN**
Indiana University Purdue University Indianapolis

## Introduction

*Every morning in Africa,*
*A gazelle wakes up;*
*It knows it must outrun the fastest lion,*
*Or it will be killed.*
*Every morning in Africa,*
*A lion wakes up;*
*It knows it must outrun the slowest gazelle,*
*Or it will starve.*
*It does not matter if you are a lion or a gazelle,*
*When the sun comes up,*
*We'd better be running.*

This little scenario, uttered by Alfredo de los Santos, depicts our dilemma; to survive we must compete, we must run, and, in the process, we must change.

Human nature instinctively resists change. Whether it is a new idea, a new artifact, or a new procedure, the potential loss of familiarity, the loss of control and power, or different ways of doing familiar things all contribute to resistance. For the most part, faculty are no exception and often remain entrenched in a culture utterly resistant to change (Boschmann, 2003a). In Chapter 3 we caught a glimpse of this entrenchment and the importance of strategies to effect and lead change within instructional design teams.

Most developments struggle for acceptance, as did electricity, the car, and radio in the late nineteenth century. More recently, the computer, gender equality, and teaching at a distance also struggle, not only having to answer critics, but having to convince the neutral masses as well. But when such developments are successfully accepted, they obviously have embraced change, widened their influence, and removed barriers. Thus, when students of the Greek philosophers began using papyrus to record the lectures, their teachers objected on the grounds that it would destroy the art of oratory. However, besides providing a means for later review, these notes also made lectures available to those who could not attend. They widened the circle of influence.

It is the premise of this essay that a revolution is at hand and that capitalizing on its promises can bring about sweeping changes not only to education, but by extension, to the world economy. In fact, if exploited properly, this revolution can affect more people world-wide than virtually any other transformation.

While the learner is always central to any discussion, this chapter will consider fundamental concerns that we share from the larger perspective of the academy, the institution, and even society itself. The previous chapters have dealt mostly with the "how" of DE in general and with respect to the sciences. This chapter now also touches on the "why." We will first look at the barriers to distance education, both formal and informal, and the vision necessary to overcome these barriers. Next we will look at various opportunities that distance education affords, especially with the enormous capabilities of information technology. Finally, we must consider the barriers yet to be overcome.

## Barriers

As humans advance, develop, and call for change, barriers are always in place. Thousands of years ago the culture of India developed a unique educational technique. A guru hand-picked children to live with him, and he moulded them in totality; morals, ethics, values, reading, and writing. These were wonderful opportunities for the few chosen ones, but excluded most children. For millennia the tribal storyteller in the Americas provided the only means of education. The tradition of the apprentice in Europe who wandered the country stopping to learn his chosen trade from the masters he encountered has similar elements. While they provided the best education for the time, these examples are also rife with barriers of elitism, gender, time, and distance.

Similarly, prior to the invention of the printing press, the professor came into the classroom with 'the book,' read (lectured) from it to the class and held on to his privileged prerogative of control of knowledge. Aside from barriers such as time and place, that system also imposed the barrier of insisting on just one learning style: auditory. The availability of mass-produced books had the potential to influence many students, yet it took a century after the invention of the printing press for the book to have a significant influence on education — due to two barriers: most people could not read and there was no system of mass distribution of the book.

The creation of residential schools, primarily for the social edification of rich, elite, white, young gentlemen, was utterly exclusionary. What barriers! The subsequent emergence of public colleges and universities institutionalized higher learning, but still discriminated in favor of the elite upper classes. The democratization of higher education, especially in the United States through the development of the land grant institutions, the post-war enrolment surge, and the expansion of state universities and the community college system, broke down a number of barriers and opened the halls of learning to the masses. But with this rapid expansion new barriers were created: the increased isolation of the student from the master, and the 'delivering' of knowledge, rather than engaging the student in the pursuit of knowledge. Yet not only was education made available to the masses, but many other existing barriers were removed or at least reduced: cost, gender, religion, and race. Similarly, the introduction of the blackboard in the 1850s, as with the emergence of any new technology, was hailed as the harbinger of an educational breakthrough: it introduced the promise of a new visual learning style. As time goes on, barriers are removed and often new ones appear. With the exception of a brief mention in Chapters 11 and 12, the topic of barriers to learning has not yet been explicitly articulated in this book. We look at it now, because it is at the heart of why we might choose alternative approaches to teaching and learning.

What follows is a list of barriers which is not meant to be exhaustive or detailed in description.

### Cost and access

The relative ease of economic accessibility to education in industrialized countries is not the norm throughout the rest of the world. On a global scale, tuition increases much faster than family income does. The same thing is true with physical access to a campus: global population increases at a much faster rate than does the increase of new campuses (see Daniel, 1997).

### Gender

The bias against women in school is well on its way of being eliminated in the industrialized countries; however, it remains a reality in much of the world. While we think it illegal to engage in such discrimination, it is part of the culture and tradition in many countries. Perhaps it is not overt discrimination, but a rather informal way of discouraging women by not having many female faculty members and administrators, by counseling women into just a few areas of study, or by having few toilets for women.

*Religion and race*
Again, while the Western world has essentially eliminated such discrimination, there remain countries where a quota system is established to safeguard both a religious and racial imbalance.

While many of the barriers mentioned above have been eliminated in industrialized nations, some barriers remain in all societies.

*Age*
To be in a class as one whose age is far out of range from the average age of fellow students may be intimidating to some; others may sense a real bias against them.

*Family and work*
Seeking re-education while at the same time carrying the responsibility of a family and work becomes a barrier when institutions do not make allowances for such obstacles.

*First generation student*
Students who come from families without a higher education tradition can experience barriers in both the lack of understanding by family members for the need for higher education and the lack of moral and academic support from them.

*Terms and length of study*
Many institutions continue to place their own needs before those of the students. Thus, setting the beginning and ending of terms is a carry-over from the farm days when harvest demanded that students be at home during the summers. Then they accommodated students, today they do not. Similarly, students' varying abilities are ignored when the length of study is prescribed and their personal schedules are ignored when starting times are set by the institution.

*Learning styles*
Few professors are trained to teach according to the varying learning styles of students. Instead, professors generally teach as they were taught, expecting students to learn by the auditory, and/or visual method — and the faculty member decides which is used when.

*The medium is the message*
Marshall McLuhan (1964) in his book entitled *Understanding Media: The Extensions of Man*, discussed how technology affects human beings and their relations to one another. Any extension, be it a gun or e-mail, amputates other human abilities, such as archery and penmanship. With his phrase that "the medium is the message" he said we become what we behold. This can be a barrier unless we make sure that the medium *serves* the message.

*Entrance requirements*
It is a matter of discrimination when someone who wishes to enter an institution cannot due to prerequisites which the person chose not to or could not obtain earlier in life. Schools must consider accepting such students, although proper performance should be expected once in school.

*Academic culture*
Human interactions, especially in the business world, change frequently in response to changing environments. Half a century ago grocery stores were staffed by clerks who filled orders from behind a counter. As society became more demanding and insisted on self-selection, self-service stores arose. Most institutions are very slow in responding to changing times, even when their own research points toward new directions. For instance, why does so much teaching still 'deliver' knowledge when all research shows that the student needs to be 'engaged' for there to be a true and lasting positive impact on learning? (See Opportunities.)

*Lack of vision*

There are other barriers, not the least of which is lack of vision. The overhead projector was invented in 1876; by the 1930s it began to be used in bowling alleys, but it was not until the 1960s — 80+ years after its invention — that it began to appear in the classroom.

Not so long ago, when 80–90% of us worked on farms, we laboured with our hands and were assisted by our minds; today the reverse is true. It is a fact that as the industrial revolution gives way to the electronic revolution, education becomes a global necessity since the work of the mind becomes increasingly important. Those who accept and manage this change will not only be successful in helping fellow citizens, but will also help in overcoming barriers.

*It is the vision of this chapter that these obstacles can be overcome.*

In his book *An Agenda for the 21st Century*, Rushworth Kidder (1987) and a team of thinkers considered the challenges for the twenty-first century. After much discussion they listed overpopulation, the increasing gap between haves and have-nots, the arms race, nuclear annihilation, destruction of the environment, and decay of public morality as top challenges. However, these six challenges can all be overcome, according to Kidder, if the seventh one is addressed properly: namely, education.

If education is the key, then how can we approach the challenge of properly educating the masses? There are two very helpful phenomena that will be of paramount importance in the task: the existence of global unifying factors and the multipliers of human capabilities.

Centuries ago, when people lived in isolated communities with very little travel from place to place, when self-sufficiency was completely dependent on local resources, when local costumes and traditions defined and remained in the community, global unifying factors were both unheard of and unnecessary. However, since those days our global melting pot has brought about much unification. Developments such as a common system of weights and measures, the metric system, common clothing styles, uniform musical notation, the use of electricity, radio, and television, a common computer language, and acceptance of English as an official language of communication all make it possible to go from country to country and fit right in. Such unifying factors have smoothed the path to addressing the need for mass education.

The second happening is the introduction of multipliers of human capabilities. Robert Dierker (1995) cites Vinod Chachra, who amplified an idea outlined by William McKeefrey that the impact of a given technology can be quantified by determining the extent to which that technology multiplies human capabilities of accomplishing a given task. Thus, compared to walking, the horse produced a 2-fold increase in capability, the car a 15-fold increase, and the jet airplane a 150-fold increase. The plow and fertilizer each produced a 10-fold increase, thus ushering in the agricultural revolution, just as the steam engine with its 1000-fold increase in human capability ushered in the industrial revolution. According to Chachra, the telegraph, radio, and computers each have achieved a million-fold increase in human capability and thus have ushered in the electronic revolution.

Therefore, with the advent of unifying factors and multipliers of human capabilities, there are now opportunities that provide a dramatic impact on education and learning.

## Opportunities

Peter Drucker (1992) predicted that in the next 50 years, "schools and universities will change more drastically than they have since they assumed their present form 300 years ago when they organized themselves around the printed book." Much as the agricultural and industrial revolutions made quantum leaps of progress in their fields, so the electronic revolution can bring about a huge increase in human capabilities of educating the masses. We have the opportunity to create a student-centred environment where the student picks the most appropriate learning style, chooses a convenient time frame, and has no worries about access. This revamped and scaled-up educational system can take a great lesson from the business world, where mass production no longer means low quality, but instead, produces consistently high-quality products — at very low cost.

*Personal attention*
The electronic revolution holds the promise of educating the masses while at the same time providing individualized attention" The late Ernest L. Boyer, former President of the Carnegie Foundation for the Advancement of Teaching, used to tell of an incident when he visited a school for handicapped children working with computers. When he noticed a boy sitting in front of his computer in tears he walked up to him to inquire. The boy just pointed to the computer screen and said, "It is the first time anybody ever told me I did something right." When Boyer looked at the screen it said: "Terrific job, Johnny, you got it right!"

Both reach and richness are possible because information technology allows learning for all to be highly interactive, individualized, and adaptable. It can foster peer communication and group learning, and provide a mechanism for increased student-teacher interaction and feedback. (More detailed discussion around student interactions can be found in Chapters 1 and 2.)

*Access*
For millennia students had to go to the source of knowledge, but now, information technology allows knowledge to come to the student. Correspondence courses, used since Biblical times, peaked during the century prior to the 1950s (Daniel, 2005). And many lives have been transformed, especially in South Africa, through the use of radio courses (Naidoo & Potter, 2007). However, the element of interactivity is lacking and can only be present for the masses with information technology. India is currently the world

leader in open and distance learning; with China certainly coming next. Today students are more in the presence of Bach and Mozart than anyone in the eighteenth century ever could have been. And students can use computers to study the details of gas laws by varying the parameters of volume, pressure, temperature, amount and kind of gas, and particle speed, without ever leaving their home — and they can do it at no cost. Information technology is quick, student-centred, completely safe, repeatable, and cost-free! It allows knowledge to come to the student!

*Flexibility*
Correspondence courses had wonderful flexibility never achieved by traditional institutions. While there were some guidelines for length of study and ending times, the student had considerable say-so in these decisions. But the student had no opportunity for flexible learning, such as a combination of face-to-face and information technology tools. What if the student does not have the required prerequisites? Can that student enrol?

Students today can choose the place, the length of study (to some extent), and the beginning and ending time of study, as well as the level of interactivity with other students and the faculty member. In fact, students can enrol even without the necessary prerequisites, as long as the course performance is acceptable. For science laboratories there are, however, serious challenges as to how and where practical work is performed. Pioneering work is being done with a blended approach using laboratory kits sent to the student (see, for example, Chapters 5 and 7), video/DVD prepared experiments, and very excellent Internet experiments, with the student being responsible for all data collection and reports (see Boschmann, 2003b).

*Worldwide distribution*
More than any other area of knowledge, appreciation and understanding of science lags far behind its development. Perhaps this is

due to its mathematical nature, perhaps because the advance of science depends on experimentation and laboratories are out of reach for many persons, perhaps it is lack of interest, or perhaps scientists are to blame for making the fields unnecessarily obscure.

Science literacy can be improved dramatically by taking a radically different approach. In addition to classes, lectures, textbooks, laboratories, conferences, and seminars, the reach can be increased manifold through films, museums, or the Web. Celia Henry Arnaud (2007) writes of hosting videos on *YouTube* that are audience-participatory and go a long way toward inquiry-based science education. Such videos must be short and to the point, they must be entertaining, and the audience must have the opportunity to choose from an array of options.

Science publications made available through open access for all and for free not only improve visibility, but also speed distribution of findings, and often lead to worldwide collaborations. Some disciplines are already making great strides with open access publications.

Drug companies faced with tough research problems post these on the Web with an invitation to submit proposed approaches to solving them. This open competition in resolving stubborn problems not only receives instant worldwide distribution, but gives clever researchers everywhere the chance to solve a given problem and earn some money.

The time-honoured procedure of faculty having their publications peer reviewed, and if approved, published, may now be reversed, in that the article is first published on the Web, and then peer reviewed. Publications receive a much higher readership, honest feedback from a much larger set of colleagues, and can always be revised based on that feedback.

## *Learning styles and engagement*

Students learn differently. Some are visual, some auditory, some tactile, some prefer a blended approach, and some learn most when in the laboratory. While it is difficult for faculty to adjust to all these styles in one class, research has shown that the vast majority of students, by far, learn most when they are engaged with the material instead of the material being delivered to them. The emphasis is on student involvement, active learning, and engagement. Some quotes from the foremost thinkers on learning will make the point:

"...the most apparent need is to change the emphasis of instruction away from transmitting fixed bodies of information toward preparing students to engage..."
• Derek Bok (1986)
"Simply put, the greater the student's involvement in academic work, the greater his or her level of knowledge acquisition..."
• Pascarella and Terenzini (1991)

"...good practice encourages active learning..."
• Chickering and Gamson (1987)

"Since the 1920s, hundreds of studies point to the advantages of active learning. These findings are deemed 'the most distinguished of all'."
• David and Roger Johnson (1992)

"...the greater the student's involvement, the greater the learning and personal development."
• Alexander Astin (1996)

In the electronic revolution, technology provides a great additional tool in fostering such student engagement.

As with other teaching tools, there are two kinds of technologies: delivery technologies are those that substitute for lectures, books, and notes, such as videos, TV, CD-ROMs, etc., where the student generally remains in the passive role. All studies indicate that, in general, there is no significant difference in student learning whether or not this technology is used (see, for instance, Schramm, 1977).

However, engagement technologies such as the Web, e-mail, interactive computer programs, chat rooms, etc., improve student learning dramatically, as many researchers have found (see Kulik & Kulik, 1991). These tools remain static until the student participates. On Bloom's taxonomy (1984), most lectures, TV, videos, and CD-ROMs emphasize the lower end of his scale: knowledge, comprehension, and application; whereas at the higher end of the scale, analysis, synthesis, and evaluation are fostered by problem-based learning, apprenticeships, collaborative learning, and interactive computer programs, chat rooms, the Web, e-mail, etc.

Thus, a student could take an entire course in a traditional class, watching television, a DVD, or a CD-ROM and remain totally passive, simply taking notes. However, in a chat room, using an interactive DVD where no action takes place unless the student first acts, or in deciding how to set up virtual laboratory equipment, the student has no choice but to be engaged. Assessing the online learner will become a major thrust (Palloff & Pratt, 2008).

*Student-centredness*
There is a major shift under way from the passive student to one who is actively engaged, controls the destiny of study and seeks out opportunities for advancement. The passive student will fade, as the apprenticeships and correspondence courses have, because something much better is on the horizon. Hierarchical control will give way to collaborative support, and authority will become a shared responsibility between the student and the master.

*Affordability*
Just as computer storage capability doubles every 18 months, so equipment prices are cut as time goes on. It is no longer surprising to find computers in the US$100 range or wireless capabilities in many environments. Tuition still rises from year to year; however, many open source course materials are now available. Herein resides the real opportunity for third world countries: the

digital divide can be narrowed quickly and considerably with lower cost equipment and open source course materials. It will take another generation or so for traditional institutions to make the radical change from gatekeepers of knowledge to open access educators.

## Barriers yet to be overcome

The barriers and opportunities mentioned above, and the barriers yet to be overcome mentioned in this section pertain to traditional institutions; however, many barriers have been overcome by the creation of a few very special institutions. For example, the *Open University*, created in 1969, is today the UK's largest university. It provides distance education which is open to people, places, methods, and ideas and promotes educational opportunities and social justice for all. *Athabasca University*, Canada's leader in distance education, is committed to breaking down barriers of time, space, access, and success by acknowledging prior learning and providing opportunities for anyone over the age of 16. *Monash University* in Australia seeks to improve the human condition by advancing creativity in social justice, human rights, and a sustainable environment. These and other similar open institutions around the world have pioneered recognition for prior learning, and introduced tutorials, trainers, and assessors to overcome some of the barriers endemic in many traditional institutions of higher education. However, for many traditional institutions barriers do remain.

### *Academic culture*

Like any other institution, after centuries of tradition, academia is entrenched in its ways and struggles with change. How shall it respond to the electronic revolution? If terms of study are no longer necessary, then what is expected? What about courses *vs.* modules, student-paced competencies, or collaborative learning?

Is assessment the right route? Should collaborative learning be encouraged? Are employers true partners in these decisions? What about tuition for foreign students? Should credit be given for life experiences? How does one overcome the not-so-occasional depiction of distance education (DE) as second-rate, as just extension centre courses, or, worse, as a "diploma mill?"

What does faculty/staff advancement mean in a world of DE? Does innovation in technology 'count' toward promotion and tenure? Does a scholar who thinks deeply (and publishes) about how technology affects learning deserve the same treatment as one who publishes a standard research paper? What new role must advancement/promotion and tenure committees undertake, when their membership is made up of traditional faculty, yet the dossier before them not only is claiming instructional technology scholarship, but its content is perhaps beyond the committee members' grasp? How do you retrain such committees? Do traditional publications and the peer review process supersede all others, or is it possible that in the age of technology it may be prudent to publish first and then be refereed? Is the institution willing to fundamentally rewrite its advancement guidelines to accommodate the new way of learning, conducting research, and publishing?

It will take visionary and skillful leadership with strong backbone and convincing willpower to speak to these issues. It will take leaders who constantly think outside the box and who are able to set policy even when the vision is somewhat blurred.

New leaders must confront issues that go to the core of what an institution is and has been. They must tackle transformational changes that often go against the very grain of faculty fabric. There will be faculty who see DE as a time-consuming, money-draining fad that is intent on removing their cherished faculty-student eye contact of the classroom setting. On the other hand, there are many potential students who can only become students if DE is made available. Equally, there are many traditional students who look forward to the added dimension DE brings to their learning.

Experience shows that transformational changes will be most successful when

- there is administrative support of, and administrative practice in, the use of DE.
- advancement/promotion and tenure guidelines are rewritten.
- a new DE office stands on its own, and is not affixed to an existing office (such as an extension centre). Fundamental questions regarding the soundness of extension centres will invariably carry over to DE.
- early DE successes are assured with grants, publications, notoriety, etc.
- it is recognized that faculty training in DE is generally not successful. Faculty often feel, in the words of Winston Churchill, that "I am always ready to learn, although I do not always like being taught." Instead, highlight good examples, promote those with DE scholarship, and give salary increases to deserving faculty. Examples will change the culture.
- it is realized that transformational change will take a generation and its leadership will likely become a victim even of its own success.

## Funding

Money for DE can be a double-edged sword. On the one hand, since money brings power, it is important to make sure early attempts are properly funded so they can develop and, perhaps even more important, can be noticed. On the other hand, is it time to re-examine funding structures tied to political and educational jurisdictions? Essentially administrators must rethink "in-state *vs.* out of state" (U.S. terminology) tuition. Does it still make sense in a world of DE to insist on such division? Will the regulatory power of funders (donors and legislators) continue to steer or will they leave these judgments to institutions? Is it wise to pour a lot of money into equipment and support needs without having absolute assurance of DE's ultimate success? What about faculty who insist on start-up money or ask for released time from teaching to devote their energies to DE?

Again, educators should take a lesson from the retail world, which has found a system that is both ubiquitous and of high quality, rather than exclusionary and rare. The latter serves the elite few, the former the masses.

*Accreditation*
Will DE teaching of an existing course be submitted to the curriculum committee as though it were a new course, or will it be accepted as a new teaching method for an existing course? Not only is accreditation of new departments and divisions with a DE emphasis an issue for the administration, but global accreditation between institutions and countries becomes of monumental significance. How can accrediting bodies be sure the courses are not watered-down versions of a rigorous on-campus course?

*Testing*
This remains a major issue for many DE courses. How can security be assured? Should testing be conducted on campus only, or can an off-campus arrangement be secured that will maintain integrity? Some institutions use a local person in a supervisory relationship to the student to monitor tasks such as quizzes and tests.

*Laboratories*
Most current DE courses are non-science in order to avoid the difficult issue of laboratories. No other aspect has caused a greater challenge than the delivery of laboratory experiments via DE. Most vexing has been the dilemma of access *vs.* safety; it appears that as one improves the other degenerates. Couple safety issues with legal concerns, and in some countries a stifling situation is created.

Do students come to campus for laboratories at periodic times, do they go to local institutions, do they do the experiments at home, do they use animations on the Web, or do they use videos? What are the advantages of virtual *vs.* actual experiments? Are the principles being illustrated of primary concern, or are issues such as set-up, socialization with fellow students, the touch and feel of the laboratory environment, breakage, failed experiments, exposure to potential dangers, just as important as scientific principles?

Some institutions use a blended approach of actual experiments either at home or at some institution, DVD/videos, and the Web for virtual experiments. Virtual animal dissection, chemical experiments, the observation of physical phenomena, even the control of a telescope can all be done at a distance. (See Chapters 5–9 for more examples around laboratory delivery.)

## Conclusion

The electronic revolution is here, and it is ubiquitous (Fischman, 2008), forcing education to redefine its mission from teaching students to engaging every person who wants to learn. The barriers academia has set up over time, whether involving the use of papyrus by the students of Plato, or gender, religious, and racial quotas set up in some countries, are being eliminated in sweeping proportions.

Wonderful new opportunities suddenly spring to the forefront, such as mass distribution of science literacy in an engaging way and open access to education for all and for free. There is wide flexibility as to when and how to attend classes, using learning styles from engaged studies to chat room discussions, and giving the student control of her destiny.

*It is New Year's Day, 1895. My name is Hans. For seven generations my family has made the finest buttons in the region, using good local horn. Today I learned that the railroad is coming to our village. My friend Olaf says that cheap factory buttons will come on the trains, but that they will never compete with my craftsmanship. I think he is part right and part wrong. They will come, but they will compete with my buttons. I must make some choices: I can become a distributor for the new buttons, or I can invest in the machinery to make buttons and export them. Or, closest to my heart, I can refine my craft and sell exceptional buttons ... I cannot stop the train; I must change.*

• Adapted from a fable told by William A. Wulf in *"University Alert: The Information Railroad is Coming."* Published on the Web. (http://net.educause.edu/ir/library/pdf/erm0310.pdf)

Hans, in the fable above, is an exception; he realizes that change is coming and is unusually clever in seeing what that change means, and envisioning several scenarios for himself. But most of all, he is doing something about his situation.

The opportunities are here. Will we be clever enough to seize them?

REFERENCES

Arnaud, C.H. (2007). A new science channel. *Chemical and Engineering News, 85* (26), 44–46.

Astin, A.W. (1996). Involvement in learning revisited: Lessons we have learned. *Journal of College Student Development, 37,* 123–134.

Bloom, B.S. (1984). *Taxonomy of educational objectives.* Boston: Allyn and Bacon.

Bok, D. (1986). *Higher learning,* (p. 165). Cambridge, Massachusetts: Harvard University Press.

Boschmann, E. (2003a). The IUPUI story of change. In J. Bourne & J.C. Moore (Eds.), *Elements of quality online education: Practice and direction, 4,* (pp. 213–228), The Sloan Consortium.

Boschmann, E. (2003b). Teaching chemistry via distance education. *Journal of Chemical Education, 80,* 704–708.

Chickering, A.W. & Gamson, Z.F. (1987). Seven principles for good practice in undergraduate education. *Wingspread Journal, 9*(2), 1–4.

Daniel, Sir J.S. (1997). Why universities need technology strategies. *Change: The Magazine for Higher Learning, 29*(4), 10–17.

Daniel, Sir J. (2005). International perspectives on open learning and distance education. Presented before the National Forum on Open Learning and Distance Education The Gambia. Commonwealth of Learning 12–14 April, 2005.

Dierker, R.A. (1995). The future of electronic education. In Erwin Boschmann (Ed.), *The electronic classroom: A handbook for education in the electronic environment,* (pp. 228–235). Medford, NJ: Learned Information, Inc.

Drucker, P.F. (1992). *Managing for the future: The 1990s and beyond.* New York: Penguin Press.

Fischman, J. (2008). Distance education becomes a major part of course catalogues. *The Chronicle of Higher Education,* December 30.

Johnson D.W. & Johnson R.T. (1992). Implementing cooperative learning. *Contemporary Education, 63,* 173–180.

Kidder, R.M. (1987). *An agenda for the 21st century.* Cambridge: MIT Press.

Kulik, C-L.C. & Kulik, J.A. (1991). Effectiveness of computer-based instruction: An updated analysis. *Computers in Human Behavior, 7,* 75–95.

McLuhan, H.M. (1964). *Understanding media: The extensions of man.* New York: New American Library.

Naidoo, G. & Potter, C. (2007). Ethical issues in using interactive radio in South Africa. *Open Learning, 22,* 159–165.

Palloff, R.M. & Pratt, K. (2008). *Assessing the online learner: Resources and strategies for faculty.* San Francisco: Jossey-Bass.

Pascarella, E.T. & Terenzini, P.T. (1991). *How college affects students: Findings and insights from twenty years of research.* San Francisco: Jossey-Bass.

Schramm, W. (1977). *Big media, little media: Tools and technologies for instruction.* California: Sage Publications.

# Author Biographies

**Farook Al-Shamali**, B.Sc.(Hons), M.Sc., Ph.D. (farooka@athabascau.ca), is Academic Coordinator of physics and astronomy courses at Athabasca University. He has teaching experience in both the face-to-face lecturing and in the distance education mode. Over the years he has published in the areas of particle physics and geomagnetism. His current research interest is in physics distance education and e-learning. More specifically, he is currently looking into the applications of Learning Objects in online physics courses and also into the design of low-cost physics home lab experiments.

**Terry Anderson**, Ph.D., is Professor and Canada Research Chair in Distance Education at Athabasca University — Canada's Open University. He has published widely in the area of distance education and educational technology and has co-authored or edited five books and numerous papers. Terry is active in provincial, national, and international distance education associations and is a regular presenter at professional conferences. He teaches educational technology courses in Athabasca's Masters of Distance Education program. Terry is also the director of CIDER — the Canadian Institute for Distance Education Research (cider.athabascau.ca) and the editor of the International Review of Research on Distance and Open Learning (IRRODL www.irrodl.org). The complete text of his most recent edited book *The Theory and Practice of Online Learning* is available as an Open Access resource (cde.athabascau.

ca/online_book). More information is available on his website (cider.athabascau.ca/Members/terrya).

**Erwin Boschmann**, Ph.D. (erv@iu.edu), is Professor Emeritus of Chemistry at Indiana University Purdue University Indianapolis. He has served as Provost at the Indiana University East Campus and was Indiana University's Associate Vice President for Distributed Education with responsibility for all eight campuses. From 1988 to 1999 he served as Associate Dean of the Faculties with responsibility for 1500 full-time, and 800 part-time faculty. He has spoken, taught, and consulted widely in this country and overseas, and has published books and articles in both teaching and research. In 1983 he received Indiana University's statewide H.F. Lieber Award for Distinguished Teaching, and in 1986 he was awarded a Lilly Faculty Open Fellowship. During 1997 he served as chair of the Indiana Section of the American Chemical Society, and in 1998 he received the Distinguished Alumnus Award from Bethel College.

**Robert D. Carmichael**, B.Sc., M.Sc. in Microbiology (robertc@athabascau.ca), is the Science Lab Coordinator at Athabasca University. With now over ten years of laboratory TA experience in biology, chemistry, and physics labs and in a wide variety of lab session formats, he has presented in the areas of distance science education administration. His research in distance education is primarily concerned with the development of online science resources for students and staff.

**Avner Caspi**, Ph.D. (avnerca@openu.ac.il), is a lecturer in the Department of Education and Psychology at the Open University of Israel. He is a research associate in the Chais Research Center for the Integration of Technology in Education. He specializes in educational technologies, the social and cognitive aspects of learning and studying, and cyber-psychology.

**Edward Cloutis**, B.Eng, M.Sc., Ph.D., is Professor of Geography at the University of Winnipeg. He has designed a number of earth science courses for distributed learning. Over the years he has published extensively on the use of remote sensing for terrestrial and extraterrestrial research. He was the recipient of the University of Winnipeg's Erica and Arnold Rogers Award for Excellence in Research and Scholarship. His research was also recognized by the naming of asteroid (6081) Cloutis by the International Astronomical Union. His teaching includes development of student-led projects in geographic information systems for non-academic organizations and clients.

**Martin Connors**, B.Sc.(Hons), M.Sc., Ph.D., PPhys (martinc@athabascau.ca), is Professor of Astronomy and Physics and a Canada Research Chair at Athabasca University. Most of his teaching experience has been with distance education. He developed innovative lab materials for DE physics and astronomy courses, and a computer-oriented statistics course. His research in distance education focuses on use of web control of lab apparatus.

**Alan Farley**, B.Ec.(Hons), M.Ec., Ph.D. (alan.farley@deakin.edu.au), is a Professor and Director of the Institute of Teaching and Learning at Deakin University. He has used technology in innovative ways in his own teaching since the early 1980s and currently leads an agenda to have Deakin recognized as a leader in Flexible Education. He is currently President of the Australian Council of Online, Distance and eLearning. His research includes articles on both general higher education issues and education in his own fields of teaching, as well as publications in his original field of Management Science.

**Paul Gorsky**, D.Sc. (paulgo@openu.ac.il), is a faculty member in the Department of Education and Psychology at the Open University of Israel and a research associate in the Chais Research Center for the Integration of Technology in Education. His research interests include instructional theory and design, and the impact of instructional technologies on cognition. In addition, Paul founded and chairs a nationwide not-for-profit organization, "Science and Reasoning 2000," which offers extra-curricular, hands-on, inquiry-based activities to gifted and science-oriented youth throughout Israel.

**Dale Holt**, B.Com., Di.P.Ed, Grad.Cert.Dist.Ed, Ph.D. (dholt@deakin.edu.au), is Head: Education Design, Professional Development and Research, Institute of Teaching and Learning, Deakin University. Most of his academic development experience has been in online, distance, and flexible education. Dale has won a national teaching award in this area. Over the years he has published in areas relating to professional learning by distance education, workplace and experiential learning, leadership and management of ICT in higher education, and teaching and learning online. With colleague Stuart Palmer, he is currently undertaking a nationally funded project on the strategic leadership of teaching and learning centres in Australian higher education.

**Md. Tofazzal Islam**, B.Sc.Ag.(Hons), M.Sc.Ag., MS, Ph.D. (tofazzalislam@yahoo.com), is Associate Professor of Ecological Chemistry at the School of Agriculture and Rural Development (SARD) of Bangladesh Open University. He played key roles in establishment of SARD and launched an undergraduate program in agriculture through distance mode. His research findings in phytochemistry and molecular plant-peronosporomycete interactions have been published in international journals and books. Over the years he has also published in the areas of agricultural education at a distance. He holds both national and international research awards. His current interests include innovative distance delivery methods for undergraduate and postgraduate courses in agriculture in the developing countries.

**Anjeela Jokhan**, Ph.D., is Senior Lecturer and Associate Dean Teaching & Learning in the Faculty of Science and Technology at University of the South Pacific (USP). Her doctoral thesis in plant physiology at the University of Bristol looked at the effects of partial root drying on the physiology of *Ricinus communis* (castor oil) plants. She has been involved in teaching through both face-to-face and distance flexible learning (DFL) modes for over 20 years and her extensive experience has focused in the area of DFL course design, delivery, and administration, with emphasis on identifying and dealing with issues related to delivery in the regional campuses. Her keen interest in DFL delivery in the area of teaching and learning, from a quality point of view, has also put her work at the focal point in preparing for a quality audit at USP in February 2008.

**Robert Lyall**, FRMIT (App.Chem.), M.App.Sci., Ph.D., MRACI (robert.lyall@sci.monash.edu.au), was previously a Senior Lecturer in Chemistry in the School of Applied Sciences, Monash University, where his teaching experience included both on-campus and distributed learning. He has published in the fields of air and water pollution as well as in educational research. Robert's research in education has concentrated on the learning strategies of distance education chemistry students and the use of interactive media. He is presently continuing this research as a Senior Research Fellow in the School of Applied Sciences.

**Jenny Mosse**, B.Sc.(Hons), M. Biotech, Dip. Ed., B.Ed., Grad. Cert. Higher Ed. (jenny.mosse@sci.monash.edu), is Senior Lecturer in Biochemistry at Monash University, and has been teaching distance students for over 20 years. Jenny is particularly interested in the development of innovative methods for flexible delivery of science programs to remote students and in designing science programs of both local and international relevance. Jenny is a molecular virologist, studying antisense gene expression in HIV virus and investigating mechanisms of drug resistance in influenza viruses.

**Stuart Palmer**, B.Eng., MBA, Grad.Cert.HigherEd, D.Tech. (spalm@deakin.edu.au), is a Senior Lecturer in the Institute of Teaching and Learning, Deakin University. He is a chartered professional engineer, having practiced in consulting engineering for a decade before joining the School of Engineering at Deakin University. He lectured in the management of technology for twelve years, working with engineering students studying in on-campus, off-campus, off-shore and online modes. In 1999 he was awarded the Australasian Association for Engineering Education McGraw-Hill New Engineering Educator Award. His research interests include frequency domain image analysis and the application of digital technologies in engineering education. More recently, he has joined the Deakin University Institute of Teaching and Learning.

**Gale Parchoma**, B.Ed., B.A.(Hons), M.A., Ph.D. (g.parchoma@lancaster.ac.uk), is a lecturer in Technology Enhanced Learning and e-Research at Lancaster University. Most of her instructional design, teaching, and research experiences have been focused on technology mediated teaching and learning. Gale has published in the areas of learner-centred instruction, lifelong learning, educational leadership, and interdisciplinary applications of technology enhanced learning. Her current research includes leadership in e-learning and interdisciplinary approaches to providing Web-based support for promoting creativity and critical thinking in higher education.

**Antonio (Tony) F. Patti**, B.Sc.(Hons), Ph.D., Grad.Dip.Ed.FRACI (tony.patti@sci.monash.edu.au), is an Associate Professor in Chemistry in the School of Applied Sciences and Engineering and Associate Dean, Graduate Studies in the Faculty of Science, Monash University. He has extensive teaching experience in both on-campus and distributed learning in chemistry, soil chemistry, and environmental science. Tony was heavily involved in the development and implementation of a home experiment chemistry kit for off-campus students at Monash University and for Open Learning Australia in the early 1990s. His current research interests are focused in Green Chemistry with an emphasis on natural organic matter transformations, soil chemistry, and the conversion of biomass into useful chemical feed-stocks and fuels.

**Bibhya N. Sharma**, B.Sc., M.Sc., received his Master's degree in mathematics from the University of the South Pacific, Fiji, in 1998. He is completing his Ph.D. degree in applied mathematics from the same university. He is currently a lecturer in Mathematics with the School of Computing, Information and Mathematical Sciences of the Faculty of Science and Technology, University of the South Pacific. He is also the Coordinator of the Mathematics Division. His main fields of interest are dynamics of nonlinear systems, robotics, artificial neural networks, and mathematics education.

**Wendy Wright**, B.Sc.(Hons), Ph.D., Grad.Cert.HigherEd. (wendy.wright@sci.monash.edu.au), is a Senior Lecturer in Biological and Environmental Sciences. She has developed and taught various programs for mixed mode delivery (on and off campus) at Monash University's regional campus in Gippsland, Victoria, Australia for nearly 15 years and has published in the areas of distance education, environmental education, ecology, and conservation biology.

# Index

## A

academic culture, 244, 252, 260
access, 42–44, 109, 172–74, 176, 177, 179, 180, 229–31, 250, 255, 263
access, remote, 168–70, 173, 177, 180
accessibility, 11, 29, 65, 191, 192, 203
accreditation, 70, 75, 263
ADDIE model, 47
affordability, 259
age, 21, 31, 69, 71, 73, 75–78, 102, 251, 260, 261
agriculture, 218, 227, 229
animal behaviour, 172
apparatus, 84, 85, 87–89, 93, 97–100, 107, 122, 136, 143, 172
astronomical camera, 171
attendance, 102, 103, 110, 123, 125, 224, 225, 229
Australia, 61–78

## B

Bachelor of Engineering (BE), 69–70
balance, 89, 98, 203, 211
Bangladesh Open University (BOU), 214, 216, 229
barrier, 52, 109, 196, 215, 243, 248–53, 260, 264
BE. *See* Bachelor of Engineering
biochemistry, 85, 113
biological science(s), 109–116, 193, 202–3, 227, 238, 241
biotechnology, 113, 115
block laboratories, 113, 240
book, 42, 99, 249, 250, 252, 254, 258
book, course, 220–22, 225
Bugscope, 171

## C

Calculator-Based Laboratory (CBL), 137
campus, 76, 84, 87, 96, 105, 111–13, 116, 134–35, 167, 198, 235–36, 238–42, 244, 250, 263–64
campus, regional, 235, 239–44
Canada, 86, 90, 95, 100, 102, 137, 260
cartography, 153
cell biology, 112, 181. *See also* biological sciences
CEQ. *See* Course Experience Questionnaire
change, 40, 47, 48, 52, 61, 75, 138, 142, 200, 204, 205, 244, 247–49, 253, 260–62, 265
chemical
  flammable, 94, 98, 100
  toxic, 94, 100

chemistry, 19, 24–26, 83–107, 148,
    171, 181, 193, 196, 199–200,
    202–7, 227, 238, 248
chemistry course, 19, 240
chemistry experiment, 85, 96, 101
chemistry laboratory, 205
chemistry program, 86
CMC. *See* computer-mediated
    communication
collaboration, 10, 43, 56, 73, 172,
    179, 181, 257
computer-based simulation. *See*
    computer simulation
computer-mediated communication (CMC), 42, 67, 73
computer simulation, 74, 84, 109,
    132–3, 167, 170, 178, 192, 225
consortia, 181
consumables. *See* materials,
    consumable
contingency-based framework,
    61, 68, 69, 77
correspondence-based DE (*also
    correspondence courses*),
    40, 131–133, 215, 255, 256, 259
cost(s)
    (general) 5, 84, 87, 89, 90, 111,
        135, 137, 138, 141, 144, 180, 181,
        191, 192, 196–208, 225, 230,
        242, 250
    capital, 144, 198
    construction, 198–99, 207
    full, 197, 202
    location, 198–99, 202
    shipping costs, 90, 201–3
course difficulty, 21, 28, 30
Course Experience Questionnaire
    (CEQ), 62
course team, 220, 221

# D

delivery technologies, 258
delivery
    online, 67, 73, 238
    print-based, 238
demonstrator, 75, 92, 93, 105, 121, 239
developing country, 213–15, 224,
    225, 229–31
dialogue
    instructional, 19, 20, 29
    interpersonal, 19–24, 26–27, 29,
        31, 32
    intrapersonal, 19–21, 23–25
digital video disk. *See* DVD
disposal procedure, 92
DVD (digital video disk), 92, 93,
    256, 259, 264

# E

earth sciences, 147–203
earthquake, 148, 155
ecology, 113, 163, 203
education
    flexible, 61, 62, 64, 65, 67–9, 77, 78
    off-campus, 66, 67, 69, 73, 114
    online, 76, 265
e-learning (electronic learning),
    8, 43–45, 66, 219, 231
electrical engineering, 169
electron microscope, 171, 181
electronic engineering, 181
electronics, 74, 169
engagement, 1, 2, 12, 76, 173, 225,
    257–59
engagement technologies, 259
engineering
    electrical, 169
    electronic, 181
    food, 171

engineering education, 69, 71,
    181–85
enrolment, 66, 137, 203–5, 207, 214,
    218, 227, 236, 240, 249
entrance requirements, 252
environment
    digital, 151
    home, 87, 93, 100, 220, 225
    immersive, 11–13
    learning, 33, 43–44, 46, 63, 65–
        66, 76
    remote, 176, 180
    virtual laboratory, 132, 170
equipment, 84, 89–92, 112, 122, 125,
    133, 135, 140, 141, 143, 170, 175,
    177, 180–82, 198, 200–2, 240
    laboratory, 83, 84, 239, 259
    virtual laboratory, 259
equity, 237
European Union (EU), 181
experience
    virtual laboratory, 170
experiment
    hands-on (*also* hands-on exercise), 84, 85, 97, 131, 133, 147,
        149, 151, 192
    home, 83–107, 132, 134, 204
    internet-based laboratory, 85,
        202, 215, 256, 263
    kitchen chemistry, 85, 101
    Millikan's oil drop, 171
    practical, 83, 85
    quantitative, 90, 99, 132, 135
experimental errors, 178
external institutions, 44, 196

# F

feedback, 3, 41, 48, 50, 64, 73, 74,
    122, 155, 162, 173, 175, 195, 221,
    224, 255, 257
field trip, 155, 162
field work, 149, 151, 162, 163, 165,
    224
financing, 175
fiscal pressure, 180
flexi-school, 238, 239. *See also*
    school
flexibility, 8, 10, 64–66, 70, 112, 139,
    178, 195, 225, 230, 231, 256, 264
flexible learning, 42, 43, 67, 70–72,
    235, 238, 244, 256
full costing, 197. *See also* cost

# G

gender, 31, 249, 250, 264
geographic information systems
    (GIS), 150, 151
geography, 147, 150, 151, 161–65,
    179, 193, 245
geology, 147, 149, 152, 153, 156, 157,
    161, 164, 165, 193, 202, 203. *See
    also* earth sciences
geomagnetic observatory, 171
geomatics, 147
GIS. *See* geographic information
    systems
global unifying factor, 253
Google Earth, 152
greenhouse, 172

# H

Hawthorne effect, 175
hazardous experiment, 96, 178, 179
historical geology, 153
home experiments, 83–107, 132,
    134, 204
home experiment kit, 87, 91, 92,
    95, 103–6, 191

home lab kit, 85, 132, 135, 137, 192, 194, 197–201, 203–5
home laboratory, 102, 131, 133–38, 144, 192–94, 197, 199, 200–205
Hubble space telescope, 168
human biology, 112. *See also* physiology

## I

information and communications technologies (ICT), 13, 42, 65–67, 219, 229, 230
information technology (IT) support, 45, 46, 176, 197
interactive robotic operations, 172
institutional supports, 192, 197
instructional design, 22, 29, 175, 248
instructional development team, 37, 39, 41
instructional strategies, 27, 29, 54
instructor availability, 22
Intelligent Flexible Learning DE, 43
interaction
 student-content, 4–7, 10, 12, 13
 student-student, 4, 7–13, 173, 231
 student-teacher, 3–6, 8, 10, 255
interpretation of data, 87
interpretation of results, 105
IT support. *See* information technology (IT) support

## K

kinetics, 171
kitchen chemistry, 83–85. *See also* home chemistry

## L

laboratory
 (general), 81, 85, 93, 94, 99–101, 117, 169–70, 173, 175, 176, 181, 196, 201, 239–41, 257, 258, 263–4
 on-campus, 106, 134, 144, 182, 200, 201. *See also* residential laboratory
 optics, 181
 real, 170, 178, 179
 remote, 169
 residential, 192, 195–205, 207
 virtual, 2, 37, 84, 132, 133, 170, 178, 241, 259
laboratory demonstrator, 75, 92, 93, 105, 239. *See also* laboratory instructor
laboratory environment, remote, 174, 175, 180
laboratory environment and human interaction, 174
laboratory equipment, 83, 84, 239, 259
laboratory exemption, 65, 67, 74, 124
laboratory experience, virtual, 170
laboratory experiment, internet-based, 85, 202, 215, 256, 263. *See also* internet-based practical
laboratory instructor, 143, 193, 195, 199. *See also* laboratory demonstrator
laboratory kit, 85, 110–12, 132–35, 137–41, 143, 167, 192, 194, 197–200, 202, 203, 241, 256
laboratory kit, partial, 204, 205
laboratory program, 87, 96, 101, 110–13, 123–25, 191, 192, 194, 197–205, 207
 home, 194, 197, 199–207

on-campus, 200, 201, 207
  residential, 124, 192, 194, 201, 204
laboratory report, 103, 105, 134, 195
laboratory staff, 193, 195
laboratory work, 11, 74, 75, 86, 88, 105, 113, 151, 178, 191, 192, 215, 218, 220, 224–26, 228, 229, 241
Labview, 176
language, 13, 241–43, 245, 254
language barrier, 243
leadership, 38, 50
Learner Experience Design Framework, 76
LearNet, 181, 185
learning
  active, 63, 258
  blended, 65
  collaborative, 3, 12, 43, 76, 259–61, 164, 165, 225, 259–61
  e-learning, 8, 43–45, 66, 219, 231
  flexible, 42, 67, 72, 235, 238, 245, 256
  independent, 37, 41, 241
  individualized, 7, 9, 12, 193, 255
  m-learning, 180, 219, 231
  prior, 71
  self-paced, 10
learning management systems (LMS), 43, 180
learning style, 65, 161, 249, 250, 255
lifelong learner, 75
limits of flexibility, 65, 69, 78
literacy, 237, 257, 264

# M

manipulation, 84, 87, 98, 169, 171, 172
Material Safety Data Sheet (MSDS), 96

materials
  (general), 21, 41, 49, 62–64, 66, 72, 92, 93, 102, 149, 155–57, 161, 162, 200, 220–22, 238–39, 258–60
  consumable, 198, 200, 201, 203, 240, 241
  print-based, 72
  printed, 91, 92
  printed course, 220, 222
measurement, 88, 120, 140, 142, 170–172
media choice, 72, 218, 230
"medium is the message", 252
mega-university, 215, 231
microbiology, 113, 203. *See also* biological sciences
Millikan's oil drop experiment, 171
mineralogy, 147, 152, 156
m-learning, 180, 219, 231
mobile devices, 180
mobile phone, 230, 231
modular curriculum, 70
multi-media DE, 40
multimedia, 150, 152, 192
multipliers of human capabilities, 253, 254

# N

National Science Foundation, 181
negotiation, 38, 43, 50
Network for Education — Chemistry, 181
non-ideal result, 178
novelty, 136, 175, 180

# O

observation, 87, 88, 92, 132, 143,

Index · 279

147–49, 151, 152, 155–57, 170–72, 202, 264
Occupational Health and Safety (OH&S), 90, 93
off-campus education, 66, 67, 69, 73, 114
off-campus student. *See* student, off-campus
on-campus laboratory program, 200, 201, 207. *See also* laboratory program, residential
on-campus laboratory, 106, 134, 144, 182, 200, 201. *See also* laboratory, residential
online delivery, 67, 73, 238
online education, 76, 265
opportunity, 8, 12, 22, 41, 46, 63, 66, 73, 124, 125, 215, 216, 248, 249, 254, 256, 257, 259, 260, 264, 265
outcome
  instructional, 21
  learning, 7, 12, 54, 67, 133, 144, 149, 157, 174, 175, 185

## P

password protection, 176
PC Anywhere, 176
PC Duo, 176
PEARL project (Practical Experimentation by Accessible Remote Learning), 181
personal attention, 255
petrology, 147, 152, 156
physical props, 156
physics, 24, 26, 28, 131, 133, 135–37, 139, 143–45, 148, 169, 182–84, 193, 202, 203, 227
physiology, 112, 203

POIT-EM, 171
practical, internet-based, 74, *See also* experiment, internet-based laboratory
practical experiment, 83, 85
practical skills, 88, 114, 124, 178, 215, 224, 226–28, 231
practical work, 86, 87, 106, 107, 109, 113, 167, 220, 223–25, 230, 239, 240, 256
practicum, 169
print, 219, 220, 231
prior knowledge, 21
program
  chemistry program, 86
  home laboratory, 194, 197, 199–207
  laboratory, 87, 96, 101, 110–13, 123–25, 191, 192, 194, 197–205, 207
  on-campus laboratory, 200, 201, 207
  residential laboratory, 124
project management, 38, 46, 49
ProLearn, 181, 186

## Q

qualifier exercises, 174, 177
qualitative demonstration, 135
quality function, 62, 79
quality improvement, 63
quantitative experiments, 90, 99, 132, 135

## R

radio, 41, 219, 248, 254
recognition of prior learning (RPL), 70–71
recording, 87, 222

audio, 72
video, 19
remote access, 168–70, 173, 177, 180
remote control, 168, 181, 185
remote environment, 176
remote laboratory, 169, 170, 172–75, 178–82
remote laboratory environment, 176
remote sensing, 147, 150, 157
residential institution, 180
residential laboratory, 192, 195–205, 207
residential laboratory program, 124, 192, 194, 201, 204
residential laboratory school, 83, 113
residential school, 83, 103–6, 111, 113, 115, 121, 123–25, 249
resources
    human, 20, 22, 23, 27, 29, 31
    institutional, 179
    remedial, 177
    structural, 20–24, 29, 31, 32
risk assessment, 93–94
RPL. *See* recognition of prior learning

## S

safety audit, 96
safety consideration, 93
safety demands, 168
safety information, 96
safety instructions, 92, 96
safety issue, 90, 91, 93, 103, 263
safety requirement, 90
satellite tutorial, 238
scheduler, 177
school
    flexi-school, 238
    residential, 83, 103–6, 111, 113, 115, 121, 123–25, 249
    residential laboratory, 83, 113
    weekend, 111–13
science literacy, 257, 264
seismology, 148
self-contained site, 176
self-paced setting, 10
self-paced study, 8
self-testing, 155, 174
simulation. *See* computer simulation
SMS (short message service), 230
social capital, 7, 9, 52–4, 227
social field, 52
social negotiation, 38, 50
social software, 9, 13, 37
soil science, 147, 164
specimen, 112, 152, 171, 241
staff, 49, 63, 66, 71, 75, 76, 84, 193, 240, 242, 244, 245
Stardial, 171, 185
student(s)
    campus-based, 19, 20, 26, 27, 31
    first generation, 251
    mature-age, 69, 71, 75
    off-campus, 66–67, 72, 73, 75, 92, 104, 105, 114, 237
    on-campus, 66, 67, 72, 75, 83, 105, 106, 115, 119–21, 123
student-centredness, 259
student confidence, 114–125, 128
student performance, 10, 101, 103, 105, 106, 174, 200
subject matter expert, 45

## T

teaching

dialogic, 19–32, 38
attributes of excellent, 65, 67, 74, 124
tactical approaches to learning, 32
tactical approaches to study, 27, 32, 35
TC. *See* tutorial centre
technical support, 240
technique, 8, 9, 11–13, 54, 84–85, 88, 92, 93, 97, 98, 104, 105, 109, 124, 125, 151, 152, 165
technique course, 150
telelearning DE, 41, 43
television, 41, 191, 219, 120, 254, 259
Theory of Instructional Design, 34
Theory of Instructional Dialogue, 21
Theory of Transactional Distance, 19
time on task, 21
TMA (tutor-marked assignment), 226
total quality management, 62
transactional distance, 19
travel, 83, 84, 111, 133, 202, 203, 205, 241, 242, 253
trial and error, 25, 178
tutor-marked assignment (TMA), 226
tutorial centre (TC), 216, 220, 223–24, 226–28
tutorial visit, 238
two-way communiation, 73, 74

## U

utilization rate, 21

## V

video, instructional, 93

video broadcast, 238, 240
video conferencing, 238
video demonstration, 105, 167
video recording, 19
virtual laboratory environment, 132, 170
virtual laboratory equipment, 259
vision, 49, 93, 191, 248, 253, 261

## W

Web, the, 62, 72, 170, 257, 259, 264, 265. *See also* World Wide Web
Web camera, 172, 177
world economy, 248
World Wide Student Laboratory, 181
World Wide Web, 164, 170. *See also* Web, the

## X

x-ray diffraction, 171

# About the Editors

**Dietmar Kennepohl**, B.Sc.(Hons), Ph.D., FCIC (dietmark@athabascau.ca), is Professor of Chemistry and Associate Vice President Academic at Athabasca University. Most of his teaching experience has been in a distributed and online setting. He holds both university and national teaching awards. Over the years he has published in the areas of chemical education, as well as petroleum, main group, and coordination chemistry. His research in chemical education concentrates on the use of innovative distance delivery methods for undergraduate laboratory work.

**Lawton Shaw**, B.Sc.(Hons), Ph.D. (lawtons@athabascau.ca) is Assistant Professor of Chemistry at Athabasca University, where he coordinates all chemistry courses. Prior to his appointment at Athabasca, Lawton was a tenured chemistry instructor and coordinator at Mount Royal College, where he taught general and industrial organic chemistry courses. He was one of the first instructors there to deliver a large enrolment course in blended delivery mode. His research interests are split between pure chemical research into sonochemical oxidation mechanisms and applied educational research, primarily into the use of educational technology as applied to distance delivery of chemistry courses.